A Corner Kick
from the Middle of Nowhere

A Corner Kick
from the Middle of Nowhere

A view from the teraces, as a ruined club
survived, then escaped a football wilderness

by
Mitch Stansbury

Foreword by
Ricky George

Offside Publishing

Offside Publishing
33 Napoleon Road, St. Margarets, Twickenham,
Middlesex TW1 3EW

First published by Offside Publishing 2007
Copyright © Mitch Stansbury 2007

ISBN 978 0 9557351 0 3

Typeset by Logaston Press
and printed in Great Britain by
Cromwell Press, Trowbridge, Wiltshire

Contents

Acknowledgements

I need to say thank you to a few people.

To my Father Mitch, for first taking me to the football at an age when I must have been a real pest. We still sit together, and I am, apparently, no less of a nuisance some 35 years on.

To all the people who have suffered with me at Edgar Street and elsewhere, notably my brother, Chris, and latterly, the two Johns, Rich, Woody, Alan and Mark.

To Justin, my best mate and best man, who was there from the start, and has watched and suffered every bit as much as I have. Terminally and officially sad cases, one and all.

To the folk behind the country's best fanzine, Talking Bull, and the brave souls who keep the various Hereford United websites running, remorselessly thankless tasks, you guys are my heroes.

And, to the four girls in my life. To Sarah, Lucy and Sophie, all of whom have graciously tolerated my wandering, rambling fixation with a team many football fans would barely have heard of. Your patience, good humour and indulgence of my fascination with all things Hereford United is never taken for granted. Only my mother knows what you have been through, so Mum, a big thanks to you as well. And sorry about the language.

And for your help and encouragement along the way, and in no particular order, Alan Leighton, Justin Williams, Trevor Lonsdale, Claire Dawson, Keith Hall and Ricky George. Kind words go a long way, I owe you all a beer.

Also to Richard Prime, for repairing a script scattered with moments of madness. Your eye for detail rescued many an incoherent babble, whilst your good sense tempered the occasional rant. You have my grateful thanks. Likewise to Karen Stout for her careful reading of the final manuscript.

Cover design by the author and Andy Johnson. Cuttings used with the kind permission of the *Hereford Times*.

Foreword

As delighted as I was surprised to be asked to read Mitchell Stansbury's original account of Hereford United's nine year spell back in non-league football, I was, I confess, unprepared for the effect it would have. It is yet another unexpected bonus from the greatest day of our football lives, and it reminds me, lest I should ever forget, that a football team, no matter how small, is nothing without its loyal fans. The supporters of Hereford United and the famous team of Giant-killers that I was so lucky to be part of are intrinsically linked — together we beat Newcastle United.

A Corner-Kick from the Middle of Nowhere tells the compelling story of a supporter who had seen his team reach the giddy heights of League Division Two, now called the Championship, and then self destruct over the next twenty years to return, in 1997, to non-league football. The book charts the following nine years, as Hereford United, by now known as 'the Bulls', lurch from one crisis to another, and how this particular fan, in common with thousands, runs the full gamut of emotions associated with supporting a team at this pivotal level of football.

A Corner-Kick is not just a record of matches played, but more a story about the characters that devotedly follow non-league clubs, the characters who run those clubs, and some of the weird and wonderful locations on the non-league map. Most of all, it is about the love affair between a supporter and his team, a phenomenon that can only be understood if you are one, or when someone like Mitchell takes the time and trouble to explain it.

As the book unfolded, I found myself laughing and crying (yes crying), as I was constantly reminded what it means to truly support a football club.

Any story written about Hereford will by definition begin in 1972, although prior to February 5th of that year, the border city club boasted a proud history in non-league football. After the FA cup triumph however, things would never be the same again. Hereford United became a Football

League club at the end of that unforgettable campaign, and within four seasons had climbed to the second tier of English Football. Success and glory became the order of the day and for many, expectancy replaced unconditional support. How quickly things can change.

I have never met Mitchell, but then I haven't been able to meet the many thousands of Hereford United fans who have played such a major part in my life. Mitchell is one such — a nine-year-old in 1972 and a member of the famous Parka Army who invaded the Edgar Street pitch three times on that never to be forgotten February afternoon, when the dreams of nine-year-olds collided with the dreams of twelve part-time, non-league footballers.

His story will strike a chord with the many thousands who follow non-league football, but as Mitchell says, 'Whether you follow Arsenal or Aylesbury, if your soul lies with a football team, any team, there is something here for you.'

It is engaging and funny, nostalgic and different, and very well written.

Ricky George
September 2007

Introduction

The following is a narrative where events described actually occurred, even, occasionally, at the time and place stated. Whilst precise details may be coloured or clouded by failing memory, I was actually present at most of the matches described. In one or two cases, names have been changed to protect the innocent, whereas the guilty are exposed for the inept and useless characters that they are.

I had spent two years of watching Southern League football when everything changed. Until then, I was keen, but it wasn't a religion. Then came a day in 1972, an incredible, un-fucking-believable (at the time I said double flipping brilliant) day, so many details of which all these years later I haven't forgotten. I hope I never will. When you're nine, and flipping is your best swear-word, everything is bigger, more compelling, just better than anything sullied by the cynicism that comes with growing up, but this was a magical day that touched the lives of many people. Some of those lives were changed for ever, although in some cases changed might better be described as blighted. And looking back after nearly four decades following Hereford United, there are two questions I ask myself, the first being 'Did my Dad really have my best interests at heart when taking me to watch his beloved Whites?' Or did I, as he insists, leave him no option, due to my incessant nagging to take me to the Match. Probably a bit of both.

The second, and one that could be asked by many Herefordians of a certain age, is this.

'Did Ricky George ruin my life?' But how could Ricky, a part-timer who flitted around the lower echelons of professional football, and a player who spent just a few short months at Hereford, change, let alone ruin my life? Should I blame Ricky for all the hours (countless), miles (never-ending), and cash (don't even ask) spent following my team up and down the country? How different would life be today if he had turned down the £25 a week offered by John Charles, bona fide football legend and then player-manager of Hereford United.

Perhaps I would have grown out of my infatuation with my local team, after all, many youngsters do. I might have been cured even before I knew that there was something wrong.

If I was wavering, if there was any doubt, a cup tie on 5th February 1972 extinguished it. From that day on, I was hooked. But back to Ricky. He was substitute for Hereford in an FA Cup 3rd round replay, a huge game for a non-league side, with the aristocrats of West Ham United waiting to visit the winners. Hereford United, a semi-professional outfit with a reputation for cup upsets, had held First Division and six times FA Cup winners Newcastle United to a 2-2 draw at St. James's Park. Having already beaten two League clubs along the way, here was a case of giant-taming rather than giant-killing, but nonetheless, some achievement for the part-timers. With such an obvious gulf in class, the unwritten rule is that the plucky lower-leaguers get just one chance of a famous scalp, the Goliaths of the football world being more than ready second time around. A case of the underdog having his day, but only the one. With ninety places in the football ladder between the sides, and Newcastle eager to avenge the embarrassment of the home tie, surely Hereford had missed their chance, England centre-forward Malcolm 'Supermac' MacDonald promising ten goals by himself.

Tell that to a nine year old who obviously knew better. The five times postponed replay finally defeated the perpetual rain of that winter, and was played on 4th round day, on a gluepot of a pitch. Perhaps a leveller, in the words of a rookie BBC reporter, but realistically, Hereford remained long odds to upset Newcastle again. In a spirited and well-balanced contest, the home side were giving the First Division high-fliers an afternoon to remember when Supermac delivered the first ten per cent of his promise, heading the visitors into an 81st minute lead. This surely wasn't right, life couldn't be so cruel, today was our day, not MacDonald's. I don't think for a minute that I was the only schoolboy in a parka who just knew that Hereford would triumph against the odds, so how dare Newcastle take the lead?

Our Dads, older and wiser, weren't so sure, but 14,000 fans crammed into the Edgar Street ground weren't going to watch their team defeated without a whimper, and called for one last effort. As did dozens more, perched on rooftops, floodlight pylons, even in trees around the ground. Step forward Ronnie Radford, like Ricky a journeyman, non-league, part-timer. With minutes remaining, Ronnie unleashed a shot so true, so pure, that he could surely never before have struck a ball so sweetly. 35 yards and a split-second later, the BBC goal of the season and the FA Cup goal of the century almost broke the net. A carpenter from Yorkshire had kick-started an act of legendary giant-killing, setting up Ricky for the moment that changed both the City of Hereford and its football club for ever. Newcastle were shell-shocked, Hereford's players finding energy from who knows where, and there was only one winner from that moment on. Extra-time was not half over when Ricky turned and struck a low shot toward goal. Whereas Ronnie's shot had screamed goalwards, Ricky's rolled toward the same corner of the same net in what seemed like slow motion. An eternity later, same result, and for the second time that afternoon, hundreds of delirious schoolboys cavorted over the Edgar Street mud.

We were the Parka Army.

Match of the Day cameras were present to capture Hereford's brave but ultimately futile attempt to upset the big boys, and the aforementioned junior reporter was expecting a shock-free afternoon. It was anything but. John Motson's first TV appearance became centre stage, as he described the biggest FA Cup upset of all time, and a goal by Radford of such quality that it is still shown before cup ties today. Hereford were into the 4th round, and four days later disappointed not to have delivered a similar shock to West Ham, who held on for a draw. Although the replay was lost to a Geoff Hurst hat-trick, Ronnie, Ricky, Hereford United, and Motty were in the news. Hereford's Southern League campaign continued, ultimately gaining second place. Backed by large, vocal crowds, a forward-looking board, and in Colin Addison a player-manager of huge ability and ambition, Hereford applied that spring to play with the big boys and join the ranks of full-time professional football.

In the days when the Football League was a scandalously closed shop, a vote by existing members was the only door left even slightly ajar, the Old Pals Act saving many a league club over the years, the ballot usually a formality. But not this time. The voting was perilously close, with Barrow polling equal nominations to Hereford.

A second ballot saw three chairmen belatedly respond to their conscience, and Hereford were elected to the Football League. Barrow chose the wrong year to finish bottom of the pile, and were consigned to the Northern Premier League.

Hereford United had just two months to prepare for League football, which they did without the man who made it all possible, Ricky George choosing to stay part-time. Even without Ricky, Hereford wasted little time in adapting to the higher grade of football. Driven onwards by Addison and chairman Frank Miles, things got better and better, and supporters were in dreamland as two promotions quickly followed the nail-biting election. Within four seasons of joining the Football League, Hereford United were in Division Two, now re-branded as The Championship.

I was thirteen years old, and truly believed that to support your local team was the guarantee of a carefree life, with no hint of the despair and misery that fans of rubbish teams routinely accept as their lot. Well, why should I? We were rubbing shoulders with Wolves, Blackburn and Chelsea, and pinching ourselves, as this was just too good to be true. Whilst it was without doubt true, it was also too good to last. As the chairman and manager moved on, the fall from grace was even more startling than the ascent. Successive relegations saw a return to the old fourth division in 1978, and there we stayed, for twenty years of mind-numbingly awful football.

We were, officially, crap.

Like many kids, my team was my first love, but like many others, the fan and the club parted, physically, if not emotionally. I left the city in 1984, but whilst the boy left Hereford, Hereford never left the boy, and I became a White in exile, finally settling in West London. Inevitably we drifted further apart, although we never, ever fell out. As one mediocre season followed another, my eyes would occasionally wander — QPR were handy, likewise Brentford — and even, WHISPER IT QUIETLY, occasionally, turning to the dark side, and egg-chasing at Harlequins. Was I a football tart, or just experimenting?

I don't know, but there was never the euphoria of victory or despair of defeat that I would experience with Hereford. These matches were sterile affairs, platonic relationships that were always harmless, sometimes enjoyable but ultimately, never really satisfying. I suppose something like a date with the vicar's daughter. Then, as now, watching football without the prospect of utter dejection at the end of it just wasn't the same.

My (very) foolish heart was always with Hereford.

Two decades of serial under-achievement had seen a deep-seated malaise embedded at Edgar Street. It seemed to me that the club was happy to have found its rightful place in football's hierarchy, plodding grimly along in the basement, winning nothing, indeed becoming its longest serving member. No mean feat, but you don't even get a sodding cup for that level of consistency. We did gain something in those forgotten years, even if it was only a new nickname, as the Whites slowly became the Bulls. How I don't know — the shirt had sported a bull's head for longer than I could remember — but no matter, I liked being a Bulls fan. And we now had a big, scary mascot, even if the team were far too often the polar opposite. There was a period of genuine excitement or, more honestly put, buttock-clenching trauma in the early eighties, when bankruptcy very nearly finished the club. Hereford survived by a whisker, only to once again become a forgotten team. Whilst occasionally threatening good things, the small town club played more and more like a village side, frequently flirting with relegation. It was perhaps only a matter of time, but in 1997, Hereford United flirted once too often. Twenty five years after League football had marched gloriously into Hereford, it was gone. The club was at its lowest point in three decades. Apathy in the boardroom and on the terraces mirrored on-field performances, and expulsion from the League was the result. An unprecedented and horribly traumatic final Saturday shoot-out saw Brighton survive and Hereford kicked out of the big boys' playground.

And if that alone wasn't bad enough, we were to enter the unknown territory of the GM Vauxhall Conference with debts that had gone way beyond a manageable level. A massive financial time-bomb was ticking louder and louder. If 1976 was my nirvana, this was my nadir as a Hereford fan, and not only mine. For Bulls supporters everywhere, a large part of their world had been damaged, perhaps beyond repair, many saying that they would walk away. My wife Sarah put that very question to me. Would I still follow the Bulls, now that they were in a rubbish league? Whilst tact isn't always her strongest suit, she already knew the answer. How could I turn away when my first love needed me, needed all of us, more than ever. So now the unthinkable had happened, back to Ricky George and my ruined life. My answer, when disaster struck at ten to five on 3rd May 1997, would have been a resounding 'Yes, he bloody well has'.

Six weeks later, I was probably over the trauma of that suicidal day as far as I ever will be, when our second child was born. It was perspective time, and there are many things more important than football (and by many, I actually mean almost none), but Sophie breezed into the world much as Lucy had done two years earlier. And as I had with Lucy, I hoped she would be a football fan, a Bulls fan. No, really, I did, but was too scared to check if there were laws against that degree of child abuse. It had been a miserable six weeks, but now life was fun again. I could deal with the Conference in August. No, Ricky, you didn't ruin my life. Not much, anyway. Bill Shankly could not have been more wrong when saying that football was more important than life or death, and great sound-bite that it is, I think he knew as much when he said it. It doesn't mean however, that football can't lift you gloriously, crazily up, or kick you again and again when you're down. Especially if you follow a rubbish team. Which is why football is more than just a sport. And why we love it.

What follows is the story of the next decade from the perspective of an exiled, but rejuvenated supporter.

It's not a comprehensive record, for whilst I was and still am a season-ticket holder, I have seen perhaps half of the games played in the ten years concerned, and probably more away from Edgar Street than at home. If you crave minutiae, and have to know every scorer, every assist, every sub and every card, this may not be a story for you. And you might be just a little bit of an anorak. It is, however, a tale with characters both noble and bizarre, locations palatial and decrepit, flirtation with disaster and glory, and more than the occasional moment of comedy, both intentional, and totally, side-splittingly accidental. And this isn't just the story of Hereford United, but also of the top tier of English non-league football over a decade of radical change. And believe it or not, some of the football was actually not utter crap. Welcome to the basement. Welcome to the Conference.

1 History Lesson

3/5/1997 - Brighton and Hove Albion. Home

Twenty years of football, most of it shockingly dull fare that could rarely
be classed as entertainment, had passed since the Bulls of Hereford took
residence in the old Fourth Division. Which is a lot of Saturdays. And to
think that I used to combine the lunch-hour and tea-break my weekend job
allowed and sprint through the city centre to Edgar Street, just to watch
another rubbish nil-nil against Rochdale. Most of my workmates thought I
was mad, but worse than that, some, and I could see it in their eyes, actually
felt sorry for me. Such is your life, if you're cursed with a useless football
team. Your lot is one of frustration, disappointment, resentment and pain,
but at least, and this is crucial, Hereford United played in the Football
League, and were a proper, if still resolutely crap side. Unlike Worcester
City, Kidderminster Harriers, and Cheltenham Town, all neighbours with
possibly quite good, but absolutely not *proper* teams. Until the final match of
the 1996/1997 season, when failure to beat Brighton would see us, and not
them, fall into the abyss known as the football pyramid. And yet it was just
twelve short months before this that the Bulls, in an uncharacteristic display
of near-competent football, made the League Three play-offs.

It was the mother and father of false dawns.

The Edgar Street board had sanctioned a budget for the type of player
that didn't belong in Hereford, and that Hereford couldn't afford, and the
gamble failed, if only just. Anyone capable of kicking a ball straight was
gone and normal service was resumed, but this time with bells on, leaving a
collective of talent even more modest than usual. So there we were, chugging
along near the bottom of the country's bottom division, and haemorrhaging
cash faster than a stag-weekend in Amsterdam. As the weeks ticked by and
the Brighton match loomed ever larger, somehow our form picked up, but
Brighton's picked up a little more. The shootout we had tried to ignore,

but somehow knew was coming (for this is Hereford, don't forget), had arrived, and it boiled down to this. Beat the Seagulls, or we're no longer a proper team. Twenty years of rubbish football I could cope with, even, in a masochistic sort of way, enjoy, but turning into Kidderminster Harriers was another matter. Here was a match made for that favourite cliché, a must-win game, but for Brighton, it was simply a mustn't-lose, because they had scored two more goals. Yes, it had come down to that. Two measly, pathetic little goals were probably going to relegate my team, and I just knew they were both bloody miles offside. Before the game previewed by one reporter as like going to a funeral with the twist of discovering who lies in the coffin only when proceedings have been completed, let me tell you about the main players in our little drama. Manager Graham Turner, a once quietly reliable lower-league player, but owner of a fine CV since hanging up his boots, looked after the team. Still revered at Shrewsbury and Wolves, and with a spell at Aston Villa to boot, experience like this didn't belong in Hereford. Even so, he struggled to coax enough points out of his hapless charges to survive. Upstairs was Peter Hill, local businessman and chairman of twenty years, each of which had seen our club drift closer to oblivion. Also managing director Robin Fry, lucky recipient of probably the biggest salary at ES, and so closely allied to Hill that the two may as well have been one. The experienced business brains of Robin and Peter had one or two crucial decisions to make over recent months, the biggest of which concerned our Edgar Street ground.

'We have no future at ES', they said. 'We have to move to survive', they added. 'We have to realise the value of this prime location, and move to an edge-of-town site, it's the only way', they said. And crucially, bearing in mind we were skint, this. 'We've accepted a large loan from the Bristol Stadiums Group.' What they didn't say was that the BSG had history. They had previously got their grubby hands on Eastville, then home to the Gasheads of Bristol Rovers. As a result, Rovers spent the next decade homeless, and Eastville became a furniture shop.

What Hill and Fry also 'forgot' to mention (fortunately, Talking Bull was a fanzine suffering no such memory lapse) was that the site considered favourite for the new stadium was optioned by a company whose directors *may* have had a conflict of interests. They were called Peter Hill and Robin Fry. No, you really couldn't make it up. And one more thing. Edgar Street was owned not by the football club but by the City Council, it being a gift to the people of Hereford generations previously, and subject to a covenant stating its use for *recreational purposes only*. Note the italics, this is important. In a nutshell, here were two men trying to sell something they didn't own to a party who couldn't give a toss for anything other than profit, said party itching to turn the place into another bloody Sainsbury's, clearly not a place of recreation. (Unless you're very, very sad.) Surely there are laws against that sort of thing.

Another gem from the Hill/Fry brains trust was to make the Brighton game all-ticket. Good decision, given a certain full-house. They then sent over a third of the tickets to Sussex, including a terrace usually occupied by Bulls fans. Excuse me, but just what the fuck were the custodians of our once proud football club playing at? Sure, we're only the supporters, only the sad cases who turn up week after week, only the fools who ultimately pay the wages of our flawed heroes, and only the people who time and again are treated like something on the bottom of a shoe. To say that Hill and Fry were not popular in Hereford was an understatement, but amongst the dwindling hard-core of Bulls support, unpopular barely scratched the surface. I and every Bulls fan I spoke to, the crap on the bottom of the shoe, despised the pair of them. All utterly depressing, but there remained a football match to be won, for surely it was better to be in hock to a ruthless developer as a proper club than the alternative. So to the match, where we hoped (and prayed) that the inspiration, perspiration and preparation needed for the right result would come from GT and our lads. On the first two we were fine, on the latter, oh dear, oh no, oh bollocks. Something, and only GT knows quite what, persuaded him to drop Trevor Wood, a trustworthy, reliable, *dependable* goalkeeper, and recall Andy deBont, a chubby, erratic, *accident-prone* netman, after three months on the sideline. It was a bizarre decision by the manager, and before a ball had been kicked we were a little nearer that coffin. And so began the near two hours of purgatory we had been dreading for weeks. Which started well. We were the better side, no really, we were. We had most of the ball, and crucially, deBont was almost a spectator. And then, after half an hour, we had a goal. Thirty minutes of foreplay was consummated in glorious fashion, as a Brighton defender put through his own net.

GET IN YOU BEAUTY!! Once again we were a proper club, only an hour of fingernail chewing to endure, our destiny in our own hands. Brighton showed little coming forward, we remained the better side, and still in control, but again remember, this is Hereford. With twenty minutes left, Andy deBont horribly scuffed a clearance straight to a Brighton forward,

3

and within seconds, we were again the 92nd best team in England. And so began the Brighton party that probably lasted the whole summer, Bulls top-scorer Adrian Foster (nickname — useless offside donkey) confirming our unproperness (sic) by missing an open goal in the last minute.

So that was it, goodbye Football League and hello Stalybridge Celtic, Leek Town, and get this, Rushden and Diamonds, surely a joke and not a football team. Was there a silver lining to this misery? A few small crumbs of comfort could be found, if you looked hard enough.

Robin Fry immediately resigned, citing the drastic cost-cutting the club would now have to endure. The fact there was no money to pay a small squad of useless footballers, let alone an over-salaried useless MD might have been behind his thinking. Whilst GT also offered his resignation, Peter Hill for once made the right decision in refusing it. GT would be unforgiven by many as the man who took the Bulls out of the Football League, but you didn't have to look too deeply to see where the real blame lay. As endorsed by HUISA, our fledgling independent supporters' association, who swiftly offered GT their full support whilst giving no such commitment to Hill or what remained of his board. HUISA, under the stewardship of GFB (German Fat Bastard if you must know), a self-confessed pie-eating fat-bloke, would have a large part to play in the survival or otherwise of this ailing football club. And most surprisingly, much of the small amount of what passed for quality in the squad remained for our battles in the pyramid, along with Andy deBont, although I doubt that lucrative offers of employment were falling through the letterboxes of our fallible footballers. So realistically, what were our chances of bouncing straight back? Whilst you have to hope, the answer was pretty slim. Whilst this playground belonged to Children of a Lesser God, many of these kids were on considerably more money as part-timers than our still full-time professionals. If money does indeed talk, you can bet your life that it talks loudest to footballers. Survival would be the new name of our game.

2   1997-1998 On Loan to the Conference

16/8/97 Welling United - home

So here it is, the Conference, and here also are Welling United, formed in 1963, and a club as old as I am. A club to have graced the Greater London League, the Spartan, Athenian and Southern Leagues, and the GM Vauxhall Conference. Never heard of any of them. Our side, however, has a balanced look, pre-season has been good, and more than 3,000 Bulls fans are inside ES, a figure bettered only once last season. No prizes for guessing when. Unsurprisingly, our financial problems hadn't gone away, and with rumours of unpaid players, outstanding loans, and an ever-growing overdraft, already the outlook was bleak. Rushden and Diamonds, confirmed as a real (as opposed to a proper) football team, had helped, rashly donating £30,000 in exchange for Donkey Foster, the villain who could and should have become a cult hero against Brighton. Which was, however, small beer in comparison to the £500,000 owed to the Bristol Stadiums Group, full repayment due in two years should our new ground not materialise. Hereford United were ailing and likely to get worse, even critical, before getting any better. And would you believe it, our recently departed MD had offered his consultancy services to oversee our supposedly essential relocation. Yes, Robin 'I have a Dream' Fry was still fixated on the edge-of-town site that would save the club. Keep that man away from ES. Depressing finances notwithstanding, there was a surprisingly upbeat feel among supporters, with one optimistic, if a little cheeky, soul selling 'Hereford United on Loan to the Conference' T-shirts. Enough reasons to be hopeful, but then, if you can't be positive before a ball has been kicked in anger, just when can you, even if you're a Bulls fan? As for Welling, theirs was merely a supporting role, as Hereford took their first step towards regaining a seat at the big table, and were sure to fold under the pressure of a stadium, crowd and opponent of far greater size and status than they were used to. Of course, it wasn't like that, not even close, and as the two sides lined up, one thing stood out. Welling had a pair of central defenders that could have been chiselled from stone. They were big, and very scary. The full-backs were of the same stock, perhaps even the same family, identikit bruisers surely earning a living in the security business. Theirs was a doorman's convention, their expressions delivering a clear message. 'You're not coming in son, now piss off while you can still walk.'

I was surely seeing things, for realistically, how could a back four appear so intimidating and still possess sufficient co-ordination to even occasionally, connect foot with ball? We would soon find out, as Conference football was on show for the first time at Edgar Street.

To the surprise of some, there wasn't the gulf in class many had expected between the Third Division fare of last season and the Conference variety of this, and whilst Hereford showed a little more quality, our supposedly inferior opponents were no mugs, even if a little lacking in adventure. Passes were finding team-mates, a pattern of sorts was developing, and chances were created, though none clear-cut. Whilst the artistes (and that's relatively speaking) of the Welsh borders slowly gained control, the artisans of North Kent held firm. Hereford searched for an opening Conference goal, but the four doormen of the apocalypse were having none of it, greater finesse and experience getting nowhere against organised and highly motivated opponents. It was the type of game, and we've all seen many, where the first goal was vital, and it came courtesy of Welling Security Services. No co-ordination problems there, it appeared. Unsurprisingly, a goalkeeping error saw Andy deBont picking the ball out of his net, having been a virtual spectator up to that point, and as in his last game at ES, fingers were pointing at our netman. The Bulls' increased urgency was matched by the visitors, their confidence growing visibly, and when the second goal came, it was again deBont who stooped to retrieve. Another howler, and not for the first time I wondered just what our rotund custodian was doing alongside men who made something close to a living from the game. Whilst deBont was having a 'mare, Welling's afternoon could be summed up thus. Two shots, two goals, two nil, and even the hardy few on the visitors terrace seemed too stunned to gloat. The optimism around the ground before kick-off had dissipated, and just an hour into the new season, the despair of the old one was back. It was disastrous, even embarrassing. As the final whistle blew, the Welling players were dancing a lap of honour, firstly to their manager, then to their supporters, each and every one getting a bear-hug of joy. It was as though they had won the double, right there and then, such was the delight on display. But was it so surprising, and was this their biggest game of the season, their cup-final, an opportunity to strike a blow for the little clubs? Of course not. Although arriving from different directions, Hereford and Welling were equals on the pitch, but it later transpired just why Welling were so jubilant. In a piece of motivational genius, manager Kevin Hales had delivered a succinct but devastatingly effective pre-match team-talk. 'Get out there, and show them' was his call to battle. He said it whilst pointing at a T-shirt pinned to the dressing-room wall. It said, 'Hereford United - On Loan to the Conference'. Seven little words, and twelve pounds wisely spent by a manager who, on the day, got it absolutely right. Whilst Welling partied their way back to Kent, Bulls fans were asking themselves this. Just how long would we be on loan to the Conference?

Tell Me That's Not a Woman
23/8/97 Farnborough Town - away

Following the Welling debacle, Hereford collected their first non-league point at Hednesford Town. Another from the list of 'Who are they, where is that?' clubs that the Conference has in abundance, and a note here to any supporter of a 'big' or 'proper' club underwhelmed at the prospect of a trip to Port Vale or Northampton. Try Hednesford, and see how you like that. Little to report, apart from the return of goalkeeper Chris 'not Andy deBont' Mackenzie after a year on the injury list, and a first goal for summer signing Neil Grayson.

So to Cherrywood Road Farnborough, a ground hiding within a dozen or more eerily deserted avenues. It was a vista of low-rise plainness, the visitors' terrace six crumbling and neglected concrete steps. OK, it was small and scruffy, but Cherrywood Road had certain charm, centred around the benefit of a social club only twenty yards from the away terrace, and with a door policy that put Farnborough immediately at the top of my list of favourite unproper grounds. Maybe the reputation of Hereford's more boisterous following was yet to reach Hampshire, because the rare experience of a decent pint before, after, and amazingly, during the match was enjoyed. Surprising, but true, as a quiet word with the gateman, more in hope than expectation, allowed a half-time freshener as welcome as it was unexpected on a scorching day. And as good as his word, there he was at four o'clock to usher the lucky few back into the ground.

And how fared our brave athletes? Moderate at best, was the answer. Whilst Farnborough comfortably out-crapped (they weren't that good) Hereford, little was created in front of goal. HUISA Chairman GFB, not easily missed in the crowd of 250 Bulls fans, was taking out his frustration on any piece of terrace debris within range of his size tens when the first piece of near adequacy saw the Bulls ahead. A slick three man move ended with Fishlock heading home a picture goal the match didn't deserve. Grayson followed up with a tap-in second, and the Bulls had their first Conference victory. The win was soured late on by two random and pernickety yellow cards, administered by a referee who, up to that point, had been quietly efficient.

Wendy Toms, a trail-blazer for officials of the fairer sex, and in her second Conference season, obviously had a quota to fill, but in proving the point that referees don't have a monopoly on visual shortcomings, a perplexed Bulls fan shouted 'Tell me that's not a woman.'

It was the 86th minute, and he obviously couldn't believe what he thought he had just seen. To describe Herefordians as parochial may have been reasonable in the not too distant past, but now we were busily embracing the world outside the Shire. Or at least, most of us were. It's also probably a good thing that he didn't spy our rotund reserve keeper, his flowing locks held in check by an Alice band. The consequences for his blood pressure might have been a final, fatal straw. Andy, you're neither good enough nor pretty enough to get away with a bloody hair-band, sort it out. Whilst the occasional 'Not in my day' was muttered, the match quietly drew to a close, as, after a few sniggered requests to blow the bloody thing, Wendy obliged. We had our first win, which, whilst deserved, had been a struggle, unlike that of England's cricketers as back in the bar another pint saw a three day win over Australia completed. The Ashes victory, whilst welcome, was ultimately pointless, with the series already lost. Would the points gained by the Bulls earlier in the afternoon count for anything in the long run?

Time would tell, but it wasn't the worst Saturday afternoon I've ever had.

Dead Hand on the Wheel
25/8/97 - 2/9/97 Cheltenham(h), Stevenage(h), Leek(a)
Nine days, three matches, sublime and ridiculous. The sublime in the shape of a gritty centre-forward who runs his socks off for 90 minutes, is kicked all over the park by frustrated camels, whilst banging in goals from every

8

angle when all hope appears lost. Stand up Neil Grayson. Two cracking strikes in a 3-2 win over local rivals and serially unproper Cheltenham saw an undeserved win, and fourth place in the Conference. The ridiculous came in the shape of yet more comedy defending by our allegedly experienced back line. Having got away with it against Cheltenham, Hereford were clinically punished for it against Stevenage, 0-2, at home. This was followed by mere embarrassment rather than humiliation at Leek Town, scraping a 2-2 draw, again courtesy Grayson. The draw at Leek was the hardest to accept, for here was a bona fide village green side and also newcomers to the Conference, begging the question of just how crap the rest of last year's Unibond League must have been. Hereford could and indeed should have lost the game, with Chris Mackenzie giving a capable impression of the hapless deBont between the sticks. It was clear that if the keeper and defence didn't shape up quickly, the Bulls would soon be out of range of leaders Halifax, already looking a formidable unit. With on-field shortcomings all too visible, off-field problems, whilst less obvious, were mounting at an alarming rate. Rumours again surfaced of unpaid wages for the manager, players, even the office staff, and just four weeks into the season Hereford United were, apparently, penniless. Questions were being asked, led vociferously by HUISA and Talking Bull. If the club was failing as badly as it appeared to be, something had to change, before it was too late. All we got from Peter Hill, however, was the ever more sceptically received wittering about a soon-to-be-condemned Edgar Street, a shiny new stadium our only chance of salvation. With Robin Fry supposedly gone, it was a different singer but the same old song. I suspect our chairman hadn't been attending many games, because two glaringly obvious facts appeared to have escaped his notice. Firstly, inconsistency on the pitch had already put us well off the pace in terms of regaining our league status, and with it, the ability to access the necessary grants and funding for the 10,000 seat stadium we were rarely likely to even quarter fill. Secondly, that ES, although a little tired in places, was palatial in comparison to the homes of many of our counterparts in the Conference. The vast majority of Bulls fans could see that urgent action was needed, starting at the very top. Peter Hill had guided the club through twenty years of mediocrity and worse. He had overseen on-pitch failure, and off-pitch catastrophe. He had led us out of the Football League and into a sea of debt that was beginning to look terminal. He was, as eloquently opined in Talking Bull, a dead hand on the wheel.

So Who Are You Here To Watch?
6/9/97 Hayes Town - away

Another short trip for the south-east exiles, and a match moved to a Friday night due to the funeral of Princess Diana the following day. It was a short but surreal journey past countless groups of people walking toward central London, nearly all carrying flowers. Just a few of the millions who would pack the funeral route, all were ready for a night under the stars so they could say goodbye. I was struck by the scale of this collective demonstration of grief, for whilst a tragic loss, few of the London-bound mourners would ever have met the Princess. Far be it for me, however, to question the motives of the grieving masses, when the motives of the 150 Bulls fans inside the Church Road ground were arguably far more open to question. If the mourners were perhaps slightly out of touch, then we, clearly, were completely insane.

Here was a recurring theme for fans of crap teams everywhere. Why do we turn up week after week to witness what will often be the most dire fare, all too frequently ending in disappointment? Having suffered countless times previously, we know what's coming, so just why do we do it? Simply put, it has to be a case of the heart ruling the head. With so much emotional investment, be it over two years or twenty-two, your team becomes a part of you, whilst you in turn become a small part of that team, or at least the community surrounding it.

It's hard to explain why the attachment is so deep, but in so many of us it just is. Men who change cars, jobs, houses, even wives, sometimes without a second thought, are appalled at the thought of changing clubs. To every genuine supporter out there, it simply isn't possible.

Certainly, the less than fanatical may find their passion periodically dipping. There are, after all, other distractions. I hold up my hands, guilty in the past of turning my back on the Bulls. Test Matches, Rugby Internationals, even golf (curse me for ever with V-neck sweaters) have taken me away from the Bulls, although it was a small part of heaven on earth called Loch Lomond. But I'm not a true fanatic. That said, I could never, ever change clubs, and whenever I was elsewhere, part of me was with the Bulls, wherever they were.

But back to Hayes, and a swift pint in the Les Ferdinand Suite. Yes, the spring-heeled striker of QPR and England started right here, and Hayes had built a bar with his transfer fee. Fine player, good idea, and no, the Andy deBont Lounge isn't a likely addition to Edgar Street in the near future. Or ever. And the match itself? Subdued, unsurprisingly, given the mood of the country, let alone that of the Bulls fans. Hereford didn't start well, but before the inevitable happened, I received a nudge from Justin, once again suffering with me. 'Look to your left,' he said. I did, and standing there was a familiar face, at least to a football fan in his thirties.

The name was Bonds. Billy Bonds. Licence to Scout. Obviously here on behalf of West Ham. I couldn't resist. 'Who are you here to watch then?'

Billy was having none of it. 'One or two worth a look, mate', he replied, poker-faced.

Not one of ours, that was for sure. Within twenty minutes, the object of Billy's attention was obvious. Aided yet again by comedy defending, the Bulls were two down, and being outfought by a part-time team. Two poor sides were separated by the opportunist finishing of the one player who stood out head and shoulders above the rest. At Conference level the combination of pace, close control and an eye for goal are rare and precious, and Jason Roberts had the lot, along with two sweetly taken goals. By half-time Billy had seen enough and in all honesty, so had we. The second period was no better and the calls to sack the board had begun at the same moment any realistic hope of promotion ended. It was our third defeat in seven matches, and added to a pair of scratchy draws, it appeared there was little hope of a swift return to the Football League. It was a depressing start to a depressing weekend. As Princess Diana was laid to rest watched by millions, our season went the same way, watched by 974 spectators, all just a little bit insane, and at least one scout.

And did Billy get his man? No, he didn't. Wolves were either quicker or more generous, and within weeks Jason Roberts had said goodbye to the Conference and hello to some proper footballers.

A Horse's Tale, part one
25/10/97 Sittingbourne - away. FA Cup 4th qualifying round
One of many drawbacks found in the pyramid is in the FA Cup, where the unproper (that's how it feels, like unclean, or undead) have to qualify for the privilege of a trip to, say, Scunthorpe, or Lincoln. So where, you might ask, is the romance in that? Sittingbourne, of the Beazer Homes League, would tell you, for it is they who came out of the velvet bag just before Hereford. With a chance to slay the ultimate giant-killers, Sittingbourne had the tie they wanted. GT certainly did not. It was tough for the Bulls, desperately needing a good cup-run merely to postpone the financial meltdown coming closer

with each week. A decent month on the pitch contrasted with yet more off-field problems and ironically, Hereford's best form of the season had come at a time of enormous uncertainty. More and more supporters had had enough of Peter Hill and his board, and a HUISA-organised demonstration took place outside ES after a draw with Southport. It was encouragingly replayed on local news, heavily featuring United's very own, and it should be stressed, unofficial chantologist, 'Talking Bill' Thomas. Bill is a man with a song for every occasion, and on this one he turned it up to eleven. Peter Hill had recently labelled HUISA as 'not real fans', but even he couldn't fail to recognise the anger felt by Bulls supporters, real or otherwise. HUISA vowed to keep the pressure on Hill and his board, feeling that no change at the top would see the end of the football club, and sooner rather than later. A little respite was needed, perhaps from the FA Cup, and it was maps out again, to North Kent and Sittingbourne, home of the Brickies. This was really a game United should win, with the hosts struggling, and the Bulls finally starting to show some consistency, but we had been here before. Or at least to Hitchin, Bath, and Wealdstone, all lower-league part-timers who had humiliated Hereford in the recent past. This was categorically not the time to be victims. Defeat could have fatal consequences, and we knew it. We could only hope that the same message had reached the players. The Bulls started well, a Fishlock goal giving a deserved lead. One up and in control, the point when things usually start to go wrong. Not today, not yet anyway, as half-time arrived, bringing with it the supporters' coach, and fifty-odd very pissed-off Bulls fans. The story? A horse had become separated from its box on the M4, coming to a sticky end in the middle lane just in front of our unfortunate travellers, resulting in six hours on a coach to watch 45 minutes of football. There were probably better ways of spending your Saturday, but at least the lads were doing it out there on the pitch. Note the past tense. The horse-jacked supporters didn't bring any luck, as Trevor Matthewson headed a glorious equaliser. An interesting character, Trevor, a half-decent central defender who combined a fruit and veg business with being a non-league footballer. Not unusual, you might think, for a Beazer Homes Leaguer to mix and match careers, but Trev was ours, one of Hereford's finest. Whilst Trevor's first goal of the season had been overdue, the greengrocer had nodded the ball into the wrong onion bag. Ten minutes later, another deBont mishap saw the Bulls go behind. To be fair to Andy, it was his first real howler for two months but to be honest, he had only played in one of the last thirteen games. This was now deadly

12

serious, with more than just a cup tie on the line, and the next fifteen minutes would have a huge impact on the club in the coming weeks. No cup run for the Bulls would be a disaster, the missing revenue perhaps signalling the end of Hereford United. There was a mounting sense of panic on the terraces when an unlikely hero emerged, as substitute Gary Cook, spotted more frequently in night-clubs than football grounds, hammered an equaliser. Had GT, notoriously reluctant in his use of subs, got a vital decision right, or was the god of football smiling on Hereford for a change? I neither knew nor cared. Cook had scored. Relief more than joy greeted the final whistle, we were still in the tie, and still alive. So once again the question, was there any romance left in the FA Cup?

Oh yes. At 5.15 that afternoon, the draw for the first round was made, and this is what the suddenly romantic car-radio said. Sittingbourne or Hereford United will play.........Brighton and Hove Albion. Of all the teams, and there were 95 of them, Brighton were the ones. Less than six months after the darkest of days back in May, an opportunity for at least a small measure of revenge was presented to the Bulls. Great news for Hereford, but not so good for Sittingbourne, for there was now not a chance of them being allowed to poop our first round party, not with the despised Seagulls waiting.

Simple Minds - Promised You a Miracle
1/11/97 Morecambe - away

In the unglamorous depths of the Conference, celebrity fans are few and far between. Whilst punk violinist Nigel Kennedy has been spotted at ES, as a Villa fan we can't claim him, even if we wanted to. And we don't. Someone we do have, however, is Stan Tippins. What do you mean, never heard of him? Stan was once road-manager for glam-rockers Mott The Hoople, the City's biggest (please tell me you've heard of the Mott) influence on the music scene of the 70s. A Bull through and through, Stan was doing as much as anyone to raise desperately needed funds for the club. At a time when finding the money for the team bus had become a weekly challenge, HUISA, Stan and many others were organising auctions and race-nights, golf days and quizzes, bailing out the club on more than one occasion. And if it wasn't hard cash raised, then it was profile, with a United shirt appearing on Top of the Pops, courtesy of rock legends Simple Minds, and of course, Stan Tippins. However, amongst the famous and probably infamous celebrities enrolled into HUISA by Stan, he managed a little gem, when Debbie Harry modelled a Hereford shirt in the pages of Talking Bull. Yes, that Debbie Harry, one time Playboy model and iconic lead singer of Blondie, happily posed in the red and black quarters of our away strip, doing her bit to raise the profile of a team she had never seen and played in a league she had never heard of. Good on you, Stan.

So whilst the dedicated few were fighting to keep the club alive, and one or two Bulls fans of a certain age were reflecting on a dream come true, albeit twenty years late, what of Hill and his board? Sadly not a Baywatch Babes in Bulls Shirts calendar, but a staggeringly ill-conceived venture which served only to distance them still further from reality. They launched The Bulls 1,100 Club, the essence of which was this. 1,100 shares in a limited company would be sold to fans at £250 each. The company would then loan £250,000 to the football club, in return for a seat on the board, and 10 per cent of any profit made when ES was sold and developed. Someone remind me what 10 per cent of fuck-all is. Still tempted? Added to which, a place on the board would be a token gesture, with Hill still the major shareholder, vetoing any issue not to his liking. And has he once again forgotten who owns the freehold to ES? Did Hill and his cronies really expect people to hand over their cash to a board that had so mismanaged affairs that bankruptcy was looking ever more likely? Given also that workers in Herefordshire are amongst the lowest paid in the country, and had witnessed close-up the fiscal skills of Mr. Hill, it was asking a lot. The Bulls 1,100 Club was a dead duck, and HUISA vehemently rejected support for what they termed a failed regime, even without which it would have been extraordinary for even a handful of these shares to have been bought. We hadn't been, in the words of Stan's rock and roll friends, promised a miracle, but an investment opportunity with no chance of seeing a penny in return, truly a scheme concocted by the most simple of minds. The board had yet again demonstrated how far out of touch they were with genuine fans. If Mr. Hill was answerable to shareholders rather than to his own conscience, he would have gone a long time ago. Wishful thinking. The good news was that the protests against the board were becoming louder and more frequent, the question now being, just how thick a skin did Peter Hill have?

Oh, and Morecambe away? One of the smartest sides in the Conference, especially on their own patch, and the Bulls without the prolific Grayson, it was going to be tough to get anything up there. As things transpired it was a rout, a five-goal demolition with the sides looking at least three divisions apart. Amazingly, it was Hereford who hit five, on-loan striker Andy Milner grabbing a hat-trick, and the newest of Bulls legends, one Gary Cook, again scoring as a late substitute. It was total football of the highest quality, or put another way, not the usual crap, and boy, did we enjoy it. 'It's just like watching Brazil' is usually sung with a hint of irony, but not this time, as the Bulls tore Morecambe apart with a performance that made you wonder quite what happened at Hayes and Leek. Whilst without doubt highlight of the season thus far, it earned only the regulation three points, good enough to hold on to eighth place, but it was Halifax who were attracting rave reviews, and our next away trip. Before which, the small matter of some nasty seagulls to deal with.

Best Served Cold
15/11/97 Brighton - home. FA Cup 1st round

As predicted, Sittingbourne were comfortably despatched back to Kent. Brighton were coming, and there was no doubt how much this game meant. Football throws up many coincidences, but few Bulls fans imagined that a chance for revenge would arrive so soon, and almost everyone present on May 3rd was back at Edgar Street for this opportunity to bury, at least partially, the memory of that dreadful day. Of the players, only Brian McGorry and one other were in a position to heal some not-so-old wounds out there on the pitch, the significant other being a man who would have a nightmarish memories of the day Hereford lost its status as a proper club. Yes, it was he of the scuffed, disastrous clearance, Andy deBont. Andy was back in the side, as Andy Quy, recently signed (of course on a free) to bring some much needed quality between the sticks, was cup-tied. On the upside however, Grayson was back, after a month out injured. Was a deBont in goal worth a Grayson in attack? Probably not. The absence of deBont had seen a far happier goals-against column, but in marked contrast to the previous meeting, United fans were this time, confident. Brighton were struggling in division three, unsurprising as their temporary home was in Gillingham, the Goldstone Ground a building site. Another team might have engendered some sympathy, for this was a nightmare for the fans who had worked so hard to keep the club alive. Several thousand Seagulls were enduring a season where every match was away from home, and were a credit both to themselves and the club they loved, but this was Brighton. Grudging respect was the best I could offer, but no room for sympathy. We wanted revenge and had, I thought, a great chance of getting it. Brighton fielded seven of their great-escape eleven but, this time there would be no after-match party. Much as on May 3rd, Hereford dominated, and again struck first, Grayson, who else, doing the damage. Again Brighton equalised, once more against the run of play. Then, horror of horrors, a Brighton penalty. Same end, same keeper, different result, as the fabulous and agile deBont pulled off a fingertip save, and within minutes the Bulls were ahead and cruising. Two-one didn't flatter Hereford, the thoroughly deserved win all the sweeter for the identity of the victims. Whilst revenge is supposedly a dish best served cold, today the temperature was unimportant. Hot, cold or lukewarm, it tasted bloody great. The afternoon was wrapped up by another HUISA demonstration, this time a sit-in on the Meadow End terrace. Credit to GFB and his band, they were showing no intention of allowing Peter Hill to let the club fade quietly away. Later that evening, what should have been a bonus was delivered. Courtesy of Match of The Day, we could see it all again, a treat rarely granted to the unproper. As I say, should have been. Whilst Grayson again struck clinically, and deBont grew from zero to hero, the viewing experience was soured by the verbal diarrhoea of a man called Hill. Surprisingly enough, not Peter, but his namesake Jimmy, adeptly stepping into the role of Public Enemy No.1, at least in the eyes of Bulls fans. Jimmy's expert analysis was a condescending diatribe, rubbishing everything about our performance that afternoon. We were lucky, the penalty a poor decision, Brighton had an off-day, and victory was scant consolation for losing our League status. Our man of the match was referred to as 'that little man', or by way of variation, 'that little man again'. Wrong on every count bar one, wise pundit. Having seen enough dire performances from the Bulls to recognise another, I can tell you that today Hereford were worthy winners. The penalty was a correct decision according to no less an authority than the man who conceded it. Brighton had an 'off-day' because we didn't allow them to play, and the only luck was that which saved the Seagulls from a hiding. And that little man has a name, Ian Foster, there in the programme Jimmy, if you'd bothered to read it. There was clearly something about Hereford that Jimmy Hill didn't like, and he made little effort to conceal his disdain. Fortunately, anyone with even a passing knowledge of the game saw him for what he was that evening. A grumpy and bitter man who let an undisclosed agenda divert him from his brief. Or as one unnamed friend put it, a sad chinny old twat. What he did get it right was that our victory, though cherished, was indeed scant consolation for what happened on May 3rd. Scant, maybe, but boy, did we enjoy it.

'If they could have picked him up, they would have chaired him off'
6/12/97 and 16/12/97
Colchester United - home and away - FA Cup 2ⁿᵈ round

Too many trips to Colchester in those halcyon (who am I trying to kid?) days of proper football had ended with nothing to show for them, and it was there we would travel in round two. Layer Road is a ground which wouldn't look out of place in the Conference, hovel being a flattering description, and for a while the football on display was on a par with the surroundings. Hereford were, however, matching their higher-graded opponents, and looking surprisingly secure at the back. Which, inevitably, is when something goes wrong. Equally often, it's an old boy coming back to bite the hand that once fed him, former Bull David Gregory, now a yard quicker and considerably lighter, shooting past deBont, on this occasion blameless. The Bulls were looking at a Cup exit that could again have damaging consequences, until Neil Grayson bought some precious breathing space with a sweetly executed free kick. It was a routine worked on at the luxurious FA centre of excellence in Lilleshall, an excursion enjoyed by the players but funded by HUISA. With at the very least a replay to enjoy, it was money well spent, but yet another indication of the dire position the club was in.

The return at ES was without doubt the coldest I have ever been at a football match, but the hardy souls who braved the elements were richly rewarded. A hard-fought 1-1 draw saw extra-time, the Bulls equaliser coming from the usual source. It was now seven goals in as many games for Grayson, and quite where we would be without him didn't bear thinking about. Another thirty minutes wasn't what the fans or players would have wished for, as frostbite became a genuine possibility, but Andy deBont was showing few signs of discomfort in a display which warmed the soul, if not the extremities. Perhaps his extra insulation was proving useful, but at a time when the brass monkeys had long since retreated, Andy was assured and steady, and as penalties approached, was again the focus of our FA Cup hopes. The temperature was now beyond cruel, and many fans had left ES, feeling that if they stayed any longer, they might not be able to move, even if they wanted to. The slow death of penalty kicks began with eight conversions, incredible given the conditions and pressure. The ninth kick was saved, and the fabulously gifted deBont was Hereford's hero once again. One more spot-kick and we could begin to thaw out. It was scored, and each of Warner, Hargreaves, Walker, McGorry, and of course Grayson had done their bit to see the Bulls home. As for Andy deBont, he was becoming an enigma. Erratic, disaster-prone, and hardly svelte, he had twice performed FA Cup heroics, and done more than his bit in keeping the club afloat at a perilous time. Fair play to Andy, for whilst he undoubtedly owed us, he had again paid a little bit back.

As the players and supporters slowly thawed, I felt a tug of sympathy for the hundred or so visiting fans beginning their trek back to Essex. They had come a long way, probably taking time off work to do so, and had seen their team crash out of the Cup in the cruellest fashion. They had been colder than should be allowed in a civilised world, and by the time they got home, it wouldn't be worth going to bed. All told, this particular Tuesday evening had probably ruined their whole week. I wonder if players realise just how much investment is made by the fans in their team? Let's just say that if they didn't on a night like this, they never would. A few weeks later, the next issue of Talking Bull featured the mercurial deBont, big and bold, on its front cover. Beneath his beaming smile were the words 'If they could have picked him up, they would have chaired him off.'

Well done Andy, you chubby, useless genius of a goalkeeper.

I Can't Wait For This Season To End
7/2/98 Slough Town - away

Since the sub-zero heroics against Colchester, performances had been mixed, but mostly crap. Humiliation aplenty away from ES, with defeats at Welling, Stevenage, and Slough, where the Bulls managed just one shot on target. Not just Slough, but all three matches combined. Unacceptable on each occasion, being either out-thought, out-muscled, or both. To label these sides pub teams, as many had done, bordered on the insulting, but to be embarrassed three times in succession by part-timers was testing the most phlegmatic of Bulls fans. Contrast this with a Christmas double over neighbours Kidderminster Harriers, including a hangover defying 4-1 victory at Aggborough, where the players for once gave a five-star display just when it was needed. Another hat-trick away from home, and again it was a loan player who obliged. Thanks Richard Leadbeater, Happy New Year to you. There was a rumour (unsubstantiated) that a conversation (unconfirmed) might (possibly) have taken place after the game between GT and Richard, that went something like this.

GT - Fine hat-trick there Ledders, fancy a contract?

RL - Yeah, great, when can I start?

18

GT - Tomorrow OK?

RL - Fantastic.

GT - Good. We're strapped for cash at the moment, wages might not be what you're used to.

RL - No problem to me Boss, the football is more important.

GT - Good. See you Monday then.

RL - Ok. Uh, Boss, how much *can* you afford?

GT - Not much, I'm afraid. Nothing ,in fact. Would you play for free?

RL - Oh. Can I get back to you.

Unlikely, but all too plausible. Fortunately, we would see more of Leadbeater in the months to come, although he was unable to prevent an FA Cup exit at the hands of Tranmere. No real surprise here. To slay the giant for a third time in as many months was asking too much, although a 7,000 crowd provided more much-needed revenue. With the FA Cup now a memory, and the Conference title long since conceded, the FA Trophy was the remaining crumb of comfort on offer. The draw had been kind, and Dulwich Hamlet (uncomfortably close to a pub team) were despatched, bringing Dover Athletic to ES in round two. Beat them, and Wembley would be three matches away, a treat yet to be enjoyed by Hereford supporters. Having shown that we were, on our day, the equal of anyone in this league, hopes were now of a cup-final to round off our first season as a non-league team. We were equally aware that also, on our day, we could capitulate to the most ordinary of sides. No surprises (for this is Hereford), when on the last day of January Dr. Jekyll was elsewhere, and Mr. Hyde came to ES. It was a shameful display, and a two-nil defeat signalled the end of meaningful football for the campaign, unless of course we slipped far enough to contemplate a second successive relegation. Many more performances like that one and it would be all too real a prospect.

So with the season imploding around us, was there anything to look forward to? Clearly GT and physiotherapist Simon Shakeshaft weren't throwing in the towel. Between them, and with a little help from elsewhere, they had assembled enough football memorabilia to stage an auction, raising more than £10,000, probably enough to keep the bank manager at bay for another month. Meanwhile, the board declared the Bulls 1100 Club a failed venture, to the surprise of no-one but themselves. Despite his continued failure to take the club forward, a recently revealed achievement by our esteemed chairman came to light. Hereford United were, according to a proper club, in a league of their own when hosting their boardroom chums from around the country. All well and good, but who picked up the tab for this Premier League hospitality? Whilst the story may have been a little mischief-making, it echoed what I had been told by a former employee of the club, and many fans had heard the same. The vision of Peter Hill gently sipping Chianti with his mates whilst supporters paid for a week of decent training facilities was too painful to contemplate. He had to go, and soon. I only hope that the money raised by Shakey, GT and HUISA was kept a suitably large distance away from Hill and his cohorts, for if the only thing Hereford United could win was a Michelin Star for Boardroom Hospitality, then it might just be time to devote a few more Saturdays to gardening. And I really, *really* hate gardening.

So, to Slough, and the Rebels, a near neighbour of both Windsor and Eton, but a million miles away from both. Slough is a charmless urban sprawl, a grey town which, like United's dismal January form, seemed to go on forever. The fixture had minimal appeal, with both teams mid-table and likely to finish so, and here was the biggest problem facing the Conference. With only one promotion slot, by Christmas there was no real interest for teams safe from relegation but not placed to make a title challenge. Whether you love or loathe them, play-offs keep a season alive for upwards of ten teams and dramatically reduce the amount of dead fixtures. For you fans of proper clubs out there who don't like them, try a season without. You might not like that much, either. As for Slough Town, they were enjoying a second Conference season, a good example of a club surviving on limited resources and holding their own against sides with considerably more support and spending power. Slough were organised, committed, and unusually in this league, didn't put the ball into orbit at every opportunity. That said, if there was any flair on display, I must have missed it. Whilst the game itself could be described as dour, the Bulls' performance was closer to dire. Our first shot on target came as the ref was checking his watch, Slough already three goals to the good. There must be something about Hereford United and gritty part-timers, because we were coming out second-best too bloody often.There was for me, however, an unexpected bonus, as I was greeted by chantologist Talking Bill Thomas. It isn't often supporters get paid to watch their team, but today was one. I had entered a predictions quiz organised by Bill earlier in the year, and had somehow conjured the most correct guesses. My two pound entry had grown to fifty, and the now weekly ritual of drowning the sorrows in alcohol would be subsidised. I enquired of Bill, one of our more cerebral, if slightly insane (yes, you can be both) fans, how he saw the remainder of this campaign. Normally one of life's optimists, Bill's glass was today, half-empty.

'I can't wait for this season to end', he said. No singing today from our loudest if not most tuneful vocalist. Whilst Slough were the deserved winners on the day, they suffered their heaviest defeat, probably heaviest ever defeat, at the end of the season, and one not due to an under-par performance or goalkeeping mishap. Having finished in a creditable eighth place, Slough Town were expelled from the highest league they had ever graced due to problems over the leasehold status of their Wexham Park ground. I felt for them. To battle away for 42 matches, only to have it all rendered meaningless by some suits around a table, was clearly a scandal, yet it attracted perhaps one percent of the coverage accorded to David Beckham's latest haircut. Things weren't to get any better for the Rebels. The club were made homeless, and now grace the Ryman League, two rungs below their rightful place in the unproper pyramid. Whilst the Ryman is a semi-professional league, there are big differences, not least the fact that gates rarely creep over 400 and are often closer to the proverbial one man and his dog. I hope that the Rebels find the spirit to fight back. They certainly deserve to.

Crisis, what Crisis?
10/2/98 - 13/4/98 More Unproper Teams - home and away
62 days, during which United played 13 matches, winning 8 and drawing 5. Which makes no defeats. 18 goals scored, 7 conceded, including 6 consecutive clean-sheets. And no, Mr. Mercurial wasn't in goal. Comfortably the best and most consistent form shown all season, and achieved without Neil Grayson, sold to Cheltenham for an insulting £20,000, GT having 'no option' due to an unpaid utility bill. It was apparently a case of managing without our star striker or without electricity, and, if one were needed, another painful reminder of how precarious a situation the club was in. It was painful to see one of our few remaining assets almost given away to a local rival, but at least Grayson could now go to work knowing that he would be paid at the end of the month. It was a mystery but without Grayson, the Bulls somehow became the team we hoped they would be. Here are some of the highlights, or otherwise, of that 13 game run.

- A trip to Northwich Victoria, who boast not only the oldest football ground in the world, but also the best pub name, The Swinging Witch.

21

- A deserved draw with champions-elect Halifax. An organised, motivated team, and with flair when needed, Halifax were as good a blueprint for a title-winning side as you would see.

- Five goals in seven games for Chris Hargreaves, this after firing blanks for the previous twenty. This raised a few eyebrows, most of them assuming that his sudden return to form might just be related to the number of scouts sniffing around ES for a few more emergency sales. Sell Hargreaves or we'll turn off the taps. Not such a tough call to make, should the Water Board send one of those red letters.

- One sadly all too real departure from ES in physiotherapist Shakey, much loved by fans and players alike. The temptation of a properly resourced treatment room, higher-graded football, and better wages being paid on time proved irresistible. Good luck Shakey, we'll miss you.

At a point when on-field events were at a season's high, lest any Bulls fan find an unusual spring in their step, off the field Shit-Creek had become an Ocean. The fine-print of the deal struck with the Bristol Stadiums Group was revealed, and a realistic picture of the club's finances became apparent. Apologies if you find the details a little dry, but given the implications, it is necessary, if painful, information.

The BS Group had loaned the club £500,000 at 3½% above base rates, this, plus interest, to be repaid by May 1999. Failure to repay would see a rate increase to 5% above base.

So far so good, for the BS Group at least. Add the fact that the leases on Edgar Street, with twenty years to run, were *given* to the BS Group in return for the generosity of their terms, and it became clear just who was gaining most from this deal. We were now sub-tenants at Edgar Street. And if that wasn't enough, a joint venture arrangement was in place, to run for seven years, according to which the BS Group would take 25% of any profit if the ES site was sold, United taking 75%. Should the ground be sold *after* the seven-year period, we would get nothing. Hill and Fry had jumped immodestly quickly into a deal heavily weighted in favour of the BS Group to buy a little breathing space, but the £500,000 was quickly gone. The Inland Revenue, along with Customs and Excise, were paid part of what they were owed, brewery loans outstanding took some more, and whether or not a former Managing Director of the club received a going-away present is a question many have pondered. Who knows how big a part Robin Fry played in the negotiations. Perhaps it was just happy coincidence that a substantial amount of money came to the club precisely when he was due his final pay cheque. The whole affair didn't seem quite right, and there were many questions that may never be answered. But casting aside conspiracy theories, and to cut a long story mercifully short, the plain facts were that United owed half a million pounds, plus exorbitant interest. The BS Group controlled the leases, and had shown a chilling contempt for anything other than making money, exhibit A being the Ikea store on what was once a football ground in Bristol. As one supporter noted in a poignant message-board post, an anagram of Hereford United was 'died here on turf'.

If Peter Hill had been searching in his twenty years of control for a way to finally bury the club, it appeared he had found it. Things had never looked more bleak for Bulls supporters, all the cards being in the hands of a company who had already made one club homeless.

All the cards bar two. The local council still owned the football ground, and Hereford United still had Graham Turner. Unforgiven by many as the man who relegated their team, GT had stuck it out when most would have walked away, and in the most trying of circumstances had somehow fashioned a team that in a normal, *proper* league would have secured a play-off spot. There were also however, increasingly loud whispers that GT was prepared to buy out Peter Hill, and that Hill was perhaps ready to sell. To see Peter Hill finally out of Edgar Street would be an enormous boost, and at a time when any crumb of comfort would be greedily accepted. Whether or not GT became chairman, however, the club was still a financial disaster, lurching from one crisis to another. If GT did indeed become the major shareholder, he would be either a very brave or a very foolish man. Dark days, but there was a Saturday in early April when the sun shone, at least metaphorically, on Bulls supporters. Time to lift the mood.

A Horse's Tale, part two
4/4/98 Stalybridge Celtic - away
Two things I like about non-league football are the nicknames and the grounds. Take the Badgers of Bower Fold, and the suggestion of a genteel Home Counties country estate.

Codswallop (I love that word), as this is downwardly-mobile Stalybridge Celtic and their modest ground. Modest it may be, but with a saving grace of enough shelter for the 795 souls present, as it poured down from the start. The Celtics, like the weather, were in a depression, rooted to the bottom of the Conference and near certainties for the drop. Given the state of the pitch and the desperate need for points by the home side, a typically ugly

Conference game was expected, but the Bulls rose above the conditions, playing decent, controlled football, and deservedly taking the lead. The goal was created by a very young, very slight, but clearly talented debutant, Gavin Williams. Against the run of play, the Bulls found themselves trailing, but a brace from Trevor the Grocer, opening his account for the season in the correct net this time, were sufficient to take the spoils. Big Trev's efforts and the unearthing of a potential star of the future were enough to make this a better than average day out for Bulls fans, but for once there was more. Thirty miles west of Stalybridge, a brave steeplechaser was hauling himself and his jockey around Aintree Racecourse in conditions not dissimilar to those out on the Bower Fold pitch. Good to soft, waterlogged in places, would sum it up. But why now the interest in horse-racing? Despite the efforts of our greengrocer, the sporting story of the day was the Grand National, and for the second time this season I was being paid to be a Bulls fan. And this time, I wasn't alone. The majority of visiting supporters had a little flutter, as many do on the National, but today things were different, as we were nearly all on the same horse. One of the favourites for the world's biggest steeplechase was Earth Summit, who duly obliged over the Liverpool fences, strolling home at odds of 9-1. The reason that Hereford fans had backed this particular winner were not the black and white colours (they weren't), nor his being trained in Herefordshire (he wasn't). No, it was simply that we sort of knew his owner. OK, we sort of worshipped him, and more so than ever at just after four o'clock that afternoon. Earth Summit was owned by Ricky George, Bulls legend, and the man without whom twenty-five years of League football might never have happened. Having enjoyed his fifteen minutes of fame back in 1972, Ricky enjoyed fifteen more, the second time being substantially more lucrative than the first. Bulls fans had enjoyed a rewarding, if wet, day out in Stalybridge, paid for by Earth Summit, and Ricky. I'll answer that question again.

No Ricky, you didn't ruin my life, you made it richer, today, literally so.

You're Not Staying at My Place
2/5/98 Woking - away

Here we go again, as developments off the field overtake those on it, time for more money talk. In a moment. Before which, an innocent question that quickly became a nightmare. Whilst thousands of people pass through London's Waterloo Station every day, few are wearing a Hereford away shirt, but here was one, ten feet away at nearly midnight on the last Friday of the season. What does a fellow Bull do, other than say hello? Chances were that I knew this guy. Wrong, on all counts. Didn't know him, shouldn't have spoken to him. As he turned around, I knew I had made a mistake. Super-strength lager in hand, and what looked horribly (and ironically) like chicken tikka artistically obscuring the Sun Valley logo on his shirt, this was not a pretty sight. Now the great thing about a real, up-country Herefordshire accent is that no matter how drunk you are, it doesn't change much. That said, this chap was so far gone that anyone else in the station would have suspected he was from another planet. Having introduced myself, and declined the offer of a pint in the station bar, and not merely because it was closed, we chatted, of sorts, about the game tomorrow. Well, I chatted, whilst he repeatedly observed that 'Annie Darrabont was a flocking flat trat'. Not a big fan of our netman, I suspected. And somewhere, fatally, during this bizarre conversation, I must have mentioned that I was heading home towards Twickenham. Which was, in pundit-speak, a schoolboy error. 'Cannay stayit yoreplaysh', he asked. Oh shit. What do I do now?

'Pleeslet me, I flockinate Woking stayshun, kipped there before.' This was getting serious. Whilst I felt for him, if I took this monstrosity home to a sleeping wife, daughter, and ten month old toddler, he wouldn't be the only one looking for a bed.

As he was pleading, I was wondering how to save myself. 'Wait here mate, I'll phone home, let them know we're on our way.' Which roughly translated means 'You sit there, while I leg it to platform 11, and leave you to London Transport Security.' Which is exactly what I did.

Yes, I felt bad for betraying a fellow Herefordian, but it was the lesser of two evils. And I'm a coward. So, as promised, back to the depressing world of Hereford United's finances, where having loaned the club a further £500,000, Chelverton Properties now have a stake in our club. Given that the leases on ES had already been tossed away by Hill and Fry, the assumption is that another percentage of any profit arising from the much anticipated (in some quarters at least) sale of ES would not be going in to United's bank account. This time, GT was involved in negotiations, unsurprising given the possibility of Hill selling his shareholding and the terms of the latest loan were this time, declared up front. The deal negotiated by GT, self-confessed as 'a football man, not a businessman', is this. £500,000 to the club, interest-free, repayable in May 2003, contrasting starkly to the deal negotiated by the experienced business minds of Hill and Fry less than twelve months previously. Which again begs the question of who really did benefit from the agreement with the BS Group. Also surprising was the willingness of so many companies to dole out large chunks of cash, given that the much coveted real-estate could not in theory be developed. Unless these people knew something we didn't. Lots of questions and very few answers.

GT announced that a large chunk of the £500,000 went straight to the bank, reducing the overdraft to a mere £90,000, with most of the remainder going toward something called a CVA. A Company Voluntary Arrangement is apparently an agreement between the Limited Company that is Hereford United and those owed monies by it. As an alternative to receivership or liquidation, where creditors would get little or nothing, a CVA puts a protective bubble around the company, allowing it to continue trading under strict supervision, in order to get back onto its feet. The club's debts would eventually be repaid, either in full or, more likely, in part. United's creditors had in effect drawn a line around monies owed to them and told the club to get out there, run a tight business, make some profit and, eventually, pay them something back. Oh, and play some football, if you can find the time.

To sum up the state of our finances, and maybe then talk about football, the situation as of the last day of the season was that we owed a million pounds plus interest to two property developers, and a further undisclosed amount to various other agencies. There was a small window to allow some rebuilding and stabilisation, May 1999 being the due date for repayment of the first half million. Hereford United therefore had until the end of the following season to make some serious money, which, short of the appearance of a sugar-daddy in a black and white shirt, would take some doing. More pressingly, if United broke the terms of the CVA, they could be almost immediately wound up by their creditors. Simply put, the club would have to trade at, or very close to, a break-even figure, or face closure. The situation was a waking nightmare with seemingly not even a glimmer of hope, and with no million pound man waiting in the wings it looked like either Graham Turner or Peter Hill would have to guide Hereford United through some very stormy waters. Given the track-record of the latter, it was, to use an apt Americanism, a no-brainer. If Peter Hill was still around at the start of next season, it would be odds-on that the club wouldn't make it through to the following May. More would hopefully be revealed over the close-season — please let it be good news. On the pitch, the Bulls ended the season as they had started it, with a defeat, this time 1-3, at Woking. Apart from a nostalgic, at least in one or two cases, look at the swansong of several players in a Bulls shirt, there was little to report. And happily, at least for my own conscience, my friend from Waterloo Station had made it to the game. I'm not sure whether he enjoyed it or not, and I didn't like to ask. It would have been a shame to wake him up.

Halifax deservedly regained their League status, comfortably the best side in the division, whilst Stalybridge and Gateshead exited to the Unibond League. As should have Telford, but the problems at Slough allowed them a reprieve they perhaps didn't deserve. That said, if the Bulls had finished third-bottom and survived in the same way, I wouldn't be complaining too loudly. Lady Luck deals her cards, and sometimes you get the joker. Hereford ended the season in sixth position, twenty points and a thousand miles behind Halifax, and the Conference had shown itself as a league far harder to escape from than to enter. Next season would be no different, except that the club would be operating on a fraction of the budget it was used to, and far below that of most of the serious contenders. If we made it through to August, our sights would need to be significantly lowered. Survival would be the new name of the game, and any success on the pitch a bonus. HUISA wrapped up the season with Mike Quarrell relinquishing his Chairmanship, returning to Germany with a job offer which proved irresistible. This was not before he collected not one but two trophies in the space of a week. He was unsurprisingly voted Fan of the Year, supplemented with victory in a sponsored penalty shoot-out, this in front of his spiritual home, the Meadow End Terrace at ES. Mike had succeeded where earlier in the year professionals from both Brighton and Colchester had failed, and in slotting past Andy deBont from twelve yards personally doubled the haul of silverware achieved by the Bulls in the previous twenty years. He even managed half a lap of honour. Not a bad week for a fat bloke from Germany, or, if you like, a GFB.

That was the Conference, that was
And a season for the Bulls which was frequently disappointing, often frustrating, occasionally brilliant, but ultimately summed up in three words. Horribly bloody traumatic. Off-field problems were always to the fore, and GT and the players did more than could be expected of them in trying circumstances. With wages and bills unpaid, leases given away, and a chairman bereft of ideas, the management and players could have been forgiven for walking away to greener pastures. Without their efforts, there

might well have been a new Hereford United, finding its feet in the Midland Alliance or perhaps even lower.

The lows, well, there were plenty. Defeats at Hayes, Slough and Stevenage were hard to take. The fiasco against Welling was an even bigger blow, all of our optimism gone in less than an hour, and the spineless capitulation to Dover in the FA Trophy, just when we needed a boost, was perhaps the nadir.

Losing our best striker in order to pay a bill, and to our nearest neighbours at that — yes, that also, was a particularly bitter pill.

But over and above all this hovered the perpetual threat of the club you love, the club that has been part of you for most of your life, the club whose presence you took for granted, being taken away. It is the worst feeling a supporter could have, and one I wouldn't wish on anyone.

If there was one moment to sum up the season, it came in September during a home game with Northwich. Neil Grayson had just scored, prompting a comedic and pre-planned goal celebration. The players met in the centre-circle and turned toward the directors' box. They then dropped to their knees, hands outstretched like eleven Oliver Twists, asking for more.

They probably hadn't been paid that month.

There were, however, a few moments to lift the gloom. Total football at Morecambe, and a glorious holiday double over local rivals Kidderminster, much to the dismay of our local station, BBC Hereford and Worcester. Also a 13 match unbeaten run, sadly too late to make a difference, and twice being paid to watch the Bulls.

Gavin Mahon, outstanding throughout, was voted player of the year, and deserves a better platform for his talent. I doubt he'll be in a Hereford shirt next season.

And there was the FA Cup. Revenge over Brighton was a joy, and beating Colchester on a night so cold that any feeling had long since gone, was also a welcome, indeed vital, bonus. We might have been out of the league, but Hereford were once again giant-killers.

A final word. Credit, enormous credit, is due to the men and women of HUISA. You gave a voice to the fans when they most needed one, and in a blighted and desperate season, gave a little hope when it seemed there was none.

You, above all, deserve a team to support next season.

3   1998-1999 Not a Beer but a Deer, My Dear

15/8/98 Kingstonian - away

It's August, the Bulls are still in business, and it's a short cycle ride through Richmond Park to Kingsmeadow, home of Kingstonian Football Club. Which means we still have a team, and one with a new owner. Whilst Shit-Creek is still an ocean, our boat now has a paddle, because Peter Hill has sold his shares to Graham Turner. It was cartwheels around the garden time. The gentlemen's drinking club in the ES boardroom was no more, as Hill and his dismal, failed regime slipped away. GT has stepped into what is, however you look at it, a financial nightmare. No other suitor appeared interested, and why should they, with a seven-figure sum required merely to start from scratch? Whilst GT would have paid a fraction of that figure, he is now responsible for Hereford United, top to bottom, as both club chairman and director of football. As of June 29th Mr. Turner had himself a football club, at a cost of both a few thousand pounds and, probably, most of his marbles, putting up his home as a bank guarantee showing his commitment to what is a pretty hopeless cause. Better make that all of his marbles and, love him or loathe him, I think that Bulls fans owe GT a big thank you. That there is still a team to follow is something that was in no way guaranteed last May, and the bonus of Peter Hill being ousted enough to lift spirits way higher than we might have hoped. I truly feared that the defeat at Woking could have been the last game I saw Hereford United play, but we are still alive, ready for new battles, though still undeniably flat broke. Something all too painfully endorsed when looking at the squad assembled for the coming season. Eight automatic first teamers accepted better deals elsewhere, several at our supposedly part-time Conference rivals, and skipper David Norton had retired through injury, leaving a lot of shoes needing to be filled. Oh yes, Andy deBont. Our enigmatic shot-stopper would now be either frustrating or charming the supporters of Telford United. Good luck to you Andy, go easy on the pies. A small amount of quality remained, in the shape of Gavin Mahon, Richard Walker and Andy Quy. These three players were the filling in a sandwich of experienced (old and slow) professionals and untried (cheap and frail) youngsters with hardly a senior game between them. There was also Richard Leadbeater, scourge of Kidderminster, who signed for the season and would no doubt display mere fractions of the ability shown whilst with us on loan. Don't tell me you've never seen breath-taking loan talent morph into pedestrian also-ran the second a contract has been signed. Cynical, me? Time would tell, but back to some promising newcomers.

Kingstonian came to the Conference via the Ryman League, and have an upwardly-mobile look about them. A young club with a tidy, if characterless ground, and in Geoff Chapple, a manager who knows unproper football as well as anyone. You could say that Kingstonian were a footballing yuppie, and a stark contrast to the world-weary, faded glory of Hereford United. Today however, as of ten to three, they also had a near empty visitors' terrace. Disappointing, even when considering the perilous state of the club. Surely a few Bulls supporters had kept the faith over the summer? Ten minutes later, with a handful more fans but no sign of the players, things were looking ominous. Were they already on strike over unpaid wages? Someone belatedly found the switch to the PA system, and told us that HUISA coaches were stuck in traffic, and kick-off would be at 3.15.

It was a fifteen-minute delay to the inevitable. New faces, old story, as within thirty minutes two defensive howlers saw the Bulls trailing. For Kingstonian 1998, review Welling 1997 — there was no difference. The players huffed and puffed, but were getting nowhere against another ten-man defensive unit. On the terracing, shoulders slumped and a goalless second half saw the familiar sight of a Hereford team trooping off the pitch leaving their part-time conquerors to take the plaudits. All too often last season the Bulls conceded soft goals and then dismally failed to threaten a reply, and it appeared little had changed over the summer. There was much discontent amongst the travelling support, many of whom believed that teams like Kingstonian had no right to be on the same pitch as Hereford, let alone beat them with something to spare. A sizeable minority of Bulls fans remained steadfastly in denial, unable to accept the reality of Conference football and feeling that we were somehow victims of a conspiracy, somehow a proper team in an unproper place.

There are others who are convinced that we are now a crappy team in a tinpot division, and for them, some more ammunition. Chaps, Vauxhall agree with you. Sponsorship has been discontinued, there is no longer GM product in this league, and we now compete in the Football Conference. The management committee are currently seeking a blue-chip company to stump up the five bob required to place their name above these 22 pub teams. Or so some Herefordians would have you believe. It was a depressing start, but there were two small rays of sunshine, come five o'clock.

One being, well, the sunshine. It was a glorious day, making it difficult to be truly miserable. The second was my bike. The traffic carnage around the ground could be somebody else's problem. I would be home in twenty minutes. Or so I thought. As already mentioned, it was a short ride home through Richmond Park, with cycle tracks a-plenty to give a little extra safety to two-wheeled travellers. Tell that to the psychotic deer that hurtled toward me like a four-legged exocet. In a dispute between a mountain bike and half a ton of heavily antlered, clearly disturbed stag, there was only one winner. One unscheduled dismount and a nice collection of cuts and bruises later, the demented beast trotted off to find new quarry. Thanks Rudolf, for the icing on the cake of what had been a dismal afternoon. And there was more. Whilst I didn't make a habit of returning from matches looking as if I'd been introduced to the local Mafia, the effect was similar, as I explained to Sarah's increasingly loud sniggers how I had come home looking like a road accident. Not marauding hooligans, nor even an extra beer, not at all. It was a deer, my dear.

I wasn't expecting tea and cakes, but to not even attempt to suppress your mirth at your significant other's misfortune can be hard to take. I mean, was there a funny side to all this? For once, I failed to see it. Thanks, Kingstonian. One game into the season and already right up there in the top ten rubbish days out at the football. It's a good job we've got Leek on Tuesday.

The San Siro Stadium
29/8/98 Welling United - away

But before Welling United came Leek Town, once rashly described as close to a village green side. Village or not, they're still here, and arrived at Edgar Street sitting proudly on top of the league, courtesy of a 4-0 win over Farnborough. They would take us on from the very summit of their footballing achievements, surely poised to add more pain to the already wounded Bulls. Not this time, as for once Hereford ground out an ugly 1-0 win against the type of team that frequently embarrassed us last season,

31

and indeed last weekend. The following Saturday saw a more convincing win over Dover, courtesy of a Gavin Williams brace. Keep an eye on this teenager, was the opinion of the sage elders in the main stand. In Gavin, Hereford have a young player with more than a few tricks, and he wasn't shy in demonstrating them to the older, supposedly wiser campaigners in the Conference. Or, put another way, he liked taking the piss out of has-beens and donkeys. Any momentum, however, was abruptly halted at Hednesford, 1-3, and a red card for new right-back Chris Lane, so we travelled to Welling with an air of inconsistency and, already, a mid-table look about the team. Welling United, no doubt proud to be our bogey team, possess a ground once unkindly described as an allotment and two garden sheds. Unkind toward allotments maybe, because Park View Road is as close to derelict as any ground I have seen. A tiny, rutted pitch, one and a half small stands, and a few crumbling terrace steps just about sum it up.

'Welcome to the San Siro Stadium,' said a steward as we entered the ground. Excuse me, but you're having a giraffe, mate, as they like to say in this part of the world. Surely not San Siro as in the palatial home of AC Milan? Perhaps Welling had twinned with its natural soul-mate from northern Italy, in one of those anything-for-a-free-holiday exercises so beloved by local councillors. Amazingly enough, not true. As we took in the opulence on view, all became clear. Located across the main road was a motor showroom, towering over the football ground. San Siro Motors and, of course, a Fiat dealership, what else. But already today, another Conference first, in fact, make that a first at any football ground, as here was a steward with a sense of humour, and clearly new to the job. For the record, one San Siro has 85,700 seats in three tiers, 51 turnstiles, 35 food outlets, and a match-day staff of several thousand. The other has an uninterrupted view of a suburban park, complete with cricket pitch. Which would prove an entertaining diversion later in the day. Remember Kingstonian just a fortnight ago? Well, here we go again. Pretty, intricate football can be a joy, but there is a time and a place, and today the San Siro wasn't it, and Welling knew that they possessed neither the players nor the surface to make that particular style work. What they did possess, however, was a big centre-forward who was good in the air. One knock-down and tap-in, one bullet header, and the Bulls were two down with half an hour left. Game over. We had been here before and knew that there was no happy ending to this chapter. Which is where the San Siro came up trumps in providing a decent view of the cricketers in the adjacent park. The men in white, unlike our men in black and white, were providing some high-quality entertainment, the batsmen running riot against what you might call cafeteria bowling. Cafeteria as in you help yourself. Both had a liking for the leg-side boundary, where a very large, very unathletic fielder had been posted. The ball was fizzing past, over or through this poor chap at least twice an over, the ironic applause from the football ground doing little to raise his spirits each time he retrieved a four or six. It quickly became compulsive viewing, with more travelling supporters choosing cricket above football as each over passed. In a stroke of genius, the fielding captain moved his blighted fielder a good forty yards closer to his tormentors inside the San Siro. Manna from Heaven as, of course, the ball continued to follow the hapless fellow wherever he went. More runs flowed, but he was now able to enjoy the less than subtle Herefordian wit from close-up. And then came his chance of redemption. A towering shot was heading straight at our rotund hero. Not a difficult catch, he wouldn't have to move. As the ball fell toward our man, here, surely, was a chance for some wag to deliver a final devastating witticism, the coup de grace of comedic put-downs. We weren't disappointed.

'Spill it, Pie-Boy' was the call, and if not quite Oscar Wilde, it served its purpose. As for our favourite cricketer, he didn't let us down. The catch was fumbled, but before the ball fell to earth, a desperate dive and outstretched hand plucked it to safety. An amazing piece of agility from such a large chap, he stood up and to rapturous applause delivered a theatrical bow, followed by a single-finger salute. With such a hard act to follow, it was time to declare, now we would have to watch some football. Which is when things cheered up even more. The anticipated fifteen minutes of misery didn't happen. Of course, Welling sat back and invited the Bulls' now traditionally energetic but futile second-half pressure, but today the script was ignored. Two quality strikes arrowed into the Welling net, and it was Hereford who looked the more likely winners. We came close, but the match ended all square. Were we learning to cope with the likes of Welling and their brand of hoofball? I hoped so, but we would need to show it for more than fifteen minutes a week to achieve anything worthwhile this season. So now time for a small confession. Bless Me Father for I have sinned, and dissed a seriously unproper team, because grudging respect is due to Welling United. On gates of around 500, on a pitch of barely park standard and housed in a stadium that should be condemned, they battle away in a tough, if rubbish league, and somehow survive. A good season for the postmen, teachers, and firemen of Welling would be mid-table in the Conference and, perhaps, the 2nd round of the FA Cup. Welling are the sort of club that set the Conference apart from the full-time professionals and, if you ask me, in a good way. They will never play in the Football League, but there is a lot of heart in the club. Along with comedy cricket, available when the football becomes truly unbearable. You don't get that in Milan.

A Long Time to Hold a Grudge
12/9/98 Barrow - away

It is 9,626 days since Hereford United replaced Barrow in the Football League which, however you look at it, is a lot of Saturdays. Since the day in 1972 when the Old Boys' Network of club chairmen failed in their duty to their own and cast Barrow into the wilderness, I can't confess to giving them even the smallest consideration, but I was nine and had never heard of Barrow-in-Furness. There was only one place that mattered to me. But twenty-six years later here they are again, having secured a place in the Conference by winning the Northern Premier League with, apparently, considerable help from the pocket of owner and chairman Stephen Vaughan. Barrow arguably enjoy both a stadium and a team of a standard higher than they would expect in normal circumstances, but when such riches are dangled, who would resist? Whilst true of Max Griggs and the bankrolled Rushden and Diamonds, had Stephen Vaughan bought Barrow a place in the Conference? Best ask a Barrow fan, but the question at Holker Street today was whether the hosts would have any issues with the team responsible for their loss of League status all those years ago.

Certainly there had been muttered warnings for Bulls fans to tread carefully around Holker Street, but these were of the 'take with a large pinch of salt' variety. Perusing Barrow's fabulously titled fanzine 'Give 'em Beans', several pages were devoted to Hereford United, none of them complimentary. It was, however, laced with enough humour to suspect that the authors at least, had moved on. Yes, there was some unusual history in the fixture, but most of the 1,800 in the ground would have been too young to remember the era of three-day weeks, power cuts, and secret ballots. Just in case, however, four policemen were on duty, apparently four more than usual.

They needn't have bothered. The travelling Bulls were in peril only from the gale-force winds screaming in from the Irish Sea, or from underestimating the strength of some first-class northern brews. In fairness to Barrow, they proved excellent hosts, allowing the Bulls to take all three points back to Hereford. Gary Cook provided the stand-out moment in a modest match, manufacturing a twenty-yard chip that left the home keeper gloriously embarrassed. Cookie then demonstrated the difference between natural goalscorers and the mere mortals of unproper football by snatching at two infinitely more straightforward chances to kill the game off. That's what you get in the Conference, but we weren't complaining. It was a deserved win and a good day out, but if you're planning a trip to Barrow, be warned. It's miles from anywhere and at the end of the longest cul-de-sac in Britain. It's also bloody cold, and this is September. Check it out on a map and pray you don't get them in the cup, in January.

Island Life
17/10/98 Newport(IoW) - home. FA Cup 3rd qualifying round

The Football Association have, in their wisdom, decided that this year we will enter the FA Cup at the third qualifying round, something you could look at in two ways. A bad thing if it's Cheltenham away, but surely a good thing if, like Hereford, you draw someone from the very depths of unproperness, at home. With the Bulls showing some consistency, and on the back of an excellent win at Stevenage, the part-timers of Newport could enjoy their day out, hopefully avoiding complete humiliation, and head back to the Isle of Wight to concentrate on the League.

When Tony James and Gavin Williams delivered a two-goal cushion, the banana-skin looked set to fall elsewhere as United were cruising and, with twenty minutes left, the Meadow End choir felt secure enough to have a gentle dig at Newport's handful of followers, presumably by now resigned to their fate. 'You must have come in a kayak' was a witty variation on a common theme but out of nowhere, the visitors had something to shout about. It was a scrappy goal, but they all count, even if it was merely a consolation. Newport's players didn't see it that way, as the Bulls' back four suddenly looked vulnerable. Two substitutes were introduced, both more suited to a basketball court, and an aerial assault followed, causing fifteen minutes of sheer defensive panic. Unsurprisingly, the equaliser came, route one, express delivery. This couldn't be happening. Having controlled the game for over an hour, we were now reduced to desperate hoofed clearances, any semblance of calm having long since disappeared. And this against the poorest side seen at ES for decades. We were being run ragged by a park team, and didn't have a clue what to do about it. As Bulls supporters contemplated a midweek trip to the Isle of Wight, the question became irrelevant. Again the ball cannoned around the goal-mouth, and it again ended up in Andy Quy's net, and the unthinkable had happened, as, don't forget, this is Hereford.

'Two-nil, and you fucked it up. You're out of the FA Cup.'

Which will teach us not to mention kayaks. It was capitulation of the most depressing kind. As professional footballers Hereford had dealt with the type of game Newport played countless times before and done so properly. Today something had gone missing and the cost would be measured not only in injured pride, but in lost revenue. Hereford United simply couldn't afford to be out of the Cup at this stage. With the millionaires club of Rushden a dozen points ahead of the Bulls, the Conference title already looked out of reach, making a decent FA Cup run more important than ever. This was a disaster, its implications grave. GT had stated in August that his budget was based on gates of 2,500, along with success in the cup competitions at least equivalent to the previous year. So there it was, the rest of the season, clearly marked out. Gates, already down, would continue to fall, revenue would dry up, and the club would slide deeper into a massive financial hole. Our few remaining assets were now even more vulnerable. Like Grayson last year, insulting offers would be made for Hereford players and those offers would be accepted. With the first £500,000 repayment to the BS Group due in six months, and now, no prospect of any FA Cup windfall, it would be fair to say that Hereford United had seen better times. Newport had delivered not only a cup upset, but a blow to the football club that would again bring its very survival into doubt. It would be a long and hard winter, with no guarantee of making it through to the spring.

Beach Football
21/11/98 and 30/11/98 Hitchin Town - FA Trophy 2nd round

The Bulls' next home fixture was against Farnborough. Three dismal weeks had passed since the traumatic cup exit, weeks in which points gained matched players lost, at one apiece. Richard Walker was missing as the Bulls lined up and to much dismay but little surprise, Cheltenham were picking at the carcass of a dying football club. The fee was undisclosed, probably to save the embarrassment of all parties, but Walker *could* actually kick a ball straight and was worth more. Also missing was Gavin Mahon. Whilst he hadn't yet signed for Cheltenham, terrace gossip was unanimous and Gavin would imminently follow Walker out of ES. Whilst both players would be missed, they weren't today. Farnborough, as is their wont, did the decent thing, allowing the Bulls a comfortable victory in front of a creditable 1,788 supporters. Only 53 down on the Newport debacle, it was a small crumb of comfort. Maybe we had hit the bottom and this really was the hard-core. Time would tell, probably after our next humiliation. And so to the FA Trophy, the FA Cup of the junior school playground, which whilst offering a day at Wembley for the little guys, rarely set pulses racing until the later rounds. Having surrendered to Dover last season, the draw was again kind, pairing us with Hitchin Town. Another part-time outfit, another home tie, would it be another embarrassing day for Hereford? Very nearly, as Ian Wright spared United's blushes in a dismal draw. Released by Hull City, he was a centre-back of the old school, but possessing just enough class to stand out at this level. Probably in his mid-twenties, Wrighty could pass for a man twice his age and was without question the Daddy of the side. With his knack of scoring important goals, it was easy to like Wrighty, and everyone did. Opinion was that we couldn't play as badly again and Hitchin were unlikely to raise their own game to the level shown at ES. Safely through to the next round then, that being the opinion of, amongst others, Graham Turner. With all his experience, he couldn't be wrong, surely? Before which, Mahon's departure had been confirmed, Cheltenham having been outbid by a six-figure offer from Brentford. Gavin could play, and his departure was another reason, if another was needed, to stay away from ES.

Hitchin Town Football Club had a familiar look about it, and with good reason. Four years ago, almost to the day, the Bulls were dumped out of the FA Cup on this very pitch, one which had seen minimal investment since that miserable defeat. It was a poor excuse for a football ground, the lower reaches of the Ryman League being an almost forgotten wasteland. The stadium however, was luxurious when compared to the pitch. Several tons of sand had been dumped on the playing surface, and with hardly a blade of grass in sight, was more suited to donkey rides than football, a fact not overlooked by the comedians amongst the visiting support. It was, however, the same for both teams. Hitchin, against informed opinion, were again able to raise their game and Hereford, also against informed opinion, did indeed play as badly as they had at home. It was a spineless display by the Bulls, the 2-1 victory being just reward for the home side, and Wrighty's face was a picture of fury. Like the fans, he, at least, deserved better. The Bulls were now out of the Trophy, as well as the Cup and the League, and we hadn't yet reached December. It was another dark day in a season which had already seen far too many. Only the most spoilt of supporters would fail to accept that, on occasions, their team will be beaten by supposed inferiors. Without these upsets, little or large, there would be no point in playing and, as a neutral, there are few more enjoyable spectacles than aristocrats taking a beating from their proletariat cousins. That said, it was happening to Hereford far too often, and after today yet more fans would be turning their back on the club, perhaps never to return. Sad to say, however, that I wasn't as upset or hurt as I should have been, and by the time I reached home, I was pretty much over it. After the humiliation of Newport, I felt that the situation was as wretched as it could be. I was angry, I was hurt and I was scared. Today there just wasn't a lot of pain left, my team had used it all up. Perhaps I was becoming immune.

Crest of a Slump
December 1998 - January 1999

Two months on from Hitchin and, although it's hard to believe, the plight of the Bulls has actually worsened. Two new faces have arrived, the sorely missed Mahon and Walker being replaced by a couple of thirty-somethings, Kevin Collins and Robbie Dennison. With GT operating on the tightest of budgets, it maybe unfair to criticise, as I doubt there are scores of talented youngsters looking to be paid pennies at a ruined football club. But sod it, I'm going to. Both players were well past their sell-by date, looking unfit and, in the case of Dennison, interested only in squeezing a final few quid from his footballing life. With Dennison a virtual passenger, it was a dismal ten-game run, where a paltry four points were acquired. The sole victory was hard-earned, at Hayes, where ten men for once showed the necessary appetite for a battle. John Snape collected a red card, and this after promising the fans a goal and a win. In Snapper we have a player not over-burdened with talent, and in no way blinded by the modest amount of fame Conference football might bring. Which roughly translates to crap but honest. Always good for a chat, here was a player not frightened to put a foot in where others may baulk and, because of that, forgiven any lack of technique. Or as one B-Block regular observed in misquoting Eric Morecambe, 'I like Snapper, always plays the right passes. Just not necessarily in the right order.'

Added to which, he is a qualified electrician, signed to add a spark to the Bulls' midfield.

Sorry, couldn't resist. Snape in a way epitomised the problems facing the manager. His budget would bring him industry and commitment with little discernible ability, or once talented wasters who couldn't give a fig for Hereford United. The only players appearing both young and sufficiently gifted to progress were Gavin Williams, Tony James, and perhaps Paul Parry, a trio of Welsh teenagers still learning the game and too easily bullied by the seasoned journeymen of the Conference. After the victory at Hayes, performances went further downhill, and in a hurry. Lost, lost, lost, lost, drew (Hednesford, clearly having an off-day), lost, lost. Rubbing salt into an open wound were Kidderminster, exacting gleeful revenge for last year's festive double. Twice in a week we were embarrassed by a very ordinary side, never easy to take, particularly from your nearest neighbour, our almost neutral radio station BBC Hereford and Worcester trying, but not too hard, to conceal their delight. The Bulls were now looking nervously downward, six points above the drop zone and playing like a team fearing the worst. All of GT's experience was needed, but word escaped that his right-hand man, Keith Downing, had been running the side since September, with GT concentrating on matters off the field. If this was true, it would appear that Keith was struggling, although he wasn't helped by too many of his colleagues falling short of his own high standards of professionalism. If there was any chink of light, it came in the form of Leek Village Town, Welling Tin-Shed United, and dear old Farnborough, all of whom looked in even greater distress than the Bulls. And it would be to Cherrywood Road, home of the weakest team in the division, for the latest chapter of probable embarrassment. Farnborough were next.

Even Worse than Hereford
3/2/99 Farnborough - away

Whilst I've often pondered the same question, today was very nearly a first. Rugby on the telly, or go and support the Bulls. The fact that Farnborough was just down the road and one of the few sides below us swung it. Not to mention the threat of physical damage from Justin, already arrived from the East End, along with the promise of Hampshire's finest Real Ale. The Prince of Wales was not a disappointment. At the bar a number of fellow Bulls were already in discussion with a group of locals. 'No, we're *definitely* worse than you, shocking, abysmal.'

'But hang on, we can't score, can't pass, can't defend, we're almost in the Ryman League.'

'But we've got Robbie Dennison, we may as well play with ten.' And so continued a weirdly inverted version of 'My Dad is bigger than your

Dad', and an enjoyable if unusual way to spend an hour or two. With kick-off approaching, a truce was declared. Both sides were crap, discussion to be continued after the match, winners buy the beer. A quick team check revealed another new face and also another missing. Already christened by Talking Bill Thomas as 'Sell a Player a Fortnight Season', this time was different. Mark Druce had gone to Kidderminster, the five-figure offer for our alleged striker being a deal that GT simply couldn't refuse. That is, after he'd stopped laughing. Simply put, Druce just wasn't very good, and I doubt a single Bulls fan will miss him. Our Worcestershire rivals had paid £10,000 for a player who would have been released in a matter of weeks and the good karma enjoyed in the Prince of Wales continued. Maybe we would get something from today.

The match started unusually well, as Wrighty volleyed home. Three minutes gone, one-nil. On the half-hour, Dennison ambled goalwards, where more comedy defending preceded a serene finish, two-nil. It was the same story after the break, and the four-nil scoreline could have been many more. The new face on show was Steven Cowe, on loan from Swindon and far too good for this league. There may be hope after all, especially if he stays for the rest of the season. Steven's wages, by the way, were coming not from the club but HUISA, and on this evidence appeared to be money well spent. We left my favourite non-league ground, heading for my favourite non-league pub. As good as their word, the Farnborough supporters were there, with an air bordering on smug.

'Told you so', was their first and last word, as the argument concluded. Embarrassed at home by a side that hadn't won in months was hard to argue with. We might have tried, but it was pointless. They had let Robbie Dennison score and the debate was over. Farnborough were officially worse than Hereford. Four pints of Scruttock's Old Dirigible please, landlord, my friends have some sorrows to drown.

Hereford Reserves
20/2/1999 Cheltenham Town - home

Unsurprisingly the biggest gate of the season, not only because Cheltenham was less than an hour away and challenging for the title, but also with the extra spice of some old boys returning to ES. With emergency sales Grayson and Walker in their line-up, there would be added edge to the game, especially as United were still by no means safe from relegation. There was, however, another factor, and his name was David Norton. Which should ring a few bells. The same David Norton, former Hereford captain, who had retired at the end of last season. Yes, it was definitely him, trotting out with what the home fans referred to as Hereford Reserves. And when considering the career-ending injuries endured, looking remarkably fit. To say that the natives were restless would be an understatement. They were almost literally spitting chips. None of the venom, and there was plenty, was directed at Grayson or Walker, so what had Norton done to so enrage the home crowd? After all, Norts had, in trying circumstances, done a decent job for the Bulls. He was an honest pro with enough class to have played in the top flight. He had battled against serious injury and been under the surgeon's knife more times than he would care to remember. He was popular with both team-mates and fans, none of which should provoke such an outpouring of bile. But on his retirement at the end of last season, Norton had been given a small golden handshake in the form of half of the profits of a sports equipment sale held at ES. It was a testimonial of sorts, and I doubt that the sum involved was anything more than a token gesture of thanks from the Hereford supporters. It was, however, asking too much of the home fans to politely welcome back a man who returned with the intention of sending us a step closer to relegation. Only Norton himself will know the degree to which his retirement was a permanent decision, but I would hope, and indeed think, that Norton said farewell to ES with no hidden agenda.

The Meadow End however, were not in a forgiving mood. Each time Norts was near the ball, the ground erupted, Judas being the call for the full 90 minutes, although Lazarus would have been an equally apt Biblical moniker. Norton, as a footballer at least, had come back from the dead and, seasoned pro that he is, rose above the maelstrom, helping his team to a comfortable 2-0 win. Wherever the truth lay, perhaps Norts deserved a little stick. He didn't, however, deserve the volume of phlegm or pockets of loose change that he endured. In sinking to such depths, the abusers lower themselves to a level of behaviour below that of even the most deserving of targets and, in some cases, simply spur the individual and his team on to even greater efforts. Naked, murderous aggression, spitting and missile launching, along with racist abuse, have no place in a football ground, and all, thankfully, are less prevalent in the Conference than in the Football League. Today, however, a sizable minority of Bulls fans scored on three of those four counts, and had David Norton been black, it would undoubtedly have been a full house. Norts and his team-mates probably didn't need the extra motivation offered by the home crowd's hostility, with Cheltenham looking every inch champions-elect and the Hereford reserves just three parts of an impressive whole. They were quicker and hungrier, they attacked with flair and defended with purpose. I dread to think what they would have done to Farnborough. It would take a good side to deny them a place in the Football League.

New for Old
20/3/99 Barrow - home
The Cheltenham game was the last in a Bulls shirt for both Keith Downing and Richard Leadbeater. Keith was moving to manage the youth squad at Wolves and will be missed more than Leadbeater, the latest player sold to keep the bank manager at bay. Whilst Leaders occasionally looked the part, the £20,000 offer from Stevenage was another surprisingly good deal for the Bulls.

So they're gone, it's Easter, and we need points, soon. Earlier in the season, the Bulls had fielded five players in a game aged 32 or over. We lost. Today, at home to our friends from Cumbria, the Bulls fielded four teenagers and four more barely into their twenties. We won, and comfortably, 3-0, and Barrow were given the runaround, a tonic desperately needed after the Cheltenham defeat and the two fortunate draws gained from the subsequent four matches. Had GT decided, at this late stage of the season, that youth was the way forward? The reality was that the changes were more evolutionary than revolutionary. The steady exodus from Edgar Street had left GT with little option but to play these lads, their own development being of secondary importance to putting eleven players on the pitch who could actually run. Chris Lane, Tony James, Gavin Williams, Gary Cook and Paul Parry had been around the club for a while and loan signings Steven Cowe and Christian Roberts both had points to prove. All have picked up more matches than they might normally have done, and on the evidence of today, no bad thing. The three points gained by these youngsters today lifted the Bulls close to safety, their reward being five games in which to secure a contract for next year, should they be inclined to stay. There are again apparently, plenty of scouts around ES, and I don't think they're after Robbie Dennison. This was a good day for the Bulls, particularly so for the new generation of talent, but it would be no surprise if one, perhaps all, of these lads moved on to better things before long. There was also, possibly, some good news for the manager on the financial front. Runner-up in the half-time draw was a Mr. G. Turner. Was it Graham, and what does twenty quid buy these days? As for Barrow, their Conference dream had become a nightmare, the downside that can come hand-in-hand with a sugar saddy chairman being illustrated in the most painful manner. Stephen Vaughan had walked away, leaving the club in a financial tangle that was still being unravelled by the liquidator. In a few short weeks, Barrow lost their manager, most of their senior players and reportedly even their ground, and Vaughan's exit had left them in a sea of debt, and struggling to fulfil their fixtures. Amazingly, there is a club out there in a bigger hole than Hereford but, like the Bulls, they are not giving up. Surely here is a stark warning, to be heeded by any club tempted by a rich man and his pocket-money. Check out his motives, carefully. Short-term gain often leads to long-term pain.

Back in the Nationwide
1/5/1999 Woking - away

Don't get too excited, but we're back in the Nationwide League. The financial giant found the required five bob and are the new sponsors of the Conference, meaning a cash bonus for the Bulls equivalent to a day's salary of an average Premiership player. But with Nationwide now on board, we may see added momentum toward securing the second promotion slot, something that can't come soon enough, as yet more meaningless matches have blighted the Conference since Christmas. Although none featuring Hereford. We started those at Easter.

Having banished the spectre of relegation, the players finally found some consistency. Three wins and a draw saw the Bulls on top of the current form table, prompting the notion that we should start these meaningless matches in August next season. Or perhaps not. With attendances hovering around a thousand, revenue must have all but dried up, but there was a small nugget of good news. The BS Group indicated that the half million due in May would be deferred until 2002, and no further interest would be charged. Altruism it wasn't, and had they demanded repayment on schedule, the club would have almost certainly folded, and our leaseholders would have received nothing. Whilst GT is obliged to work with the developers toward relocation, supporters remain divided and any desire amongst Bulls fans toward co-operation was tempered by a healthy degree of scepticism. HUISA, to by no means universal approval, was establishing much closer links with the club, a move signalling an improved flow of information from the board to the fans, and a small but welcome change in the club's not so smoothly oiled PR department. In Richard Tomkins, HUISA have a chairman who, whilst not in the larger-than-life mould of GFB, appears quietly determined to keep both funds and communication flowing. Both are areas vital to the future of the football club and are intrinsically linked. Without information supporters become alienated, and consequently less inclined to give of their time and money. If this is the direction in which HUISA are headed, it may, for now at least, be in their best interests. Perhaps after the battle to remove Peter Hill, the appetite for conflict has gone and a united approach the best, perhaps only, policy that will keep professional football in Hereford.

So, with the debt repayment postponed but not going away, GT and the board came up with a novel way to bring some cash into the coffers. The club announced a raffle, complete with a West Country twist. The ES pitch would be divided into 8,000 squares, temporary ownership of each costing ten pounds. Freetown Kudos, pedigree Hereford bull and occasional club mascot, would be released on to the field, the lucky owner of the first square to be naturally fertilised by Kudos winning a car. With bullshit from the boardroom and crap on the pitch, here was a case of inserting your own punchline, so ripe were the comic opportunities. Whilst many thought that a donkey would have been more apt, Kudos did his bit to keep the club afloat over the summer. Just one more thing you're unlikely to see at Anfield. Having begun the season at Kingsmeadow, we ended it at Kingfield, home of Woking, and a little déjà vu for Bulls fans. On a pleasant Surrey afternoon we were again saying goodbye to some of the squad, discussing plans for the summer, and more than anything else, just enjoying still having a team to follow. And this time the result was the right one, signing-off with a deserved victory. In saving their best form of the season until its final month, one or two of the players may have earned themselves a contract, and they also gave some long-suffering fans cause for cautious optimism over the summer break.

Better off than last year?

Yes and no is probably the answer. With GT making conciliatory noises and the developers showing at least some desire to work with the club, football at ES appears more secure than a year ago. In the longer term, however, relocation may be unavoidable if the club is to survive. Whilst I would hate to see a supermarket on Edgar Street, if it means the Bulls are still playing somewhere in the city, I'll take it. Grudgingly.

Given the slightly improved (slightly meaning from desperate to simply bleak) outlook off the pitch, on the field, the season had been a rude awakening. As last season, only more so, it was a case of getting what you pay for. Too many players were lacking either the necessary quality or the commitment, the result being a nervous couple of months hovering just, and only just, above the relegation melee. The Rushdens and Cheltenhams of our little world enjoyed drama of an entirely different kind, and it was Cheltenham who became a proper club just two seasons after joining the Conference. Well-run and ambitious, they quickly learned what it takes to get out of this league, and I suspect they will more than hold their own in Division Three. Damn, I hate them.

At the wrong end of the table, the slots of pain were occupied by the three stooges: Welling, Leek and, inevitably, Farnborough. Whilst I would miss Farnborough, I couldn't say the same for Leek or Welling, particularly Welling. The North Kent San Siro was an experience all football fans should enjoy once, and only once, comedy cricketers or not.

Highs and lows? Let's start with the bad things. As last season, money problems immediately surfaced, with yet more emergency sales seeing most of the quality gone from the squad by November.

Two, count them, just two victories during December, January, February, and most of March.

Twenty minutes of horror against Newport, Isle of Wight, as our season ended in mid-October at the hands of the tiniest of footballing minnows. The low point of a depressing year. I hope that never again will supporters feel the way we did that day.

More humiliation, this time at Hitchin, when I thought I had, after years of suffering, finally become immune to the pain. I hadn't, of course. It was just another one of many desperate days with the Bulls.

Add to this our lowest league position in forty years, and the depressing turnouts at Edgar Street that naturally followed, and it would be fair to say that the season had been an enormous disappointment, albeit less traumatic than the previous one.

And so, to the good things.

Which are there somewhere, if you look hard enough.

The emerging talent from our youth policy, all of whom were brought into the first team sooner than GT might have liked, but each showing enough promise to give hope of better things, both for themselves and, hopefully, Hereford United.

The high comedy of cricketers at the San Siro, bettered only by a Kidderminster Harriers manager actually paying for the signature of Mark Druce.

A glimmer of light in the relationship with the developers, in whose hands lie the fate of the football club.

And a strong finish to the season, giving us all a little hope that next year might just be something to look forward to.

Player of the season?

Andy Quy was consistency personified and Mark Taylor was a dependable and almost ever-present engine in midfield. The precocious Williams and James shone brightly, and Paul Parry, had he played more, might have contended, but for me there was only one candidate. Ian Wright was colossal, week in and week out, often carrying all around him toward a hard-earned point. If the rest of the squad showed half of Wrighty's determination, we would have finished far higher than thirteenth, and if he stays, he could be the next genuine Bulls legend.

However, the highlight of the season, make that of the last twenty seasons, was a departure from Edgar Street. Peter Hill. The man who would define a crisis as the point when the boardroom Chablis was slightly under-chilled, was gone, and if there was a single Bulls fan sorry to see the back of him, he or she was keeping pretty quiet about it. We had endured a bleak nine months, but with the last of the old regime removed, there was now one less excuse for supporters to turn their back on Hereford United. Make no mistake, GT and his new board would have a long hard struggle to return the club to a position of security, let alone challenge for a place back in the Football League. The Conference had again showed that whilst there were still a handful of genuinely poor sides, you needed something special to challenge for that precious top spot.

Circumstances had changed, and drastically, but despite the clear lessons of the season, many Bulls fans were still living in the past. To them, Hereford United was the biggest fish in a small pool, and they were insulted that we had not yet made our way back to the big time. However, twenty-five years of League football was now history and, whilst no-one could take it away, it was time for a new mindset. The short-term future of the club would be measured not in silverware, but survival.

But, as twelve months ago, we still had a team, even if it was a fairly crappy one.

4   1999-2000 Party Politics

14/8/99 Sutton United - away

Two days before Hereford United lost its League status, New Labour enjoyed a better result, although not in our city. After eighteen years of Tory Government the country called time, whilst for the same period Peter Hill sipped Chianti in the comfy chair at ES, watching half-heartedly as his empire slowly crumbled. Is there a parallel here? I'm not so sure. The Tories somehow got a few things done properly before losing the plot, whereas the rancid mess inherited by Graham Turner would have been far more daunting a prospect for Tony's cronies to remedy. Two years on, and to the Member for Hereford, Paul Keetch, a Liberal Democrat and a frequent visitor to ES. Whilst he probably doesn't wear Bulls pyjamas, I doubt that he watches United for the kudos. Over the summer Paul joined the debate about the ES site, as did leader of the local council and another Lib-Dem, Terry James. Terry is apparently not a Bulls fan, but in recent months has added comment to the talking-shop that is Edgar Street and its future. Having met GT, HUISA, and also the developers holding the leases, he feels that any change of use of the site is unlikely, strongly advocating that Edgar Street be the subject of redevelopment. The crucial point, at least to us, would be United remaining at ES, perhaps as the focus of a new multi-sport facility. Here was a dramatic shift of the goalposts. For the Bulls to relocate within the county, the local council would have to break the covenant over the usage of ES, and they weren't keen, and departure from our home of several generations was looking less likely than a few months ago. Amidst the confusion, however, one thing appears certain. For any progress to take place, the developers, the council, and to a lesser extent the piggy-in-the-middle known as Hereford United would need to reach some kind of accord. From the perspective of many Bulls fans this was great news, for here was at last an influential voice committed to a redeveloped Edgar Street and a future for the Bulls, where we belonged.

But perhaps not so, if you took the more cynical point of view. To some Terry's standpoint was merely political manoeuvring, a cheap catcher of wavering votes, or perhaps a ploy to stymie HUISA, who were planning to field candidates in the upcoming local elections. Watch this space, carefully.

So, in a summer which had seen some busy politicians, what of GT?

Also busy, it would appear. Most of last season's squad were still in place, including the talismanic Wrighty, signing a new two-year contract, good news in itself, but upstaged by the signing of one Steve Piearce. 'Steve who?', you may well ask. Steve signed from Halesowen Town, one division below the Conference, hardly unprecedented even for a club with, putting it delicately, issues of a financial nature. At least until you consider that Piearce had been signed from under the noses of several clubs with significantly more spending power, Rushden included, and on a three-year deal.

Something worth repeating. A three-year deal. Quite a feat for a club who had been surviving week to week, or on occasion day to day, not so many months ago. No-one had seen it coming, but GT had somehow acquired the leading scorer in the Doctor Martens League, and, according to Halesowen supporters, a goal-machine. Little excites fans more than a proven, clinical goalscorer and, out of the blue, we now had one. No pressure on Piearce then, as long as he banged in thirty goals en route to the Conference title. Something which shouldn't prove a problem for a goal-machine, so bring on the new season, bring on Sutton United, where the Bulls new strike force of Piearce and Leroy May would deliver some revenge for the many fruitless afternoons I had spent chasing leather around the adjacent cricket pitch. Or wouldn't. Leroy, in his second spell at Hereford, was struggling and withdrawn, probably to prevent further embarrassment. Piearce also limped off, leaving Paul Fewings and Rob Elmes to rescue the Bulls from the subs' bench. And a rescue was needed, due to slapstick defending and a one-goal deficit. The Bulls had been poor, in a very poor first 45 minutes, ominous shades of Kingstonian twelve months previously. Adding to the misery was a half-time downpour of monsoon proportions. As another dismal Saturday was shaping up, salvation was at hand, as one of those moments that set the Conference apart from its bigger, supposedly better brothers arrived from an unexpected source.

As the monsoon reached top gear, a steward called to us. 'Lads, are you getting wet?' He, of course, was irritatingly dry under the main stand. A wise-guy steward taking the piss was not needed with some of the Bulls' less restrained followers unlikely to be in the mood for playful banter. 'Lads, are you deaf, or just daft?' There he goes again, this will end in tears.

It was, and not for the first time, Justin who read the situation a little better than I, and a moment later, I was being dragged towards said steward by my best mate. Assuming they'd both developed a death-wish, I pondered which of these maniacs would be the easier to fight.

I should have known better. Maniac one was shaking the hand of maniac two, and ushering us toward the gate he had just opened. A gate leading to a section of the main stand full of seats. Empty seats. Dry, empty seats. Above the din of the tropical storm still battering several hundred Bulls fans on the open terrace, you could hear the penny drop. I was almost lost for words. A mumbled thanks was acknowledged with the suggestion that we call our fellow Bulls to the shelter, and within minutes the stand was full, the visitors' enclosure empty. There were a few puzzled expressions as the players returned to the pitch to be greeted by an empty space, no doubt wondering whether they had been so bad in the first 45 minutes that the supporters had gone home.

'We're behind you', some wag shouted. It was an out-of-season pantomime moment that even Wrighty found funny, and he never smiles on the pitch. Whilst we were grateful to the steward who had obviously missed the obligatory course in how to be a miserable bastard, the players also had cause for thanks. With the roof over our heads providing acoustics as well as shelter, and now able to make a decent noise, we reminded the players why they were here. Perhaps the increase in decibels helped, but it was a much improved second half and whilst our substitute strikers didn't find the net, Tony James did, leaving Sutton hanging on for a point. We deserved our draw, perhaps more, and had achieved, hold the back page, our best ever start to a Conference season. I found our benevolent but under-trained steward on the way out and thanked him properly. He genuinely didn't know what the fuss was about, but here was a man in the wrong job. Having met one at Welling with a sense of humour, we had found one at Sutton who had a soul. Another who I doubt will be a match day steward for long.

This Allotment Looks Familiar
28/9/1999 Welling United - away

One year ago this very weekend, United earned a draw at Welling's San Siro Stadium. Sadly for Welling, the point gained was no help in keeping them out of the relegation zone come the business end of the season, and they fell into the Ryman League. Or so we thought. Given that never again would be too soon for me and Welling United to be reacquainted, why were we again preparing ourselves for the stiff necks that invariably followed a match where any contact between ball and turf is fleeting, and probably accidental? It's a story beginning nine months previously in north-east England. Toward the end of last season, United's teenagers had beaten Barrow, leaving the Cumbrians in a desperate relegation fight. In receivership since January, Barrow had fought a brave battle, preserving their Conference status with a final Saturday victory at Kidderminster. They achieved it with a rag-tag squad assembled from the depths of professional football's bargain basement, and under the guidance of a Supporters Trust hastily convened to try to keep the club alive. However, the liquidator and the trust were unable to guarantee that Barrow could fulfil their fixtures for 1999-2000. Hardly surprising, due to the carnage left by Stephen Vaughan, but enough for the Conference management committee to take action. Barrow were deleted from the list of member clubs, an action endorsed at the Conference AGM in June. Having achieved a near-miracle in retaining their Conference status, Barrow were thrown out, with no right of appeal. To many people, the Conference had acted prematurely in allowing Barrow no notice of its decision, nor any time in which to organise the required guarantees. Here was a football club with a hundred year history, abandoned by its owner and then cast adrift by the very body that could, and should, have offered a helping hand. You wouldn't treat a dog like that, but once again Barrow had been relegated in a committee room. The first time around, a club from the Welsh Borders had been the beneficiaries, but this time Barrow's loss was Welling's gain. Whilst Hereford had worked tirelessly for their moment of glory, backed by thousands of fanatical supporters, Welling had merely finished above Leek and Farnborough, backed by a few hundred disenfranchised Charlton fans who had suffered enough of the Greed is Good League and Premiership prices.

As with Telford, the mis-management committee had granted a reprieve to a club on matters unconnected with events on a football pitch, and whilst I felt no sympathy for Barrow's previous eviction by show of hands, I certainly did this time, and for two good reasons.

Firstly, it was wrong, plain and simple. Secondly, it meant another trip to Welling Tin-bloody-Shed United. This was my second visit to the San Siro, for many travelling Bulls a third, but after today, most would need a lot of persuading to venture there again. It was an inept performance against a side who delivered precisely what was expected, with the obligatory burly striker causing all of our problems. Ritchie Hanlon had already notched two goals following some, let's call it relaxed, marking. That was merely a curtain raiser, however, when compared to the goal which finished us off. Ian Wright had taken a knock but stayed on the park, a one-legged Wrighty being a better bet than some of our two-legged substitutes. So quite why Paul Sturgess chose to play a cross-field ball five yards behind his hobbling colleague seconds later, only he will know. Needless to say, Mr. Hanlon was handily placed to stroll past our wounded skipper and slot calmly past Andy Quy, with enough time to autograph the ball en route to his hat-trick. Sunday league defending again, which was a pity for Sturgess, as he had been steady up to this point of the season. Perhaps after five games in a Bulls shirt he was getting the hang of how an organised back-four worked, Hereford style. Ten goals conceded in five matches, at least half of them due, according to Talking Bull, to Keystone Cops defending, saw the Bulls languishing in 13th place, with five points. Currently the whole was not adding up to the sum of the parts and, with Stevenage ten points clear, the season already had an ominously familiar look. And Welling, well, they were just being Welling. Not pretty or skilful, but again too clever for Hereford. No doubt they will struggle in or around the relegation zone, only to survive with a final Saturday victory, just to ensure we come back next season. Today was a day of should-haves. Welling should have been playing in the Ryman League, we should have marked Ritchie Hanlon rather than gifting him the easiest hat-trick he will ever score, and I should have stayed at home. There is apparently a tradition at the other San Siro, where visiting supporters are, to put it delicately, introduced to the bladder contents of the Milanese stationed in the tier above. Whilst the home of Welling United doesn't possess an upper tier, the Bulls now had something in common with the great names of European football. Whilst we had remained mercifully dry, it was nonetheless a case of being pissed on in the San Siro.

No-One Could Say We're Dull
14/9/1999 Forest Green Rovers - home

Lies, damned lies and statistics, and here are two. So far this season the Bulls had scored more goals than any other Conference side, a healthy 17. We had also conceded more, a leaky 16, and were, unsurprisingly, placed in the middle of the pack. But still in better shape than Forest Green Rovers, currently in the drop-zone, with three points. And at nearly four goals a game, the neutral could have few complaints about the entertainment on offer, although quite how anybody neutral would have business anywhere near a Conference match would be a mystery. Unless they were one of those strange creatures known as ground-hoppers. Or perhaps a referee. In both cases, possibly a few cans short of a six-pack. So, whilst our defence looked a little wobbly, our strike-force was on song, led of course by the goal-machine.

Er, no. Steven Piearce had notched just twice, three times failing to last 90 minutes. Whilst showing glimpses of the form that routinely destroyed defences, the downside to Piearce was that already he appeared a little fragile. Yes, strikers in this league take a kicking most weeks, but the good Conference goalscorers were the resilient ones, the departed Neil Grayson a fine example. Piearce would need to toughen up, and soon. Our surprise package, and finding the target with ease, was Robin Elmes. Signed, like Piearce, from Halesowen, there was no pre-season hint to suggest that Elmo would prove such a sensation, looking every inch a park player. With the turning circle of a barge and the touch of a Sumo wrestler, he was frequently outpaced by the linesman, and would invariably be wheezing long before the end of a game, glancing longingly toward the dug-out. Enough reason to wonder how Elmo had carved out a career in professional football, but the truth was, he hadn't. He was head of languages at a Midlands school and football was his hobby, his pocket-money. Training two evenings a week and a run round the school grounds of a lunchtime went a long way toward explaining his less than athletic presence, so what exactly did Elmo bring to the pitch, come Saturday afternoon? Simply put, he used his head, and not merely to nod the occasional cross into the net. Here was a player who knew absolutely what he was and wasn't capable of, a player who made more out of limited talent than anyone I can recall, and whose speed of thought would frequently get the better of a more fleet-footed opponent. Like Wrighty, it was easy to like Elmo, and we did. We liked his lumbering runs, his comical jumps, and his anguished, fruitless pleas for help from referees yards quicker than himself. But what we liked about Elmo more than anything was the shocked, goofy grin that would light up his face when he hit the back of the net.

So, with a schoolteacher leading the attack, let's introduce our sheep-farming goalkeeper. Stop laughing at the back, it's true. Mark Jones had been brought in as cover for Andy Quy, and like Elmo, undoubtedly for reasons more economic than athletic, with neither player planning early retirement on the basis of their football earnings. Tonight's clean sheet was the farmer's second in three starts, but in a throwback to the good old days, a stray dog escaped on to the pitch. No problem to our shot-stopper, as Joner had him under control and, in seconds, expertly herding the ball goalwards. OK, so I made that up, but like Elmes, our part-time keeper looked every bit as comfortable out there as his full-time colleagues, in some cases more so.

With electrician Snape and physiotherapist Ian 'Dodge' Rodgerson completing the part-time contingent, a Bulls side with just seven footballers was a thirty-year low. I don't know how many of the visiting players were part-time, but I suspect it was more than four. In their second Conference season Forest Green Rovers remain a part-time club, almost another village side, being both small and sufficiently remote from civilisation. If there is a team more deserving of the country-bumpkin tag than Hereford, Forest Green is it. Swiftly christened Forrest Gump, or the Gumpers, here was a team with two nicknames for the price of one. A team with little history, existing on gates of around 600, who had still comfortably survived their first Conference season, finishing one place and three points higher than the Bulls. How did they do it? I'm not sure, but how did the real part-timers fare against the part part-timers? Very well, nearly. The hitherto free-scoring, all-conceding Bulls hit an entertainment cul-de-sac, not helped by a rugged, organised, but charisma-free visiting team. A charmless nil-nil was beckoning until a late rescue by the goal-machine. Steven Piearce was the Bulls' saviour, but not in the way he might have envisaged. Once again breaking down, his replacement Paul Fewings promptly struck the only goal of the evening. Not unprecedented, as only four days previously at Southport, Piearce limped off, allowing Fewings to steal a 1-0 win. Paul Fewings turned an ugly draw into an ugly win, which, whilst appreciated, would not live long in the memory of any but the most masochistic of Bulls fans. Another gear would have to be found by Saturday, when all-conquering Stevenage Borough would visit.

Swede Worship
16/10/99 Burgess Hill Town - home. FA Cup 4ᵗʰ Qualifying Round

And when they did, the Bulls failed to find that extra gear, and this time failed to get away with it, in a lacklustre 2-1 defeat. There was however, a neat role reversal for Paul Fewings, who did get his start and another goal before predictably limping off. Something is seriously amiss with our strikers at the moment, as almost every week at least one has been lost to injury. Only Elmo would appear to be sufficiently robust to stay the course, although he is usually gasping like an asthmatic on Everest long before time is called. So how is it that Hereford are currently the highest-scoring professional football team in the country? Whisper it quietly, but crap Conference defending might be part of the answer. The Stevenage defeat was followed by one of those capitulations that the Bulls have been liable to produce since joining the Conference, and not for the first time, Dover were the beneficiaries. Whilst Barrow may be a long way to go for a football match, Dover is too far, by about 220 miles, to watch your team roll over and have their tummies tickled. GT must have introduced some teacups to some dressing-room walls in the four days between a wasted trip to Kent, and the destruction of Rushden and Diamonds. Here was a club most Bulls fans would not have heard of before joining the ranks of the unproper. In fact, before 1992 no-one would have heard of them at all, because they didn't exist. They were formed by a merger between Rushden Town and Irthlingborough Diamonds (where, who and what the fuck are they?), Max Griggs spending a few of his Doctor Martens millions to provide the club with a luxurious ground and a group of players who placed the lure of an oversized wage packet above the glory of playing in the Football League.

In most cases I wouldn't blame them, but they had inevitably acquired a tag as a team of mercenaries. Given their status as the rich and spoilt new kids on the block, the rest of the Conference despised Rushden, taking huge delight in turning them over. It was of course envy, plain and simple, but if it gave supporters an added incentive to turn up, or an opponent some extra motivation, then why not? How much extra motivation our team needed we'll never know, but they produced some sparkling football to outshine the Diamonds (I know, I'm sorry), demolishing their high-flying rivals in a four-goal thrashing that could easily have been more.

'Can we (bankrupt cloggers from a tin-shed) play you (pampered palace-dwelling greedy bastards) every week?' sang the Meadow End choir in a resonant, almost tear-inducing split harmony which, due to the stadium acoustics, came across more as 'You're shit, and you know you are.'

Whichever, for the first time in our Conference life we had reached mid-October and the FA Cup with our title aspirations still alive, if not exactly flourishing. Sixth place, and the leaders still in sight, just, was somewhere near where we deserved to be. Having endured the Isle of Wight experience twelve months ago, a home draw against an even more villagey outfit was, this time, good news. Burgess Hill Town, club motto 'Jumpers for Goalposts', were a team that made Hitchin look big and important. Fewings performed his now customary party-piece, hobbling off after scoring, allowing a cameo from the goal-machine. Piearce replaced Fewings and added his name to those of Williams and the increasingly impressive Parry on the score-sheet in a comfortable 4-1 victory. With a place in the first round secure, this might be a good time to describe just what passes for pre-match entertainment, West Country style. Along with the rest of the planet, Hereford approached the Millennium with an eye to the future, a good time perhaps to move on from the stereotypical images of combine-harvesters, hop-picking, rough cider, and a city that would only awake from its slumbers every Wednesday, when the cattle market hit town. Was it finally time to ditch the quaint but tired picture of a community rooted in centuries-old traditions? And would the football club decide that parading a Hereford Bull around ES was anachronistic and just not 21st Century? Whatever the club or the city had in mind, HUISA took a pro-active stance, and it was they who organised today's pre-match entertainment. So maybe they could explain quite how six fully grown men found themselves on hands and knees on the ES pitch, paying homage to a small, painted vegetable. The object of their attention was a swede, placed on the centre spot, painted, of course, black and white. If that alone was not surreal enough, the six, having completed their worship, then passed the swede back and forward over the ES turf, heading toward the sparsely populated home terrace. Equally bemused and amused would sum up the atmosphere, as applause and laughter greeted the HUISA stalwarts. Six yards from goal, a final precision ball, or should that be precision swede, found an unmarked worshipper who side-footed gloriously wide of an empty net.

Oh dear. Much finger-pointing and shaking of heads ensued, along with a brief chorus of 'You couldn't score in a farmyard'. Obviously not meant to be part of this bizarre ritual, the errant vegetable was retrieved and once again a pinpoint swede rolled across the box, this time duly despatched into the Meadow End goal. An embarrassed high-five later, the vegetable worshippers were gone, replaced by a slightly more professional crew who happily, found far fewer problems in placing the spherical object into the onion bag.

So what, you may ask, was that all about? Decades previously, swede worship had been part of the pre-FA Cup routine enjoyed by United supporters, supposedly bringing huge amounts of good luck to the players. A HUISA member plucked it from an ancient memory bank and thought it worth resurrecting. Quite how planting a swede in a goalnet would bring luck, good or otherwise, is beyond me, but be thankful for small mercies. It is said, albeit mainly by visiting fans, that some of the farm-related rituals supposedly enjoyed by we not-quite-but-very-nearly-in-Wales folk would be strictly post-watershed when compared with an innocent piece of swede worship. Who knows what our Sussex visitors made of it but as a pre-match diversion it was different, if a little yokel, and yet another thing you wouldn't see at Anfield. Hereford in the new millennium? Yup, still a hundred years behind the civilised world. Unless, of course, HUISA were a little smarter than they were given credit for, and had pulled off a small but appealing PR stunt. No such thing as bad publicity, especially when fighting for your very existence. And there could be no argument with the 100% record enjoyed by the swede. Which leaves just one question. Why didn't they bring the bloody thing out a year ago? Newport would have had no chance.

One Fit Striker
30/10/99 York City - home. FA Cup 1st Round

If you're struggling in the third division, probably too good to go down and even more probably not good enough to go up, the greatest cup competition in the world is a perfect fillip to spice up your season. York City were one such club, hoping to avoid disaster en route to a shot at one of the big boys. What they got, however, was the tie they probably least fancied. One of the less-crappy non-league sides away from home, with an unmatched reputation for giant-killing and running into some decent form to boot. By contrast, GT would be looking forward to the prospect of another David and Goliath contest at ES. Perhaps the television companies would be interested, the £75,000 fee being more than welcome to our ever-patient bank manager. Sadly, the poor and needy of some other tin-pot club got the television money, and there would be no larger an audience than the 2,800 thrill-seekers present at ES on a miserable October day, joined by 75% of the Bulls' striking options. Missing from action were Elmo (hernia), Fewings (ankle), and goal-machine (broken, several parts required), although Piearce had the privilege of a view from the dug-out, in all likelihood to avoid the embarrassment of an empty space on the substitutes' bench. The rapidly maturing Gavin Williams was in truth a midfielder, which left fourth-choice front man Leroy May, recalled to enjoy only his third start of the season, along with a media furore rarely seen in the Conference.

In the week preceding the tie, Leroy generated more airtime and column inches than the Bulls had enjoyed since the Brighton shoot-out. Almost all was of the nudge nudge, wink wink variety, with nothing to do with Leroy's talent, or lack of, as a footballer, as it was Leroy's other job that had the media in a frenzy. Like many Conference players, Leroy supplemented his football income elsewhere. Most called it their day job, but in Leroy's case, it was a night job, and apparently a nice little earner. Alongside Jones the Sheep, Snapper the Sparky, and Elmo the Teacher, we now had May the Flash, Leroy May being professional football's first, and perhaps only, male stripper. Well, why not? Leroy was a good-looking chap who apparently had all of the other requisites for a man in his sideline of work. Perhaps the pubs and clubs of the West Midlands saw more talent from Leroy than we ever did — on the evidence of the season so far, not difficult. That said, on FA Cup 1st round day, Leroy May was in all senses of the word our one fit striker. It was Leroy's destiny to become the hero of the hour, and on the hour, he was precisely that. The vital piece of anatomy today was his right foot, which touched home the game's only goal and dumped York City out of the Cup. It was a reporter's dream, the double entendres coming thick and fast, their jobs made all too easy by the goalscoring stripper. But cheap gags apart, today Leroy and his team mates deserved their win. Add York to the long list of League sides to crash out of the FA Cup at Edgar Street, look forward to the 2nd round draw, and maybe another team who wouldn't relish the prospect of a trip to Herefordshire. Today had been a good day for the Bulls and a good day for Leroy. And it was the day that a male stripper stole the headlines from a sheep-farming goalkeeper and a bunch of swede worshippers. Which is a line that you probably wouldn't expect to see in the story of a non-league football team. Get those velvet bags ready.

A Hundred Grand Doesn't Come For Free
21/11/1999 Hartlepool United - home. FA Cup 2nd Round

GT must love the FA this year. Another home draw, and perhaps another League scalp for the Bulls. This time Hartlepool were the potential victims, and the two clubs knew a little about each other.

Hartlepool seemed to pop up at ES for pretty much the whole of our residency in the Football League, the Monkey-Hangers seldom threatening anything other than dreary, bottom-dwelling survival. Little has changed for them, including, like the Bulls, a monthly struggle to pay the wages, but today saw a welcome cash bonus. Sky television were no longer able to resist the lure of swedes and strippers, and the tie was moved to a Sunday lunchtime for a nation to enjoy. Or, if not enjoy, be entertained sufficiently to stay awake after a lunchtime pint. Cue black and white wigs, daft inflatables and two thousand Bulls fans who suddenly remembered where Edgar Street was. Some might call them our sleeping fan-base or fairweathers, whilst others might be less polite and suggest that they were glory-hunting posers who want to be on the telly. Whichever, their presence made ES a noisier, more cosy place than it had been for a good few years. I was happy to see them. Hopefully a handful would be back next week for the Trophy game against Barton Rovers — not, I promise, a made-up name.

The match was a re-run of the previous round, although Leroy only made the bench, replaced by a fit-again, loosely speaking, Elmo. It was he who took the glory, nodding cleverly home after half-time, but whilst Elmo grabbed the headlines, it was again Mark Jones and his defence who were the real heroes. Wrighty was just being Wrighty, but his partner and apprentice Tony James was proving a fast learner, and the Hartlepool strike force must have wished they'd stayed on the bus. Today, Jamer was magnificent and whilst not big, he is blessed with great speed, an astute football brain and an ice-cool temperament, rarely wasting the ball once he had won it. Whilst Parry and Williams seem to be sharing most of the attention, Jamer goes about his business without fuss, and I wouldn't be surprised if he goes further in the game than his two Welsh team-mates. The television money plus a few extras meant around a hundred thousand pounds that GT wouldn't have budgeted for. HUISA, and who can blame them, claimed a little of the glory, putting it to council leader Terry James that the football club had generated more publicity for the city with a painted swede than the combined forces of twenty odd local councillors.

Mr James apparently had no comment, but it would be fair to say that national exposure for the city, along with a hundred grand for the football club, didn't come for free. It cost 83 pence at the local greengrocer. The Bulls were in the 3rd round again and, like any club with a million pounds of debt and property developers as landlords, were hoping for the big one. That, of course, being a trip to Old Trafford. Once again, get those velvet bags ready.

Nearly but Not Quite
11/12/99 Leicester City - home. FA Cup 3rd Round
We didn't get the trip to Old Trafford, but the odds were stacked against it, given that Manchester United weren't in the draw. The country's biggest team didn't enter the World's oldest cup competition, their presence in Brazil for the World Club Championship deemed more important. The FA Cup holders had declined to defend their trophy. Much criticism has rightly landed at United's door, but what, precisely, are the FA dicking around at? The World Club Championship is a big name for a glorified PR exercise, the winner of which will be forgotten by Easter, and a global equivalent of the very unproper Spalding Cup. Even Woking fans have forgotten that one and they're the holders. Could United not have fielded a reserve side? That would surely have been preferable to the farcical scenario of a 2nd round loser parachuting back into the draw to fill the gap left by the now sunbathing Mancs. I suppose if you ask the wrong question to the wrong blazers, you may get the wrong answer. Rotherham or Rio in the middle of the English winter? Don't be silly dear boy, now toddle off and book some flights to Brazil. First Class.

As it happened, Darlington were the team given a second bite of the cherry, a trip to Aston Villa their reward for 2nd round defeat. Patently a nonsense, but it seemed that only the FA, and a few misguided directors at Old Trafford, thought otherwise. What if Hartlepool had won the losers' lottery and been drawn at Hereford again? Here was a billion pound business being turned into a joke, but with the holders elsewhere, was it a good draw out for us? In typical Hereford style, we did get a big one, but a small big one, as Leicester City would come to ES. Not the most glamorous of clubs, but currently the fifth best team in England and a guaranteed full house at the Street for what was effectively a no-lose tie. But before Leicester came wins against Barton Rovers, no doubt featuring a striker called Roy, and Southport, 1-0 and 2-1 respectively, and we would entertain Leicester on the back of four consecutive home victories. And with Leicester came Motty. John Motson has remained a friend of the Bulls some twenty-eight years after his first brush with fame but realistically, what were the chances of the Bulls becoming the first Conference side to defeat a Premiership club? Obviously, very slim. Woking, Stevenage and Rushden had achieved heroic draws in recent seasons, but the gap between the haves and have-nots had widened hugely since 1972. In a squad containing 15 million pounds worth of talent, Leicester fielded nine full internationals, both pitch and weather were fine, and there was no army of parka-clad schoolboys to distract the visitors. Although the swede was this time despatched with aplomb, it would take something special to cause what would be the last giant-killing of the millennium.

It was Martin O'Neil who scored first, psychologically at least. His Leicester side were led on to the ES pitch by captain Matt Elliott, a man-mountain towering above Wrighty. He was followed by Taggart and Walsh, even bigger. Then came Emile Heskey, nickname Bruno, thighs about the size of Paul Parry's, well, about the size of Paul Parry. They were huge men. Tony Cottee followed the monsters on to the park like an infant schoolboy somehow lost in a remand school exercise yard. They say that size isn't important, it's how big you are that counts. If true, this was a no-contest. For twenty minutes, it appeared that way, as a succession of Leicester crosses, headers and shots battered Mark Jones and it seemed merely a matter of how many, rather than when, the visitors would score. But they didn't. Slowly our midfield clawed themselves into the match, with confidence visibly growing as the game remained goalless. The back four began looking for white shirts, rather than simply launching the ball away from danger, Fewings and Elmo saw a little action in Leicester's half of the pitch and, amazingly, Hereford finished the half the stronger. There were a few brave Bulls fans willing to venture that we might even nick a goal after the break and really make things interesting. As the second period began to take shape, Hereford, if anything, raised their game even higher, showing little evidence that nearly a hundred teams were placed between the two on show, and it was Leicester who now appeared the more anxious and frustrated side. As the contest entered its final quarter, there was a genuine belief around Edgar Street that we could get at least a replay. And then came the nearly-but-not-quite moment. Paul Parry took a pass on half-way and set off toward goal with, for once, support on either side. A player with pace and touch will always scare defenders, and Parry had scared more than a few in the Conference. This was the same but different, as this time proper players retreated, reluctant to jump in and embarrass themselves. Parry ghosted past two markers and was one-on-one with Tim Flowers, England goalkeeper. As well as pace and touch, Parry has a tidy left foot, and with it launched a shot that beat Flowers with room to spare. Agonisingly, it cannoned back from an upright and was cleared to safety. The width of a post had denied Pazza the moment which would have drawn comparisons with Ronnie Radford all those years ago and Motty would again have been there to call it. It was the last chance of the game, and it was the Premiership side who were more relieved to hear the final whistle. There was a strange atmosphere around ES as the players took their applause, a kind of subdued bedlam. Yes, we had held a superior team to a deserved draw and given them a fright along the way, a fantastic achievement in itself. You could see in the players' eyes however, a sense of frustration that amidst the glory, a far bigger prize had been inches away. This was, however, without doubt the best day of Hereford's two and half years of Conference life. Non-league players rarely get the chance to pit themselves against the cream of their profession, in essence, the people they have always wanted to be. On the rare occasions when they do, it too often ends in a harsh reality check and bitter disappointment. But not today. Hereford's players had raised their game magnificently, and fully deserved their chance to have another go at some real footballers, and this time in a decent stadium.

They had also earned themselves a little bit of history, as the last unproper players in the FA Cup this century, and were in the draw for the 4th round.

Not Quite, but so Very Nearly
22/12/99 Leicester City - away. FA Cup 3rd Round Replay

I don't know what Leicester is like on a balmy May afternoon, but on a dismal Tuesday night in December, it's a pit. Which didn't stop nearly four thousand Bulls fans buying tickets to witness our almost certain elimination from the FA Cup, raising the question as to where they were when we were shit. No matter, it was a fabulous turn-out for a fabulous game, before which this, a genuine telephone call to ES, coming from the Arsenal office. Awaiting the winners of the tie, they politely enquired which potential replay dates best fitted the Bulls' calendar, should we both defeat Leicester at Filbert Street and draw at Highbury. Nothing wrong with being thorough, but the highly improbable was here being stretched into the realms of sheer fantasy. Little did we know how close the Bulls would come to fulfilling at least the first part of that unlikely scenario. And this is how they so nearly did it.

It began with the swede, Leicester generously allowing the worshippers into a new church, although it must have felt more like a cathedral, a gesture most Premiership clubs wouldn't even have considered once they'd stopped sniggering. But by half-time, they may have been regretting it.

From the kick-off, Hereford matched their opponents in every area of the pitch, each of the eleven making the most of their big day. And in Gavin Williams, the Bulls had the man looking most likely to make something happen, more than once making international players look foolish. When on song, Gavin, particularly at our level, is on a different plane, and today he was in the mood, but the most astonishing goal scored by a Hereford player in nearly three decades was nothing to do with Gav. Parry collected wide on the left and ran at Robbie Savage. Pazza had half a yard on his marker which in the Conference, would be all he needed. Savage, however, was every bit as quick, which in this instance cost him. As Parry crossed, Savage slid in, deflecting the ball in a harmless arc toward the Leicester goal. No danger here for the exotically named Pegguy Arphexad between the sticks. Or so it seemed, until Pegguy called for the cross.

'Keeper's. No, yours. Oh shit.' As Pegguy dithered, Paul Fewings nipped in to score with a delicate back-header in front of the Hereford support. We were stunned, silent, unbelieving (for this is Hereford) that Fewings had scored. Offside surely, or maybe a foul. We knew it wouldn't count. So why, then, was Fewings buried under a pile of team-mates, and why was the referee pointing to half-way? Because it *did* fucking well count, that's why. Chaos erupted in the visitors' stand.

As we were about to congratulate ourselves on being still in the game at half-time, Leicester were kicking off a goal down, and not against the run of play. The half-time break flew by, but we knew the next 45 minutes might just seem like a lifetime. Over the two plus hours of the tie, the Hereford players had shown passion, commitment and no little skill. Now would be the time to show courage.

And how they did. Leicester poured forward, driven on by Savage and Izzett, an unsung but ferociously effective midfield duo. The Bulls were pinned back for long periods, clearly tiring but holding firm. O'Neil was apoplectic on the touchline, not allowing his men even to consider defeat.

We knew, however, that at some point Leicester would get a chance, and they did. With time crawling by and twelve minutes remaining, 10,000 Leicester fans finally took a breath. A diagonal ball found Graham Fenton unmarked on the Bulls penalty spot. His header was well saved but not held by Mark Jones, the rebound falling perfectly, horribly perfectly, for Matt Elliott to tap into an empty net. Fuck fuck fuck.

We were twelve minutes from an insane amount of glory, so where had Elliott come from? He's a centre-half. And wasn't there a hint of offside? Probably not the most neutral of juries, but it was a unanimous verdict. He was off, yards off. The only juror with a vote, however, kept his flag down and said not guilty. It was a goal that hurt more than any since Robbie Reinelt scored for Brighton, but there was no time for feeling sorry for ourselves, we could do that on any Saturday. It was time to get behind the team. We were still in the match and still the last unproper club in the FA Cup. Whatever happened now, the Bulls would be in the headlines, we just didn't know yet how big they would be. Full-time arrived without further fright. An hour and a half had passed, with another thirty minutes to follow. Would we see the agony of penalties? I think many of us believed we would hold out and then it would be a lottery of nerves, tension, and unbearable pressure. It wasn't to be. Ten minutes into extra time, a Bulls corner was cleared to Robbie Savage, running like it was the first minute, not the hundred and first. No Hereford player got near him as he sprinted upfield and placed a pinpoint cross onto the head of Muzzy Izzett. Jones had no chance. It was a goal created by the speed and endurance of two exceptional players and it was enough to win the match. It was a heartbreaker, yet still the players ran, as the supporters sang. Both knew, however, that the dream was probably over. Izzett's goal was the last action of any significance, on the pitch at least. Shoulders slumped in despair, with several players on their knees, exhausted. They had given their all, only to be beaten by a side whose extra class, technique and, vitally, fitness, didn't really show until the last, extra half-hour. And by a goal scored by a player with four Zs in his name.

Amidst the anguish of the next five minutes came the abiding memory of the whole night, for me at least. Long after their own players had left the field, perhaps three-quarters of the home fans remained in the ground, delivering a prolonged ovation to an electrician, a schoolteacher, a physiotherapist and a male stripper. And, of course, a few footballers. Proper fans, proper manager, proper football club. I hope they give Arsenal a hiding. It had been an incredible night and very nearly the biggest Christmas present ever. For the second time in eleven days I was proud of my team and once again the players could justifiably be proud of themselves. Two hours later, it finally sank in just how close we had come to a historic victory. Sarah had taped the highlights and do you know what? Matt Elliott *was* offside. All the Bulls had to show for their endeavours would be some fabulous memories and a reminder to the country that football does still exist outside the Premiership. That and a pile of cash which would see at least one chairman enjoying a few less sleepless nights. Whilst the holders of the greatest cup competition in club football had done their best to demean it to that of an unwanted trinket, Hereford United had brought some magic back into the FA Cup.

Newport Isle of Wight? Never heard of them.

No Guts, No Glory
15/1/2000 Billericay Town - away. FA Trophy 3rd Round

Our last cup tie of the last century contrasted starkly with the first of the new, as the Bulls were paired with Ryman Leaguers Billericay Town, and a return to grass-roots football. Whilst Filbert Street isn't quite the Nou Camp, it's a rare treat for the Great Unwashed of the Conference, and a glittering palace relative to Edgar Street. Whereas New Lodge, Billericay is, well, it's a field, with changing rooms and a couple of sheds. And the players? Muzzy Izzett is a genius next to Wrighty, much as we love him, and he in turn stands head and shoulders above the estate agents and van drivers of Billericay. It is, however, a matter of degrees, and Billericay are probably a lot closer to Hereford than Hereford are to Leicester. A shock result today would be relatively minor and certainly wouldn't make headlines outside the Hereford Times or Billericay Bugle. Which is just as well, because Hereford didn't turn up, or at least not the players. The two hundred travelling Bulls no doubt wished that they hadn't bothered either, as by 4.30pm Hereford were 3-0 down and out of the Trophy. From the kick-off the home side were sharper, more inventive, and vitally, more motivated. Not for the first time, our players were outfought and outrun by eleven lads who train two evenings a week. There was simply no passion, and if Leicester's players had shown even a hint of the lack of determination shown by the Bulls we would have today been thirty miles west of Billericay, taking on Arsenal. After the gutsy, committed performances in the FA Cup, we exited the FA Trophy without a whimper. The Bulls were jeered off the pitch, and the same players who lapped up the adulation after the Leicester games were feeling very different emotions today. Sure, Billericay had raised their game but yes, to a man the Bulls had let themselves down, and badly. Not without precedent, with Newport and Hitchin still painful memories, and with countless others before, if any Bulls fans were shocked by the result, they should get to know their team a little better. Whilst Hereford United are carving out a niche as the masters of cup upsets, we are almost as often the victim as we are the victor and although today's upset would barely trouble the Richter Scale, it's happening far too often. The trite cliche about teams now being able to concentrate on the league sadly, doesn't apply in the Conference. Not when there are ten teams between yourselves and the coveted spot that delivers one fortunate club into the promised land, a privilege being disputed by Yeovil and Rushden, both with shiny new grounds and money to burn, whereas we had pride, currently wounded, and one or two contracts to play for. Season over then, unless, of course, Hereford start their meaningless matches next week and storm through the pack on a twenty-game winning streak. Stranger things have happened, but not at Edgar Street.

Rushden, and Other Meaningless Matches. Again
Christmas - Easter 2000 Eleven Opponents - home and away
Beginning with the match following Leicester's escape, and ending with another Edgar Street horror story, the Bulls won five and drew six of the following eleven league games, moving from fourteenth to third in the Conference. Typical Hereford, becoming the league's form team three weeks too late. The Christmas double-header against Kidderminster saw two 1-1 draws, 9,000 fans, a few red cards and a Danish scouser almost imploding. The man with the strangest accent in football, perhaps even on the planet, is Kiddy manager and former Liverpool midfielder Jan Molby. Never a player who could be described as svelte, since hanging up his boots Molby is now almost as round as he is tall, surprising given that he probably covers more miles within the technical area than he ever did with the whole of the pitch as his playground. Whilst it would be hard to fault his passion, someone really should hide the key to the pie-shop, for here is a man on a fast road to the coronary care unit. That said, Jan's

team looked one of the better prepared Conference outfits and to share a couple of draws with them was no disgrace. Drawing a veil over our trials in Essex, and also over another encounter with David Norton, this time in Forest Green colours, our next away trip saw a single-goal victory at Hednesford, yet another Elmo header rewarding the patience of the 150 travelling Bulls, who had to make their own entertainment for the first 45 minutes.

Why so? Because at three o'clock, the home side didn't have a goalkeeper in the ground. They were also a pair of centre-halves, a winger and most of a midfield short. Or so the story goes. Transport problems maybe, but we didn't have too many problems making kick-off time, or coping with the distraction of a pint or two en route. There's nothing like a good conspiracy theory, and many of them floated around the terraces on a grey afternoon, but remember, this is still, if only just, professional football, not a park kickabout. The few Bulls fans still in denial of our status gleefully jumped on Hednesford's timekeeping problems, tinpot team in a tinpot league being the gist of their griping. Maybe they had a point, but perhaps it was finally time to face facts. Football at this level will throw locations, characters and events towards its followers that wouldn't even be recognised, let alone encountered, in the Premiership. Which to my mind, wasn't such a bad thing.

I was getting used to the Conference, with its rickety stands, tin-shed changing rooms, crappy pitches and dodgy referees. More than that (confession time again), I was starting to quite like it.

Well, what's not to like? You could turn up at five to three after a pint in the social club, you could often change ends at half-time, enjoy decent banter with opposition supporters, and merrily abuse the players whilst actually hearing what they had to say in return. And then there are the players. They were less fit and less talented than their Premiership counterparts, but a whole lot more human. They were more like us. Especially Elmo. Here is a chap with a nine to five and, like us, a football fan. But a fan who on Saturday afternoons lives the dream instead of watching it. And more like us because we knew that he would be back in his classroom on Monday morning, as we would be in our offices, shops or vans. As I've said, Elmo is easy to like, and we liked him even more when he notched another two against Hednesford in the return at ES. With twelve matches remaining there was the occasional whisper suggesting that if Rushden and Kiddy were to suffer a wobble, the title was not out of reach. Yes, I did say Kiddy, but what were our much unloved neighbours doing there? Where had they come from? Whilst hard to take, under the hyperactive Michelin Man Kiddy put a run together better than that of the Bulls. Yeovil had faded, leaving the Harriers free to battle it out with the Max Griggs ego-trip at Rushden. Whilst no-one in the Conference liked Rushden, neither side were loved by Hereford supporters, the local radio station re-christened by Bulls fans as Radio Harriers and Worcester. Not that I'm suggesting any bias here, but if GT signed Zinedine Zidane, Harriers and Worcester might just cover it after revealing in-depth details of the new carpet in the Aggborough boardroom.

But back to football. GT had lifted the side out of a potential slump, but it was a loanee who made a big impact, as neighbours Shrewsbury deemed Scott Cooksey surplus to requirements. They must have a couple of very good keepers up there, because they'd sent us a little gem. Or, more accurately put, a huge gem, as with seven clean sheets in his first eight games, Cooksey appeared the perfect goalkeeper. Commanding, confident and an excellent shot-stopper for such a big man, he was an instant crowd favourite. Tidy, as they say in North Herefordshire, and here's what happened in those eleven meaningless games. The highlight was a trip to Rushden, and Nene Park. Fabulous, fully covered structure, perfect surface, first-class refreshments, ample parking, good access, well signposted, a description more befitting an edge-of-town shopping mall than a football ground. And were it not for the thousand (yes thousand) Hereford supporters, it would have had the same atmosphere. The game itself was that rare beast, a decent goalless draw, but more important events were happening off the pitch. HUISA had taken a party of local councillors including Terry James to the game, as an opportunity to show just how important the Bulls were to Hereford and Herefordians. It was a stroke of genius. What the councillors saw at Nene Park was something that focused a group of their community in a way that nothing else could, for here were a thousand passionate Herefordians, united in a cause and absolutely magnificent. Fantastically vocal, high-spirited but peaceful, and a credit to both club and city, it would be a hard heart that remained unmoved by United fans that afternoon. Added to which, the Rushden board wined and dined their guests royally, not taking a penny for their efforts. More than generous, but it rankled with me. This sort of civilised behaviour just wouldn't do from these Johnny-come-lately, money -no-object pantomime villains of the Conference, as we now had to go and find other teams to despise. With a little help from Doctor Martens, HUISA had shown an influential part of Herefordshire Council that 21st century football was nothing like they had imagined, clearly demonstrating that there was enough passion for the club to move its future well-being significantly up their list of priorities. Whilst once again showing the Edgar Street hierarchy how a small but determined group of people could win friends and influence people, HUISA had also shown impeccable timing. Had they entertained their Council guests three weeks earlier, a very different picture would have been painted. It was another awayday and as in most towns, a roadside sign offered a warm welcome, in this case to Nuneaton. And why not? If your day isn't complete without an edgy stand-off in a nasty pub, police dogs ushering you into a dingy stadium, increasingly menacing insults traded on a crumbling terrace, culminating nicely in a drunken ruck as your half-time entertainment, then welcome indeed, the Nuneaton experience is one not to be missed. Your reward for surviving this assault on the senses is the dubious pleasure of a police helicopter sixty feet over your head for the entire second half, not to mention the twenty minute lock-in after the final whistle, purely to enable unfriendly natives more time to set their ambushes. Yes, Nuneaton had more than their share of idiots who were there purely for conflict, but it takes two to tango. The day became a nasty mess because a small section of Hereford followers, and no, they aren't fans, chose Nuneaton as the venue for this season's piss-up and fight party. They weren't disappointed.

Was that really me, waxing lyrical about the quaint Conference grounds, unsegregated terraces, decent banter, and low-profile policing? What was I thinking? Whilst the Conference is, for the moment at least, a much friendlier place than the Football League had been, many more days like that foul Saturday would see a sadly revised opinion. No, I don't get it, and I never will, but this was another contender for the top-ten all-time rubbish days out at the football. And we won that one.

Lino on the score sheet - Twice
14/4/2000 Woking - home

Ever seen a match between three teams end in a score draw? Today, 2,216 lucky punters shared with me that unique experience. In the more traditional sense the Bulls went down 4-2, but two of Woking's goals were credited to a linesman who had clearly not seen a football ground in his life, hence the never-before-seen scoreline of Hereford 2 - Woking 2 - Officials 2. I've held fire until now on the standard of refereeing in this league, but here is something that needs to be said. The Conference must recruit officials almost entirely from the ranks of those rejected by Sunday morning park leagues. Usually equally clueless toward both teams, today they plumbed new depths. The linesman, or, if you insist, the assistant referee running the Bulls defence was literally all over the place, and getting plenty of fully deserved stick. The more abuse he received, the more flustered he became, until every decision he made was wrong, with even the players struggling to keep a straight face. That was, until he scored for the visitors. A through ball found a Woking striker in acres of space, and at least ten yards offside. He, of course, slotted the ball home and couldn't believe his good fortune when the goal was allowed. There was uproar from Bulls players and fans alike, whilst the handful of Woking supporters were busy checking that Christmas hadn't come early. Shortly after which, they were checking again, as another remarkably similar goal followed, this time even further offside. The hapless flagman put in a cameo performance of staggering ineptitude, ending any slim hope of a late title challenge. And whilst the men in black had put in an absolute stinker of a performance, the men in black and white were, in truth, almost as bad. Meaning another term in the Conference for GT and his troops.

Whilst on the pitch the Bulls meandered toward their summer holidays, things were warming up off the field. Having built bridges with the local council, HUISA did not ultimately field candidates in the local election, again showing a preference for co-operation over conflict. For now at least it appears a wise move. Terry James retained control over the council and published plans that would see a large part of the city centre redeveloped. Vitally, this included Edgar Street, complete with a new main grandstand and a rebuilt Meadow End terrace, incorporating the long overdue multiplex cinema. No-one, however, was holding their breath. It was also rumoured that the Bristol Stadium Group were having financial problems to make our own appear like loose change, the likely result being the entirety of our 1.3 million debt being taken by Chelverton. Probably a good thing, when remembering how Bristol Rovers were almost destroyed by the BSG. And we now had until May 2003 to satisfy our landlords, perhaps enough time for Terry James to get things moving.

A fans' forum saw our manager and chairman in an unusually chatty mood. As well as announcing that Scott Cooksey had signed a two year deal (good news), and that Gavin, Jamer, and Parry had also extended for two years (potentially lucrative good news), GT informed us that Steve Piearce had again broken down in training (no news at all). Specialists from several hospitals had tried and failed to help Piearce, prompting some wag to quietly suggest that a mechanic might be better able to get the goal-machine up and running. GT also stated his continued belief that there would before long be a second promotion place available to the Conference. He may be right, but it is something which can't come soon enough. The better Conference sides are more than able to compete in the Football League, endorsed by the success of Cheltenham and Halifax. In a fair and just world there should be consistency through all divisions, and we would have three, if not four, promotion places already established. Sadly, whilst fair and just are noble ideals, money talks, and persuading turkeys to vote for Christmas is hard work. The extra promotion slot is, however, a cause which will no doubt be championed by our very own new national newspaper, devoted entirely to football in and below the Conference. Imaginatively entitled The Non-League Paper, on the evidence so far it is staffed by writers and editors absolutely on a par with the less than gifted athletes on whom they report.

As an unproper paper for an unproper game, it was perfect.

Another Season gone

And you couldn't call it quiet. The Bulls didn't achieve promotion but realistically it was always a long shot. For a short week or so there was a hint that we might just be in with an outside chance, and it was a good feeling to have, while it lasted. In a season with hardly a dull moment, we had been to both ends of the feel-good scale, so let's take the positives first.

Eighth position was an improvement, and 74 goals scored at ES was great entertainment, even if too many went into the wrong net.

Hereford's players showed that they were capable, on their day, of matching any team in this league, the thrashing of Rushden being our best 90 minutes, but there were several days when football was made to look a surprisingly easy game.

The FA Cup run was a joyful and lucrative bonus, the near miss at Leicester being the highlight of our short life in the Conference.

The continued development of Tony James, Paul Parry and Gavin Williams, and their signing of new contracts, was probably the best news Bulls fans received, apart perhaps from the extension of our debt repayment to 2003.

The more promising outlook over the redevelopment of our Edgar Street ground also gave us hope that Hereford United would have a future further into the new Millennium than we once feared.

Taking the Holy Trinity of on-field success, financial viability and a secure future, progress had been made. Whilst large question marks remain, things are looking better than a year ago, and a relative orgy of champagne and caviar in comparison to the year before that.

But it wasn't, of course, all good news.

Like the little girl in the story, when we were good, we were very, very good, but when we were bad, oh dear. Billericay and Dover were just two examples of our simply not turning up, something still happening far too often. Whilst we had our share of near-adequate football and, also encouragingly, a few more ugly one-nil wins, there were still far too many disappearing acts. Until GT sorts out that aspect of our game, we will be going nowhere.

The Conference as a whole was, I think, a little stronger. Kidderminster continued their winning streak and cruised to the title, nine points clear of an imploding Rushden. It galls me to offer a pat on the back to our nearest rivals, but you can't argue with the margin of their triumph. I genuinely hope they enjoy it up there with the big boys, just not enough to stay more than a season.

At the wrong end of the table, we lost Sutton, who were poor, and Altrincham, not a lot better. They were joined, joy of joys, by Welling, our nemesis from Kent losing out on goal difference to the Gump. To the few fans of Welling United that still care, not many teams know the feeling of being relegated by a couple of goals, but we do and you'll find that life goes on. Just don't pawn the San Siro to a property developer.

Replacing these teams would be Boston United, Leigh RMI, and Dagenham and Redbridge, the latter being one club, not two.

Of the three sides, Boston appeared the most serious of the Football League wannabees. With good support, decent infrastructure, and a chairman with deep pockets, they may provide a serious challenge next season. Or so says their manager, one Steve Evans, someone who doesn't appear overburdened with either tact or modesty.

And where, by the way, is Leigh RMI? Or do I mean what is Leigh RMI? We shall see, sometime after mid-August.

HUISA ended the season with a new chairman. Richard Tomkins had deftly steered his group into a position where they had the ear of the fans, the club, and the local council. No mean feat, Richard, you deserve a rest. Kevin Wargen takes the reins and he appears to have a team behind him who are not prepared to let things drift quietly by. HUISA once again presented their awards and player of the year was a surprised John Snape. Whilst not the most gifted player, he is one of the gutsiest. My vote, however, was for a man who never hid, often moaned, but always enjoyed the fact that he was playing at a level I doubt he suspected he would reach. He also knocked in a couple of goals, usually when they were needed most. I hope Elmo is around next year.

Our Millennium season had been mixed, but was a small step in the right direction.

Along with a little less rubbish than recent years, it also saw goal-scoring language teachers, exotic dancing centre-forwards, ritual worship of a root vegetable and a keeper who could only play if the sheep were safely in. I'll be watching carefully, but if this summer's European Championship has any of those, I'll buy Peter Hill a drink.

And if, at kick-off time, a team should be missing their keeper and five of his team-mates, I'll buy one for Robin Fry as well.

5   2000 - 2001 Rocks and Poppies

22/8/2000 Kettering Town - away

Ten, yes ten pre-season friendlies, after which GT was probably none the wiser. New signings were introduced, notably player-coach Phil Robinson, and helping with coaching would be former England striker and Black Country legend Steve Bull. We, of course, pondered the chances of Bully donning a Bulls shirt, a question met with an emphatic 'No chance' by GT. Too bad, it would have been good to see two goal-machines on the Edgar Street pitch, although the chances of both Bully and Piearce being fit at the same time would be slim. Another new face had arrived, and one with a story. Released by Luton, Michael McIndoe came with whispers of gambling and drink problems, something all too common amongst footballers, although rarely at this level. Christened Merson-Adams Syndrome by some particularly cutting (probably Spurs) fans, how much substance existed behind these rumours was uncertain, but the briefest view of views indicated a player whose natural level was several rungs above the Conference. McIndoe could indeed kick a ball straight. Although not straight enough to trouble Southport, as the season opened with both a goalless draw and more touchline tantrums, the visitor's new manager doing his best to out-perform the insanely hyperactive Jan Molby, as another former Anfield legend became the human equivalent of a nuclear melt-down. Today's guilty party was Mark Wright, a man for whom the term fiery redhead was surely coined. His team were a tough and well-organised outfit, but one that nobody could call pretty, and one that more than most, reflected the man at the helm.

Whilst the Bulls drew a blank against Southport, three days later saw them find both Kettering and the back of the net for the first time. Kettering Town inhabit Rockingham Road, surely the toughest ground name in the Conference. Contrasting acutely, or perhaps just cutely, to the least intimidating nickname, as the Bulls took on the Poppies. Rockingham

Road may have been a culture shock to Robinson and McIndoe, but they bossed the midfield so completely that Scott Cooksey was a virtual spectator. When the inevitable goal came, however, it was from an unlikely source, as Chris Lane broke his United duck in style, netting a glorious thirty-yarder. A late second followed, scored by recently acquired substitute Kerry Giddings. Whilst Lane had taken eighty matches to hit the net in a Bulls shirt, Giddings took just eight minutes, some start for a striker plucked from the local league obscurity of Stourport Swifts. Had GT found another youngster with that little bit extra needed to make a career in professional football? Impossible to tell in fifteen minutes, but it had been a better day than a mere three points suggested, with a shape and purpose about the Bulls that hinted of better things to come. Robbo had added industry and steel, McIndoe the quality that would embarrass Conference defenders with ease. And just maybe, a rookie striker with the potential to become a goal-machine. Poppies versus Bulls suggested a mis-match and, tonight, it was just that. It might be a long season for Kettering.

Something Borrowed, Something Blue
2/9/2000 Woking - away

Saturday lunchtime, the short trip to Woking and a chance to reflect on four Conference games and no goals conceded. A 2-0 win at Hayes replicated the Kettering victory, followed by stalemate at home to Northwich, a scarily perfect clone of the Southport match. Obviously the defence is looking strong and our forward line, well, they're getting there. So yes, you could say that most Bulls fans were in a buoyant mood heading towards Kingfield. Where I was faced with a decision. Joining me was Tim, a Rugger-Bugger, despite which he was still a good friend. Should we sit in the stand (great view, adjacent bar, dry), or should I drag him over to the travelling Bulls (crap view, no beer, wet)? It was a tough one. My head said 'Sit down, idiot, and enjoy a half-time pint.' Good logic and hard to argue with. But, and isn't there always a but, my heart said the reverse. 'You're not an old man yet. So what if it rains, get over there and sing a few songs for your team.' It was ten to three and, on the horns of my Bulls dilemma, I did what any true supporter would never have contemplated and left it up to my mate. Now Tim is an easy going guy who knew I was inching toward the terrace. Until the clouds burst. 'Seats it is then', he said. I didn't argue.

'I suppose that makes you a fair-weather', he added. I feigned deafness, as the real Bulls fans got soaked. This was wrong, and uncomfortably so, but something else was badly amiss. As Wrighty led the Bulls onto the pitch, two hundred Herefordians did a double take. Our team emerged in the most hideous excuse for a football shirt I had ever seen, best described as a fluorescent toothpaste blue. Obviously borrowed from the home side due to a clash of colours, I can only imagine that the shirts were purchased by a colour-blind kit-man, or someone with a seriously warped sense of humour. Adding to the shock was the fact that they probably belonged to Woking's youth team, resulting in what you might call a snug fit. It was a sight to disgrace any catwalk, and attracted hoots of derision from the home support. I asked Tim what he made of it, when he eventually stopped laughing. 'Camper than a row of tents', he offered. I couldn't argue and just hoped that the players didn't succumb to the migraine-inducing strip they had been forced to wear. I needn't have worried. The Bulls dominated, taking the lead courtesy of Gavin's tap-in. Just after half-time the same player was felled by the exotically named and already cautioned Dante Alighieri, for a cast-iron penalty. Chris Lane converted, a case, if ever there was one, of London Bus Syndrome. Having waited two seasons for his first Bulls' goal, his second in ten days made him joint top scorer, and he was enjoying it. Alighieri was fortunate to stay on the pitch, but the referee had been less generous or perhaps more spiteful than we thought. The poor chap was petrified of making a tackle from that moment on, a fact seized upon by Gav, who for the next thirty minutes condemned Dante to his own hellish inferno. Like a cat who has snared a mouse, Gavin tormented his victim, the only surprise being that just one further goal resulted, Rodgerson converting one of his many immaculate crosses. Three-nil and fully deserved, it had been an excellent afternoon for Bulls players and fans alike, as five games into the season we were still to concede a goal. Was this the beginning of something special? A few Bulls fans apparently thought so, launching into song as they left the ground. 'Graham Turner's aquamarine army' was their chorus. I didn't see Talking Bill, but I suspect our chantologist wasn't far away.

Lucky Numbers
5/9/2000 Telford United - home
1 - There is a one pound increase in admission prices tonight, payable when United occupy a top three position. Edgar Street is still one of the cheapest grounds in this league and once in a while we actually get something close to our money's worth. I wonder if there's a discount if we hit the bottom three?

2 - Promotion places available from Conference from next season. Probably. A play-off system is likely, according to the mismanagement committee.

3 - Sightings of Steve Piearce, fleetingly spotted on the subs' bench. Yes, the goal-machine is still broken.

8 - Thousand pounds, the amount given in grants and sponsorship to each Conference club this season. Contrasting to the three hundred thousand available to third division sides.

11 - Thousand pounds, now due to the Inland Revenue. For once not a disaster, GT stating that he doesn't need to sell a player to pay the bill.

18 - Professionals currently registered at ES, three of whom are part-time. Not enough, given that 16 are needed each match day. An injury or two would again see the embarrassing sight of a half-empty substitutes' bench. Which revisits the question of one Stephen George Bull putting his boots on in an emergency. Rumour has it that the Tipton Skinhead is registered as a Hereford player. Bully for the Bulls? Don't bet against it.

50 - Free seats at ES, distributed to local schools for each home game, and a too rare piece of positive PR by the club. More please.

90 - Percent of petrol stations which remain closed due to blockades by fuel protesters, perhaps explaining the almost-empty visitors' terrace today. And Telford is only a few miles up the road. But, then again, maybe they just couldn't be arsed.

152 - Thousand pounds. The total amount paid in transfer fees by third division sides this summer. A figure dwarfed by spending in our league, with both Boston and Rushden individually spending more, in the case of the latter, on a single player. A stark reminder, if one were needed, of the gulf between the haves and have-nots in the Conference this season.

986 - Miles, covered by supporter Jon Wells, cycling from Lands End to John O'Groats to raise money for the club. Good on you Jon, genuine Bulls fan, genuinely nice guy.

2,000 - Pounds, raised by Bulls fan Gary 'Tango' Smith, in a two-minute act of ultimate sacrifice. In front of a packed (to a quarter of its capacity) Meadow End, Gary's trademark golden mane was shaved off. Gary's loss was HUISA's gain and whilst a two-grand haircut is no longer the sole preserve of Mr. and Mrs. Beckham, HUISA continue to keep their profile high and funds coming in.

18,000 - Pounds. The cost of the new electronic scoreboard at Edgar Street, the first sizeable amount of money spent on our decaying ground in decades. You may think a new scoreboard something of a luxury for a club in our position, but somewhere out there is a generous fan who thought it necessary, donating the cash solely for the purchase of said technology. Fancy seeing your name in lights forty feet above the Blackfriars End goal? Well now you can.

400,000 - Pounds. The amount of money supposedly lost by Kidderminster in achieving promotion last season. Try that little stunt when you're in a CVA.

1,300,000 - Pounds. A big, very scary number and the amount still owed by the Bulls to developers, repayable in May 2003. Which, unless a Bulls fan wins the lottery, isn't going to happen. Six lucky numbers on the right ticket would be, well, just the ticket.

And here's another number for you. Today, Scott Cooksey kept a clean sheet, making it six in a row. Further upfield, Robbo and Snapper opened their accounts for the club and season respectively and, quite honestly, Telford never looked like scoring, leaving Hereford as the only club in senior Britain yet to concede a goal. Scarily close to proper football.

Handbags, and a Handbag
3/10/2000 Kingstonian - away

Fifty minutes into our next game, Scott Cooksey was re-acquainted with an almost forgotten feeling, Hednesford's Neil Davis slotting home, and for the first in five months the Bulls were behind. Wrighty's header spared further embarrassment, but a point was all that we deserved.

Four days later, Nuneaton also had the temerity to beat Cooksey, but Giddings and Dodge maintained our perfect away record and second place in the Conference. Nine matches into the season saw the Bulls finally come up short, disappointing but not unexpected, as all we ever get at Doncaster is wet. Follow that with two points from nine and the Bulls had avoided a clean sheet for six matches, precisely the number they had managed to stay blemish-free. The vessel was leaking, and with Yeovil and Rushden forging ahead, an urgent return to early season mode was required. Kingstonian, suffering what could kindly be described as mixed fortunes, might be the place to put some wheels back on the tracks. Just over a hundred Bulls fans ventured to Surrey on a damp Tuesday evening, including Alan, a Bulls fanatic introduced to me last season. Alan and I, it transpired, had attended the same Hereford College, so it was strange that we had never met in those days, being only two years apart in age. Even more so that we hadn't connected on our travels with the Bulls, given that for the last eleven years we had lived no more than 500 yards apart and shared the same local. And it's supposed to be a small world. So we headed toward Kingston (bus not bike), musing on the chances of being both moderately entertained and finding a much-needed win. Little did we, or the 831 others in attendance, suspect that we were about to witness the most bizarre ninety minutes of football that any of us had seen. This was on the surface a game to tempt only the most devoted (or desperately sad), and for twenty minutes was a match living up fully to our lack of expectation. At which point the referee, showing all the traits of a top Conference official (inconsistent, pedantic, whistle-happy, useless), took centre stage. Mr. Rumery blew yet again, giving Hereford, correctly for once, a potentially dangerous free kick. Up stepped Chris Lane, and scuffed horribly wide. Again please, indicated Mr. Rumery, although only he knew why. Michael McIndoe pushed Lane away, and curled a beauty into the top corner. The already tetchy home players were justifiably furious, and a niggly ten minutes saw a rash of yellow cards, along with an already struggling referee completely losing the plot. The only surprise about Elmo's header on the half-hour was that Rumery had allowed play to continue for long enough to see a decent chance both created and finished. The Bulls then assumed a degree of control that the referee could only dream of, but he was not to be denied further glory. A dubious penalty decision sparked yet more outrage in the Kingstonian ranks, whilst we scratched our heads in puzzled amusement. Lane once again scuffed his shot, Farrelly saving comfortably. Obviously, all eyes were on Rumery as we waited for the re-take, but surprisingly, it didn't come, and it was still two-nil. A quiet interlude of around 90 seconds followed Lane's mishap, before everything, and everyone, kicked off. Literally. Robbo tangled with Geoff Pitcher in midfield, and several already frayed tempers snapped. The louder Rumery whistled, the more the players pushed, shouted and shoved. Only Farrelly in the home goal and Colin Luckett appeared to keep both their heads and a safe distance from the melee, but handbags were eventually downed, and the lectures began. The wise old heads belonging to Pitcher and Robbo blended into the night as Rumery reached for his cards. Amazingly, no yellow was flourished for the twenty-player punch-up, but one man, amongst all the red mist, saw red. Staggeringly, the only outfield player who appeared not to be in the thick of the mayhem was selected and Luckett was on his way. Mild amusement gave way to guffaws of laughter, for this was now categorically a joke. Well, it was for us, safely ensconced in the visitors' enclosure. Everyone else, I suspect, failed to see the funny side. As half-time came, the good folk of one of West London's more placid suburbs were in a collective rage, the focus of which was cocooned within a small army of stewards heading toward the tunnel. As I had suspected last season, Kingstonian were blessed by the absence of a lunatic fringe, a good thing for the hapless Mr. Rumery, who surely would have been in mortal danger. Perhaps a half-time cuppa would cool things down. Forty-five minutes of entertainment, the like of which you can only dream about, had flown by, driven by a referee of such woeful incompetence that you could but wonder just where he learned his trade. If this game was on videotape it would be a best-seller, and without question a comedy classic. So, could any second half live up to what we had just seen?

Initially it appeared not. But whilst act two began quietly, we suspected that more was to come, and on the hour, Rumery pounced. Fearing we had forgotten his first half exploits, the man in black was back and oh, how he had saved his best until last. Steve Farrelly, England semi-pro keeper, launched a punt downfield, closely monitored by Gavin, and in one of those what-happened-next moments, Rumery delivered his coup de grace. Gav left a leg mischievously close to Farrelly as he followed through, said leg barely touching the home keeper's foot, but nonetheless, Gavin crashed to the floor. The consensus here was that Gav had fouled Farrelly and, as Rumery blew once more, might see a yellow card for diving. But remember, this was no normal referee, and as Gavin's non-existent injury was attended to, the lecture was for the home keeper. 800 people held their breath as Alan, a sage reader of body language, called the next play. 'Farrelly's gone.' And he was, as another flash of red emerged from the pocket of Mr. Rumery. Which is where poor Steve Farrelly lost the plot. Without the intervention of players from both sides, we might just have witnessed a keeper administer a right-hander to a match official. Goalkeepers are by definition mad, but Farrelly was by now way beyond that, apoplectic being a conservative description, with further stewarding required to save the linesman from a hiding. This was train-wreck drama, so far removed from normal fare that it was easy to forget the football match taking place beneath the main event. Whilst several Bulls fans were close to tears by this point, I felt sorry for Farrelly, for he had been well and truly done. A theatrical tumble and the world's worst referee had ruined the night, probably the whole month and maybe even more, of an honest chap just doing his job. With half an hour remaining and both teams realising that a softly-softly approach was the only way to guarantee a continued part in the drama, there was little left for Mr. Rumery to do as Gavin rubbed salt into the wound, applying a crisp finish to another perfect McIndoe assist. Three goals, a missed penalty, a million yellow cards and two reds, a twenty-strong punch-up and a homicidal goalkeeper merely hinted at the scale of drama, comedy and incompetence on display. But there was more. As the players made for the dressing-rooms, Farrelly re-entered the fray, unsure whether braining Rumery before or after dismembering Gavin was the best course of action. Whilst both were well protected, both would have been well advised to lie low, or risk leaving the ground in an ambulance. As Mr. Rumery left the pitch, this time with a double helping of security, the temptation became too much for one lady of Kingston. Showing huge athletic prowess, a brief sprint was followed by the launch of a handbag. Like most of her intended victim's decisions it was wide of the mark — probably a good thing for the home club's sake. Can there ever have been so much outrageous entertainment on a Conference football pitch in one helping? It had been 90 minutes of pure theatre, a match with everything bar a half-time cameo from The Beatles. And all for nine quid. The postscript came in the supporters' bar after the game from a Hereford player topping up supplies for the journey home. A Bulls fan observed that it had been a lively evening, a statement akin to observing that the Titanic had minor buoyancy issues. With a four-pack of lager in each hand, we were treated to an insider's view of events. 'That, mate', he replied, 'was fucking mental.'

He had a point and discretion will conceal his identity, but I can tell you that it wasn't Gav.

He, apparently, was being smuggled on to the team coach in Scott Cooksey's kit-bag.

The Not So Mighty Quinn
October - December 2000

The season had taken a familiar turn for the worse and, with Yeovil and Rushden imminent, was unlikely to get better soon, four points being a minimum from these two matches if any hope of a challenge for the title was to be retained. A cracking match with the former saw four goals shared at ES, but the signs were clear. Yeovil were clearly less crap than the Bulls and unlucky not to have taken three points back to Somerset. In comparison, the Diamonds of Rushden looked one-dimensional, but were still able to pinch a one-nil win from an even more ordinary Bulls side, bolstered by international superstar, Northern Ireland's Jimmy Quinn.

OK, superstar may be overdoing things just a little, but bolstered is surely reasonable. Sadly, no. The only thing being bolstered would be a bank account, name of J. Quinn. He was four years older than me and looked it, and many fingers were being crossed in the hope that the loan wasn't a long-term arrangement. If this was the best GT could find, we were in trouble, and on a familiar slide towards yet more meaningless post-Christmas fixtures. We needed a lift as Dover came to ES and, happily, we were enjoying ourselves again. After eight minutes, however, it was Dover having all the fun, as two gift-wrapped goals were handed to the visitors, witnessed by the first sub-2,000 crowd of the season. For once, though, it was the stay-aways who got it wrong, as did the handful who had seen enough by half-time. The last straw for them was our fifth missed penalty of the season, Quinn this time the guilty party, although you might think his effort striking the woodwork a shade unlucky. Until you consider that the woodwork in question was an advertising board wide of the goal. Twenty fucking feet wide. It was a horrible miss to cap a dismal 45 minutes for the Irishman who literally couldn't put a foot right. Quinn probably failed to appreciate the irony of his wayward spot-kick, but a few Bulls fans were reaching for their mobiles during half-time, the board in question directing the desperate and depressed towards the friendly voice of the Samaritans. The writing, it appeared, was on the wall, literally so for the no longer Mighty Quinn. He left the pitch to a crescendo of abuse, although whilst Quinn had been woeful, his team-mates had been almost as bad. Only a few days had passed since Kingstonian, but it felt like a lifetime. Could the second half be as bad ? No, as within fifteen minutes the reality that football and cliché can be more than cosy bedfellows had been perfectly demonstrated, the match becoming the ultimate game of two halves. Elmo replaced Quinn, bringing much-needed, if only comparatively, pace and mobility to the front line. Gavin and McIndoe woke from their slumbers and United were a new team. Within forty seconds Matt Clarke had broken his United duck, like Chris Lane, after two years of trying. Wrighty notched an equaliser, shortly after which Elmo added two more, and the Bulls coasted to victory in a half of near perfect, almost proper football. It might not be such a busy night for the Samaritans after all. That, thankfully, was the last we saw of Quinn, without whom the 4-2 scoreline was repeated at Scarborough and followed by a 3-1 win at home to the Gump. We were scoring for fun but, crucially, no nearer to either Yeovil or Rushden.

And so ended a goal-feast and began the famine. The Bulls had a blank Saturday after victory over the Gump, due to a defeat and FA Cup exit three weeks previously. And how we needed that cup money. The unwanted holiday preceded a run of five winless matches, including a first visit of Boston United and their voluble boss Steve Evans. Evans left ES with a point and the impression of a manager happy only when his players were putting either the ball or, preferably, an opponent, into orbit. Evans has an uncompromising attitude, reflected in his team and without the benefit of some surprisingly competent refereeing might have taken more than a solitary point. Sadly for Boston fans, the day was soured by a mini-fracas and a stolen drum. I would have been all for borrowing the damn thing and handing it back at five o'clock, but that was going too far. The famine continued, the next five games producing three points and the collector's item of a goal from Steve Piearce. The goal-machine made his seasonal debut at Morecambe, leaving the bench to net an undeserved but high quality equaliser. True to form, Piearce was then absent for the traditional home defeat by Doncaster and failed to impress in a dire nil-nil with the utterly crap Poppies of Kettering. What, I wonder, does GT now think of his wonderkid striker, the man who continues to baffle medical science with his startling range of injuries and ailments? Let's just say that if the agent who brokered the goal-machine's three-year deal shows his face anywhere near Edgar Street, he would be wise to ensure that his own health-care premiums are up to date. Unless he could somehow convince the Bulls that a penalty kick presents a reasonable opportunity to put the ball in the back of the net. Against Doncaster, another effort failed to find its target, Robbo this time the culprit. Some wag suggested that the club fly the German Fat Bastard over every Saturday, as specialist penalty kick substitute. Not such a crazy idea. Was it not GFB who slotted a perfect six out of six at ES just a few seasons ago? No doubt a dream come true for Mike Quarrell, but a sad day for Steve Perrin, larger-than-life keeper of Forest Green Rovers, who would no longer be the owner of the best beer-belly in professional football. But more of Perrin and his spare tyre later. December had again been a miserable month for the Bulls and was rounded off in depressing mode with a Boxing Day defeat at Chester. Our early-season form was a distant memory and the FA Cup exit at Woking looking more significant with each dropped point and missing spectator. The club was obviously losing money and although a host of Christmas fund-raisers were helpful, it wasn't enough. Rewind to the start of the season, when GT stated that there was no need for emergency sales. Well, that was then, and this is now.

Another bill had arrived, apparently marked overdue and with a covering letter detailing winding-up procedures should it remain unpaid. With a five-figure sum urgently needed, the January sales began early at ES, and a tearful Chris Lane departed, in return for £12,000 and a profit share if he ever made a big money move onwards. Southport got themselves a decent right-back for their money, and the Bulls a little breathing space, along with a cancelled court appearance. Lane's departure was a serious concern, for we were now back in a scenario where players were being sold in order to keep the lights on. It was a clear signal to any club with spare cash to go shopping in Hereford and make a joke offer for one or perhaps all of our remaining assets. Michael McIndoe, Tony James and particularly Gavin would be hard to hold on to for much longer, unless there was a dramatic turnaround. It was perhaps a blessing that Paul Parry had missed most of the season with damaged ankle ligaments. Despite the slump, there were often more scouts than visiting fans at ES and our youngsters were consistently demonstrating quality that deserved a bigger stage. Bigger even, perhaps, than Southport.

So here's a question. Can football fans genuinely feel pressure?

Whilst there was clearly enormous pressure on GT and his staff, could we, the fans, admit to feeling it as well, given that each defeat was, simply put, just another game? Whatever the outcome on a Saturday afternoon, none of us would be defaulting on our mortgage. So obviously the answer is no. In comparison with the pressure felt by the players and management, how could we, mere supporters, be stressed, or worry, or lose sleep, or hair? We lose a match, we go home, have a beer and life goes on, just a couple more points we might have earned but didn't. But look at it the other way, and it is the genuine long-standing fan that has most to lose when things go so badly wrong. Another poor performance, another hundred supporters turn away and another handful of tenners don't reach the bank manager. And so another player is sold for peanuts. And on it goes, until all that remain are Dodge, Snapper, Elmo and a handful of YTS boys. With the Bulls back in the nightmare scenario of week-to-week survival, I would say that yes, real fans do feel the pressure, and more so than any player.

If our creditors, our friends in property development or our bank manager decided to pull the plug, there would be a team somewhere for each of United's current squad, something which couldn't be said for us. For where would we go? Not bloody Kidderminster, that's for sure. A huge hole would appear in many lives that would never be filled. Just ask a die-hard supporter of Maidstone United or Bradford Park Avenue. And what would I do if United ceased to exist?

A question that doesn't bear thinking about and, at the same time, is always lurking at the back of the mind. Here's my answer, and not necessarily in order of importance. I would play more golf, spend more time with the kids, rejoin my old cricket club, maybe even find a team in need of an ageing but once moderately competent goalkeeper. All agreeable ways to spend an afternoon, so why does the very real prospect of no more Hereford United bring such a sense of dread? Maybe it's that the Bulls and Edgar Street have been part of my life for such a long time, and that so many people, places and memories exist for me purely through my team, that it would be like losing a limb. If something that had always been there and I thought always would be was suddenly taken away, it would leave a gap that I doubt would ever be truly and completely filled. And I'm only a part-timer.

There are many Bulls fans out there, as there are for all clubs, whose team *is* their life. God knows what they would do. The future of Hereford United is in the hands of GT, who has kept the club alive before in similar circumstances and not all that long ago. We have to trust him, simply because there is no-one else. He says that he's in it for the long haul and I hope he's right, because the alternative doesn't bear thinking about. It's pretty safe to say that yes, of course we're feeling the pressure.

As is the boss, whose patience finally snapped in the case of one of his employees. Already with a reduced squad, the last thing GT needed was another Piearce sick note, but that's what he got. Tamworth took pity and signed Piearce on a month-long loan deal, unaware that this particular goal-machine didn't come with a warranty. Nine starts in eighteen months was a wretched return on the club's investment, and Piearce can count himself fortunate that he wasn't a racehorse. You could safely say that by now he would have been retired. Permanently.

You write it, we print it
13/1/2001 Dover Athletic - home. FA Trophy 3rd round
Lane's sudden departure, announced with no indication that finances were again critical, was for many Bulls fans the final straw. Forums and fanzines raged at the manager and whilst some of the criticism is justified, GT has a job, or is it two jobs, that you wouldn't wish on your worst enemy. Competing

with the wealthier clubs in this league must be like boxing with one arm tied behind your back, but somehow the Bulls remain in fourth spot, so GT is clearly doing something right. But, and it is a very big but, Mr. Turner and the club let themselves down, and badly so, from a PR perspective. The Chris Lane sale was just one example of poor, sometimes non-existent, communication between club and supporters. Perhaps Richard Tomkins, previous HUISA Chairman, was a more skilled solicitor of information than he was given credit for. Or perhaps GT has so much on his plate that he simply hasn't got time to keep the most vital part of the football club updated on a matter that concerned them more than any other. If it's the latter, it's not an excuse and needs to change. Recent months have seen yet more race-nights, quiz-nights, cycle rides, plant-sales, head-shaves, penny collections and more, each putting desperately needed cash into the kitty. All are efforts from Bulls fans not prepared to let their club slip away quietly, and they deserve better. Yes, even the person who suggested that the club should fold and start from scratch. Express and Star West Midland League, anyone?

The most bitter, polarised point of view, however, came from a group known as New Meadowender. A four-page diatribe appeared in Talking Bull, pinning the blame for everything bar foot and mouth and the fuel crisis firmly at GT's door. According to this collective, both our diabolical penalty record and Steve Piearce's catalogue of injuries would somehow have been avoided with a different manager. Whilst some of their points were valid, how exactly is a missed penalty the fault of someone sitting 60 yards away? Talking Bull has a strap-line, 'You write it, we print it', and rightly so. Whilst the editors are generally pro-GT, they have never shied away from printing pieces critical of the management, but they also have a sense of humour. The New Meadowenders were allowed sufficient column inches to position themselves as constructive critics of GT, all in one moderately well-considered page. And then take three more to become a laughing-stock. Come on Turner, be a proper manager, get on there and slot home a penalty or two. Or at least keep us in the FA Trophy, starting today with Dover. Once again, a must-win game would take place at ES, a cup-run now essential to keeping interest and cash-flow ticking over. So says GT in his programme notes, belatedly explaining why Lane had to leave.

'It's money again folks, really sorry Laner is gone, but hey, Matt Clarke, can revert to his best position, the 'leccy bill is sorted and we've one less mouth to feed.' My words, not his, but you get the gist. Sod's law then prevailed, as a knee injury ruled Clarkie out of today's game. Also missing in action would be Steve Bull. Yes, Bully became a Bulls player as a late sub at Northwich. An England international partnering a West Midlands schoolteacher would make interesting viewing and I'm sure that Bully could teach Elmo and, more importantly, Gavin, a trick or two. What knowledge our schoolteacher could impart to Bully is another matter, unless of course he needs help with his complex Germanic pronouns. Unlikely, but GT brought perspective to our situation, pointing out that since relegation he had collected more than £400,000 in transfer fees. In the post-Bosman era of freedom of contracts this is a staggering sum, without which the Express and Star League might already have had a new member. Something overlooked by New Meadowender, but why let the facts interfere with a good whinge?

The must-win game was far from a classic, but Gavin gave the ever-present scouts more food for thought with another man-of-the-match display, along with the only goal.

Like him or loathe him, we remain in the hands of Graham Turner and it appears for the foreseeable future that if Hereford United continue to exist, GT will be at the helm. An unsackable manager doesn't sit well with me, and is no more palatable than the Chairman picking the team, but at Hereford United we currently have both. That GT is answerable to no-one is something his critics are unable to see past, but there is a bigger picture to consider and I, for one, am happy that GT is sticking it out. Despite his imperfections, without him I doubt that we would have a club, a fact that might upset his critics slightly more than a few missed penalties. Because Graham Turner is, in fact, answerable to a decent and honest, if over-worked, chap, and one with a conscience. Fortunately for Hereford United, GT is answerable to himself, and thankfully there remain enough Bulls fans out there with the ability to see the bigger picture. And, on a lighter note, guess which full-back scored on debut for Southport today?

Civil War
3/2/2001 Leigh RMI - home. FA Trophy 4th round

Time to find out who and what, if not where, Leigh RMI are. Yes, Leigh Railway Mechanics Institute really is a football club and they visited ES in the next instalment of the Trophy. This was no easy match for a squad missing Parry, James, Wright, Bull, and Piearce. Only four substitutes were named, two of them unfit, present only to avoid more embarrassing gaps

86

on the bench, and if more than one player was forced off through injury, reserve keeper Matt Baker would be showing his paces as an outfield player before we had seen him between the sticks. In a season that had gone rapidly downhill, the light relief provided by a sub keeper playing centre-half would have been a welcome diversion, but it wasn't to be, the two sides playing out a flat nil-nil draw. Although the FA Trophy isn't the biggest of prizes, it was all we had left to play for in this now wretched season, and vital to keep both interest and revenue alive. So just why the players turned in their most lacklustre performance in months is anybody's guess. It had been a bleak afternoon for Bulls fans and no doubt the last straw for a few more die-hards. 1,493 were in attendance, including a cab full from Leigh, a good effort given both our recent form and the lure of rugby on television. The thirty-point drubbing inflicted on their Welsh hosts provided a small crumb of comfort for the English contingent, myself included, being one quarter Welsh except on rugby days. Whilst there has never been anything more than friendly banter between English and Welsh supporters at ES, the same can't be said for the anti-Turner lobby and those standing by him. The war of words between the two camps has escalated to such an extent that the internet forum was temporarily closed due to the level of abuse, including threats of physical violence. There was even, at Telford last Saturday, a stand-off between two groups of United fans, almost coming to blows over their difference of opinion. Like most civil wars, the two camps appear so entrenched that handshakes and a cordial agreement to differ are clearly not on the horizon.

Because Graham Turner was the man who dismantled a league three play-off squad, replaced quality with crap, and took our club out of the Football League. His inability to motivate players, his cut-price selling of our remaining assets, his baffling tactics, even his failure to convert a penalty, were all sure signs of a manager who has lost the plot. Many people, and the number is growing, dislike and distrust GT, and want him out of ES. But they also have something else in common. Not one of them has proposed an alternative.

Go ahead, have your revolution, overthrow the chief.

What happens then? For this is the same Graham Turner who inherited a squad and was given wages to pay less than half of them. He somehow coaxed enough goals and points out of a poor side to survive in any season bar the one that mattered. And the same man who put his money where his mouth was, taking sole responsibility for a basket case of a football club and keeping it alive when anyone of remotely sound mind would have walked away. He even, occasionally, gave us hope that better things might not be too far away. Our previous crises have seen supporters rally behind a united front, but not this time. The situation is as depressing as I can remember, and frankly, we're in a fucking mess. If we don't get past RMI in the replay, it could be time for the last man out to switch off the lights. That is, if the power hasn't already been cut off.

Spot On
27/2/2001 Morecambe - home. FA Trophy 5th round replay

Two trips to Lancashire within a week (no, of course I didn't go) saw another Tuesday night cup tie at ES. The first was a visit to Leigh, a rutted, frozen pitch, players barely visible through the fog, and a committed, thoroughly deserved win. So why didn't they do that at home?

The second excursion to the north-west was to Christie Park, home of Morecambe, a decent goalless draw, shaded by the Bulls and another Trophy replay to enjoy. Recent weeks have seen a big improvement in form and attitude, including a comfortable 3-0 win at Hednesford and a first goal from Coventry University student Jimmy Quiggin. Jimmy joined on a part-time contract and looks a half-decent player, although the PA announcer gave a few Bulls supporters a fright, mishearing our newest signing as Jimmy Quinn. No, not even in our current depression are we that desperate, although Quiggin's arrival filled a gap in the Bulls line-up caused by another departure, once again required to keep the CVA intact and the club trading. The latest sacrificial lamb was Michael McIndoe and this time it was Yeovil who sniffed a bargain. £25,000 was a better deal for them than for us, the extra five grand payable if he helped them to promotion — still a long way short of what Michael was worth. As with the Lane sale, 25% of any future profit would come to the Bulls, but what no-one explained is where this bonus money would go if the club no longer exist. McIndoe's departure would leave the Bulls short of a quality midfielder but at least this time the sale wasn't out of the blue, GT warning that both Boston and Yeovil were chasing McIndoe and that he was probably on his way out of ES. A good deal by a good manager, as Colin Addison was McIndoe's new boss. A local legend and a man who, thirty years after leading the Bulls into the Football League, still lived in Hereford. So here's one for you. How many clubs have a street named after a rival manager right on their doorstep? At least one, as a wayward clearance over the Meadow End roof (or perhaps a Quinn penalty) would end up in Addison Court. It might be a while before we see a Turner Terrace, but if GT can somehow get his club back into the league, it would be an achievement to more than match that of the current Yeovil boss. Softening the blow of losing McIndoe was the news that this season's forgotten man was close to fitness. Paul Parry was in training and would fit neatly back into his role on the left flank. With Parry, Quiggin, Gavin, Giddings, Elmo and even Bully around, GT wouldn't be short of options going forward, and it was Steve Bull who poached a 93rd minute equaliser against Nuneaton last week, something that we had been hoping to see since August. Fortunately, GT's assessment of Bully's chances of playing were wide of the mark and, whilst not match-fit, he's prepared to risk limb, if not life, to help out an old friend. Thanks Bully, here's to a few more goals, perhaps even today, in the FA Trophy.

Having dominated at Morecambe, Hereford did anything but at ES and it was the visitors who looked likely to break the deadlock. Even when the Bulls were awarded a penalty, it was difficult to see where a goal would come from. With the failed spot-kick count now at seven, and GFB hastily lacing his boots, Gavin somehow located the back of the net. Grown men cried and old ladies fainted as Hereford scored with a penalty kick. The question now was, could we survive 45 minutes, keep the season alive, and enjoy a televised match against Burton Albion? The answer (and don't forget, this is Hereford) was no. Morecambe deservedly equalised, leaving, to the delight of 44 Morecambe fans and the dismay of 1,400 Bulls, a penalty shoot-out. The New Meadowenders had probably gone home, knowing too well our record from the spot, but hold on. Were we not on a fabulous run of one consecutive successful penalty kick? In a tie that could have been won at Morecambe, but should have been lost here tonight, our season was entrusted to a series of shots from twelve yards and a question of who could hold their nerve the better. Oh ye of little faith. Morecambe missed, whilst Gav scored again. A Cooksey save was followed by a James conversion. Mark Quayle then almost outdid Jimmy Quinn in blazing wide, but was followed off course by our own James Wall. Drummond finally converted for the visitors, but little Jimmy Quiggin spared the fifth volunteer, slotting calmly home, and Hereford United still had a purpose to the season beyond mere survival.

Penalty shoot-outs must be the most gruesomely compulsive form of sporting entertainment devised, especially if you're English. The stress levels in these duels must be amongst the highest in professional sport, so it was interesting to see that today, all four of the Bulls volunteers were rookies, possessed of far less experience than their team-mates at the back of the queue. Sturgess, Robbo, Dodge, Snapper, even Bully, players who had been around the block at least once, were all happy to let the novices step forward for either glory or anguish. All four should be proud of themselves tonight, including James Wall. Yes, he missed, but he was there when others were not. Bring on the Burton.

Teacher on the Telly. Again
10/3/2001 Nigel Clough's Burton Albion - home. FA Trophy Quarter Final

Yet more tales from the Trophy, for which I make no apologies. Our league season has long since been an irrelevance and with progress on an extra promotion place stalled, this may not be the last time we endure these meaningless games. But this is one that matters. Burton Albion are a club on the rise and came to ES sitting on top of the Dr. Martens league, having already disposed of Scarborough and Yeovil on the way. They also have a manager whose profile is higher than his club, as today sees yet another Anfield legend in the visitors' dug-out. In comparison to the touchline antics of former team-mates Molby and Wright, Nigel Clough is almost comatose, but he appears to have inherited enough of the infamous Clough DNA to produce a decent side, and one looking likely to grace the Conference next season.

Today's game was the next in a series of must-win matches and the 3,000-plus crowd were made to wait eight minutes before Elmo nodded home the game's only goal. Our language teacher loves the TV cameras, as a perfect copy of last season's FA Cup header hit the net and, once again, Elmo had scored a goal worth much more than merely progress into the next round.

He had kept our season alive, and a cup final at Villa Park was now only two matches away.

Yes, Villa Park is the new Wembley, at least until the New Wembley is built, and a cast-iron certainty to host the Bulls this year. Because we are one of the (very) few teams never to have graced the hallowed North London turf, and (for this is Hereford) are sure to qualify just as they move the whole shebang to bloody Birmingham.

Ever Heard of a Lawnmower?
31/3/2001 The Gump - away. FA Trophy Semi-Final. First leg

So now we know where Leigh is, try this one. Where on God's Green Planet is Nailsworth?

Eight miles north of Tetbury, if that helps, served by the G37 bus. But be warned, it's a slow road. In a car, however, Nailsworth is 50 minutes from Hereford, on the western edge of the Cotswolds, and home to Forest Green Rovers. This was a good draw for the Bulls and almost as good as playing both legs at home, as Hereford had sold close to two thousand tickets, each one to a Bulls fan desperate to see something positive from this now depressing campaign. Most were cautiously optimistic, but one member of the Gump's staff knew his opponents intimately, and would be delighted to outwit his former colleagues. Having beaten United with both Cheltenham and Yeovil, David Norton had yet another chance to damage the team with which he left league football, although today his role was that of assistant manager, due to injury. But not to worry, we can hurl abuse at someone else, the justifiably maligned Adrian (useless offside donkey) Foster is leading the line for the Gump, he'll do nicely. Yes, the former Bulls striker who blew his chance to keep Hereford United in the Football League is still searching for his natural level, and may have found it here at The Lawn. Perhaps by ten to five we'll have a better idea, but as of ten to three, we still hadn't found it. The Lawn, that is.

Avoiding Nailsworth City (sic) centre where apparently Bulls fans were running riot, Justin and I were merely running late. I could say that this was an isolated incident but the truth is, it happens all the time. Rushden and Stevenage this season, Leicester bloody City of all places last year (made it with 30 seconds to spare), and too many to count before that. Alan, who if you recall lives around the corner, now steadfastly refuses a lift after one too many missed kick-offs. Wise move by a wise man, but when British Rail is more reliable than your mates, something is badly wrong. This time it was due to a marathon pool match, loser buys lunch, and also to what is known as a bum steer from a local. 'Up tharn little hill lads, two minutes' was the guidance from a friendly native, one whose perception of both topography and time were some way removed from that of the rest of the human race. For a start, 'tharn little hill' was no such thing, a fact alluded to by the name plate adorning the first house we passed. There was no hint of irony about the abode named Base Camp, and confronted by an endlessly rising track and no sight nor sound of a football ground, we were in trouble. Again.

A gale howled into our faces and the drizzle had become freezing sleet. Great. We now had eight minutes to conquer Everest without oxygen, or suffer another missed kick-off.

'Maybe she said two minutes in a helicopter' was Justin's offering as we marched upwards.

I couldn't reply. The air was getting thin. As you may have gathered, the home of the Gump is the highest point in Gloucestershire, or if not, pretty damn near, but we made it. The referee blew his whistle as we beheld the majesty of The Lawn. It was a truly breathtaking spectacle, or would have been if I'd had any breath left. The stadium reminded me of Farnborough's Cherrywood Road, in that it wasn't big on terracing. Or seating. Or even roofing for that matter, but we've been in the Conference for long enough to realise that sometimes this is what you get. However, The Lawn, like Welling's San Siro, was surely inviting prosecution under the Trades Descriptions Act, for here was a playing surface the like of which I'd never seen, as players' feet were disappearing, such was the length of the grass. Having enjoyed the dubious pleasure of council facilities in Herefordshire and beyond, I'd seen a few dodgy pitches, but all of those had seen action from a mower at some point in recent history. Here at the Gump I honestly wondered whether they possessed such equipment, unless it was a deliberate and disgraceful ploy to nullify the quicksilver feet of Parry and Williams. Dotted patches of sand finished an effect that would appeal only to the most sadistic of green-keepers, for The Lawn today was more akin to a particularly cruel golf course than a football pitch. Plenty of deep rough, a generous helping of bunkers, but no fairway and no greens. The effect was completed by four corner-flags, all of which were, due to the wind, almost horizontal. Given the state of both pitch and weather, here was a match where any decent football would be a bonus, but in fairness to both sets of players, they produced a cracking game. With wind behind in the first half, United battered the Gump's defence, only to be denied by a chubby comedian in a yellow shirt. Steve Perrin, the keeper with a twelve pack, produced a string of fine saves, showing remarkable agility for a man possessed of a physique more suited to darts than football. Of course, he was abused constantly by the travelling support, Sumo-Baby being the most original, but to his credit Perrin gave as good as he got and kept his team in the game, all done with a smile on his face. Even he, however, couldn't do much with Elmo's volley just before half-time, but there was a feeling that a solitary wind-assisted goal might not be enough. And it wasn't. FGR introduced Frankie Bennett, who gave a master class in how to terrorise a full-back. Sturgess and Clarkie were given the runaround and, with Cooksey looking worryingly nervous, it was now Hereford who were being battered. On the hour, Bennett took advantage of Cooksey's dithering and chipped in a beauty, the knee-length grass proving no obstacle to his silky running. So much for conspiracy theories. With twelve minutes remaining, Elmo converted a Parry cross for an undeserved goal, but the lead lasted just three minutes. Adrian (double useless offside camel-donkey) Foster tumbled in the box after a Jamer challenge and Meechan converted, making Foster's position as public enemy number one more secure than ever. After a rescue by the crossbar, time was called with honours even. We were cold and wet, but above all relieved. Away goals don't count in this competition and the tie was reduced to a one-off at ES next Saturday. Surely now the Bulls were on their way to Villa Park.

The Forest Green experience, in terms of professional football, is probably as far away from Highbury or Anfield as you could get. An excuse for a pitch, in a shabby ground on top of a hill, and a brace of goals scored by a German teacher against an overweight dwarf goalkeeper is the stuff of park football. And yet it was a match which makes you glad to be a fan at this level.

A blood and thunder game of two halves, backs to the wall defensive heroics, two teams battling against the elements as well as each other, ultimately earning a share of the spoils.

So five (count those beauties) in one sentence may be cliché overdrive, but anyone who left the Lawn today feeling they hadn't got good value for their ten quid should try spending three times that on a tedious premiership nil-nil. I've done that and it's not much fun.

A final word on Gloucestershire's highest peak came from Justin, as we left the ground. 'Do you think, on a clear day, I could see my house from here?' he asked. I'm not sure whether he meant the one in Hereford or the one in Hackney.

Always Ends in Tears
7/4/2001 Forest Green Rovers - home
FA Trophy Semi-Final Second leg

We should have bloody well known. Cup finals just don't happen to Hereford, not even the crappy Villa Park ones, and the end-of-season party would take place without us. The Gump came to ES as big outsiders, yet they worked tirelessly, stuck to a gameplan, rode their luck and robbed us of our day in the sun. A 4-1 defeat sounds like a hiding, yet the Bulls wasted huge possession and countless chances in a match where the visitors converted four of their five shots on target. If you take your chances you win games and today Forest Green did just that. Good luck to them, I hope they win at Villa Park, although I can't see it being a sell-out. I hope as well that they win their battle to stay in the Conference, because for what is basically a village green side, Rovers have achieved a small miracle. As for the useless offside… ah, you know the one, who today scored the fourth goal, I don't care if I never see or hear of him again.

In fact, right now I don't care if I see another football match, at least until next season.

For months we had held on to a belief that the Trophy would bring some joy to ES, but the huge disappointment felt by all Bulls fans in many cases here quickly turned to rage. It was scapegoat time again and GT was copping most of the considerable amount of abuse flying around. The season's final Talking Bull was a cover-to-cover outpouring of frustration and anger, with many previously restrained contributors joining the chorus demanding that either Turner went or they would. It appeared that even the most moderate of United fans had reached the end of their rope, but as before, not one of them articulated an alternative.

Whilst over the season GT's relationship with the supporters had deteriorated, he was big enough to stand up for himself at a fans' forum a week later. He spoke calmly in the face of some fierce questioning, making the point that the players were every bit as upset as the fans and were distraught at missing out when so close. He may well believe it to be true, but I'm not so sure. Supporters of thirty and forty years were turning away from their team, unable to take the hurt any more. Who knew when, or indeed if, they would be back.

As Low As We Can Go?

The remaining nine games of the season produced just two victories, in typical Bulls style, against the strongest sides in the league. Rushden were again well beaten at ES, handing the initiative to Yeovil in a two-horse race for the title. And then, in a neat turnaround, a last-minute thunderbolt from Dodge condemned Yeovil to another season of unproper football, after a 3-2 away win that no-one would have predicted. It was a goal which, ironically, gained Hereford a couple of meaningless points, but cost the club £5,000, as Michael McIndoe would now not be tasting league football with the Glovers. Frequently one person's loss is another's gain and Max Griggs finally saw his expensively-assembled dream realised as Rushden were crowned champions. An all-time low crowd of 867 saw a pitiful goalless draw against Kingstonian, a match with absolutely nothing to commend it, payback perhaps for the spectacular events of the reverse fixture in October, but neatly encapsulating just how far our season had disintegrated. This was a season which started so well, and we were still very much in contention approaching Christmas. The dream however, quickly became a nightmare, kept alive only by the prospect of a trip to Not Wembley and I don't want to go over that again, thanks.

A final position of eleventh place was of course disappointing but in this league the rewards are the same whether you're second, eleventh or, like Morecambe, nineteenth. Falling below Morecambe and consequently out of the Conference were Kettering, Hednesford and Kingstonian, all of whom looked vulnerable from early in the season. The Gump survived, comfortably in the end, although they went down to a single-goal defeat to Canvey Island at a deserted Villa Park.

New to the Conference next season would be Barnet, victims of a last-day shoot-out identical to the Bulls-Brighton match of four years ago. There would also be trips to Margate and Stalybridge and, great news, my second favourite football team. Yes, Farnborough were back.

The highs and lows?

Obviously, our best ever start to a Conference season. For a while we believed that the Bulls could seriously challenge and that Scott Cooksey was unbeatable.

The Rumery-inspired madness at Kingstonian, in the match with everything.

A sublime forty-five minutes against Dover, when football was suddenly a ridiculously easy game and four goals could have been eight.

The continued development of Gavin and Tony James, I can't believe they're both still with us.

And the fact that amidst our end of season traumas, the players found it within themselves to beat both Rushden and Yeovil.

Player of the year was Matt Clarke, showing everyone precisely what a full-back with pace and a decent delivery should do. Of Elmo's seventeen goals this season, Clarkie must have provided at least half of them.

And the lows. It's a long list, but here we go.

A miserable December, with a solitary point gained and a league season over.

Our inability to get results from tight matches. Of thirteen Conference defeats, only Boston beat us by more than one goal. Which perhaps served us right for stealing their drum.

More players sold at knock-down prices. Chris Lane and particularly Michael McIndoe were necessary but worryingly cheap departures and, whilst the most recent, are unlikely to be the last.

Our hooligans running riot at Rushden and Forest Green. At a time when rampaging around the country on behalf of your home town seems a pastime in decline, our brave lads appear determined to carry on regardless.

The Trophy semi-final at Edgar Street. Say no more.

Paul Parry spending most of the campaign on the sidelines.

And the most depressing of all, supporters fighting amongst themselves, in some cases almost literally. I've never known so much disharmony, anger and abuse amongst fellow Bulls fans. HUISA is ploughing on, but with goodwill toward the club at an all-time low, their job is almost impossible. I doubt that there is a Bulls fan out there anything other than delighted that the season has ended, including the 1,001 who went missing between Southport in August and Morecambe in May.

There remain some decent players under contract at ES, but GT's power to add to the squad over the summer would be severely limited. Two McIndoes, a younger Wrighty, a fully-fit Parry, a left-sided Clarkie and a striker in the Neil Grayson mould would do for starters.

Never would a magic wand be more appreciated, but fairy godmothers appear to be as thin on the ground as sugar daddies.

Especially in Herefordshire.

6   2001-2002 Say We are Top of the League

18/8/2001 Barnet - home

No honestly, we are. Four years after our ghastly re-introduction to non-league football, the Bulls reached its pinnacle. And stayed there for a whole three hours. But we'll take it, given that the victory over Barnet was less than convincing. Three first half goals in as many minutes completed the scoring, the Bulls holding on despite resuming normal spot-kick service, Gavin being today's culprit. Barnet, like the Bulls, didn't get the start they wanted on returning to unproper football but, again like the Bulls, also have problems off the pitch. The club that enjoyed or perhaps endured the larger -than-life antics of Flashman and Fry have financial worries, seemingly a compulsory feature of relegation to the Conference. With issues over their tiny Underhill ground and in dispute with their local council, Barnet just may be the only club who Hereford wouldn't swap places with at the moment, particularly with the Bulls occupying the sole promotion slot, albeit briefly.

Yes, that is the sole, single, solitary and only promotion slot available from the Conference this season. The non-league football story of the summer was that of the second promotion place. Intense lobbying by the Conference, supported from many quarters, the FA included, led to renewed hope that the 72 league clubs would do the right thing, even if it was a close call. It wasn't. Indeed if Colchester, Wycombe and Rushden hadn't voted in favour, it would have been a complete endorsement of the status quo. Sixty-nine turkeys couldn't bring themselves to vote for, as they saw it, Christmas, the greediest having the nerve to demand millions in compensation for any extra relegation places. Shame on them all, particularly those whose clubs had been promoted via play-offs and yet more shame on our recently elevated Conference opponents, Halifax, Cheltenham, Kidderminster and Macclesfield. May you all soon return to the realms of the unproper. Talking Bull was packed with righteous indignation, the issue sufficient even, to divert New Meadowenders from their ritual haranguing of GT, although I doubt they'll be distracted for long. Here is a scandalously closed shop, but one into which we need to get, and soon. To this end, the Conference Board, in an uncharacteristically smart piece of thinking, informed the FA and the Football League that they would, despite the rebuff, employ a play-off system for the coming season, the Conference champions earning nothing more than the opportunity to beat the winner of a play-off between the next four clubs. Whilst prompting outrage from many sources, perhaps John Moules and his board were for once ahead of the game. Of course the FA kicked the plan into touch, immediately finding themselves accused of double standards. Whilst they had voiced support for extra promotion, they sat on their hands and did nothing to help. When confronted however, with a move towards an unfair, even ridiculous idea, they acted, swiftly outlawing the proposal. They were right to do so, as were the Conference in pointing out the hypocrisy so clearly in operation. And with a red-card protest delivered at today's game by both sets of fans, at least the casual viewer of Sky TV will now also be that little bit better informed about the injustice of the situation.

Hereford and Barnet were chosen to showcase live non-league football to the nation, hence the noon kick-off. Until now this has been an inconvenience peculiar to proper clubs, but an inconvenience compensated by a decent chunk of rich Uncle Rupert's fortune. So far so good. Today's missing few hundred would spend their lunchtime in the pub, whilst the two clubs could figure which bills most urgently required help from the Sky windfall. Sadly, not so. Hereford's share of the television cash was just £3,000, barely covering the lost revenue from 200 fans. More in keeping with normal service, the Conference had struck a deal that was actually costing the clubs money each time they featured on live TV. John Moules had again given ammunition to the many fans who felt he was ill equipped to run a pub league, let alone the country's fifth division, which is, despite the opinion of many, not quite one and the same thing. But we weren't grumbling too loudly. Each time live TV had been to ES since relegation the Bulls had won, and the money from both the Brighton and Hartlepool matches had gone a long way toward keeping the club alive, so let's compromise. The BBC are welcome anytime, along with their £75,000 and guaranteed FA Cup glory, whilst Sky can keep their miserable three grand, along with their noon kick-offs. Unless, of course, it's in some depressing backwater that I would never have gone near anyway. Fair? Maybe, but what else of the summer? Three players were released, Sturgess, Gardiner and Giddings, being respectively the wrong age, wrong speed and wrong consistency, although many thought Kerry Giddings a rough diamond who would benefit from a little more polishing. Clarke and Wrighty signed new deals, as did keeper Matt Baker. Scott Goodwin joined from Hednesford, and Daniel Davidson arrived on a part-time contract and may prove as useful off the pitch when his accountancy qualifications are secured. Another Scott, this one Voice, signed on a two-year deal from Bilston, apparently inhabiting the lower reaches of Doctor Marten land. Voice netted an incredible 47 times last season, but will no doubt reveal himself as this year's Kerry Giddings, or perhaps even another Steve Piearce. Who, incidentally, was spotted outside ES walking without the aid of crutches. It won't last, even if true, and needless to say none of these signings involved a transfer fee.

Finally, a question. When did a football club last win three medals in a day without kicking a ball? This summer, when three United connections were honoured in the Queen's Birthday List.

Hereford's greatest ever player John Charles, forever known as King in these parts, was awarded a CBE, whilst Bulls director Grenville Smith gained an MBE for some spectacular charity work. The trio was completed with an OBE for our favourite commentator and sheepskin-clad champion of football anoraks everywhere, the incomparable Motty. It would be nice to welcome either John back to ES this season, the one because it would mean he is winning his battle with illness, the other because the Bulls would be on TV. Proper TV, that is.

Sow and Ye Shall Reap
27/8/2001 Margate - away

Three fortunate points against Barnet were followed by two performances to live long in the memory for very different reasons. Firstly, another horrible trip to Nuneaton and abject surrender on the pitch, where we were not good enough in every position, and equally embarrassing off it, as again a small but belligerent group of Herefordians found themselves at the centre of the type of mayhem that most of the country grew out of back in the eighties. Thank God they don't come out to play every week. Celtic served to cheer the heart when four days later the Bulls did turn up, the recalled Elmo striking both goals in a deserved victory. Celtic, of the Stalybridge variety, was everything Nuneaton wasn't, with a better ground, better football, better beer, better weather, and better banter with friendly locals. If football was like this every week there would be little need for the Premiership, at least not in Hereford where every Saturday coaches depart for Old Trafford, Villa Park and the like. Yes, there is still fun to be had in a world where lesser mortals compete with less precision for smaller prizes, all in front of an audience who pay a lot less but appreciate the occasional treat a whole lot more.

And now down to Margate. As non-league treats go, does it really get better than this? A seaside Bank Holiday weekender at a new ground, fabulous weather, and Germany versus England later in the day. Of course it does, but approaching half-time at Hartsdown Park, for the Bulls contingent at least, there wasn't a lot wrong in the world, as Gavin was in the sort of mood to make Conference defenders wish they'd taken up tennis. Such was his dominance that the two-goal lead was surely merely an appetiser in the most one-sided match I'd seen in a long time. But remember, this is Hereford. Only we could turn riches into rags with such frequency, and the process began just before half-time. New striker Danny Davidson wasn't having as good a day as his colleagues as, with almost his first touch, he tripped over the ball with an open goal at his mercy. Whilst Gav has probably created more than his fair share of golden chances which end in disaster, this was a shocker. Having left a trail of defenders in his wake, he presented Davidson with enough time to enjoy a cigar before slotting home from three yards. Having failed in comedic fashion, every time Danny touched the ball from then on, he endured laughter from the home fans and abuse from the visitors. Or at least enough of them to destroy any confidence our rookie striker may have had. Even after Danny had helped create the second goal, the boo-boys continued and, as his confidence deserted him, his frustration grew. Here was a player desperate to make a good impression being abused by his own supporters, incredibly, whilst his team were cruising. Not content with fighting Nuneaton fans last week and amongst themselves for much of last season, a depressing number of Bulls fans today sank to a new low. With a minute left in the half, Danny's frustration saw a retaliatory swing at the home captain, in full view of the referee. He had to go, but I felt for him. Whilst on this showing he was far from the finished article or, as one of our less erudite followers loudly put it, was a fucking clueless muppet, the point is that he was our muppet and his failings were not through any lack of effort. Davidson's red card prompted further scorn and the assertion that we would be better off without him. Famous last words. GT reshuffled the pack, replacing the goal-machine with Scott Goodwin and creating another first. Whilst Piearce invariably fails to last 90 minutes, today was probably the first time he left the pitch under his own steam. I wonder if it will be the last.

One of New Meadowenders' frequent grumbles is GT's almost non-existent use of substitutes, a reasonable point assuming that our subs were actually any good, which frequently they weren't. I wonder how they felt when, 30 seconds into the half, the newly-arrived Goodwin was easily beaten and Margate were back in what was now an entirely different game? The voices declaring us a better side without Davidson were strangely quiet and inevitably the equalising goal arrived, with time remaining to add a winner. Some desperate defending saw the Bulls hold on for a point, but it was one that should have been three. I wasn't the only one who held an element of our support responsible. Surely if we had all got behind Davidson instead of barracking him he wouldn't have lost his game so completely, or his head so catastrophically. There are fanzines, chat-rooms and of course the pub, all excellent forums in which to discuss the merits or otherwise of players, all available to each and every supporter. Which is what makes it hard to understand quite why so many visiting fans today ruined what should have been a great day out. Sure, have your say, but save it for a place where it may not be so damaging to the team, *and completely fuck up the day for the rest of us*. Thanks.

Sow and ye shall reap, for today a good number of our own supporters cost us a deserved away win and, as pointed out in Talking Bull, probably didn't even realise the part they had played in our downfall. Hereford United, even in these worrying times, have retained a hard-core of supporters that the club can rightly be proud of, devoting themselves to a cause many had deemed hopelessly and irretrievably lost. Without their dedication, the club would have withered and died, and still might, despite their efforts. Sadly today a vocal minority ruined what should have been a great day out. It would take a quite magical performance by England later that evening to lift the mood but amazingly, that is exactly what we got. A Michael Owen hat-trick destroyed Germany in their own backyard and the woes of life in the Conference were temporarily forgotten. England's stunning victory was as welcome as it was surprising and incredibly, Emile

Heskey somehow contrived to score against the best keeper in Europe. Something he had dismally failed to do only recently against a sheep-farmer from Wales. I wonder if Mark Jones was watching.

Dynamo Fox and Hounds (versus Athletico Pathetico)
29/9/2001 Hayes - away

It's happening again. A miserable month (don't even ask) has placed a depression over ES, and it's still only September. Yes I know, we've been here before, but anything less than victory at Hayes would see the twin straws of a good run in the FA Cup or Trophy being desperately clutched at. It sounds all too familiar, with dwindling interest and attendances driving the club dangerously close to a point where emergency sales would be unavoidable. Watching Gav humiliate hapless Conference defenders was the only remaining pleasure for many Bulls fans, and the thought of selling him to Cheltenham for peanuts was unbearable. Fortunately, Hayes were suffering every bit as much as the Bulls, struggling to adjust to another spell in the Conference and, surely, a great chance to kick-start the season. Wrong, and all too predictably so. Another wretched performance was endured, the 4-1 thumping our biggest unproper defeat and surely the nadir of GT's leadership. The Turner Out brigade were more vocal than ever and Church Road was not a pleasant place to be, anyone daring to ask quite what the anti-Turner faction proposed as an alternative risking serious physical damage. As it was, three Hayes supporters found themselves very much in the wrong place at the wrong time, taking a hiding they didn't remotely deserve, and Hereford's reputation for being amongst the nastiest supporters in the division went up another notch. I've looked for excuses, but there aren't any. Today was the worst day I've ever had watching the Bulls. A small group of genuine fans were joined for a post-match pint by Elmo, but there wasn't much even he could say. What can you, when your club is haemorrhaging money and support, eighteen months away from a 1.3 million pound eviction notice, and being stuffed by Dynamo Fox and Hounds?

If Hereford United were to have any sort of future, it was becoming clear that something had to change, and soon.

Man Friday Promoted - Robinson in Charge
20/10/2001 Scarborough - home

Something did actually change after the shambles at Hayes, as GT announced the handing of all playing concerns to Phil Robinson. Robbo's job would be to garner sufficient points to avoid the relegation scrap, GT's the small matter of remaining within the terms of the CVA. I don't know which was the more miserable, although Robbo made a flying start in despatching Farnborough by four goals to two, but then, everyone beats Farnborough. More significant was the number 1,205, the day's attendance, and an indication of just how Bulls fans viewed both the club and the season. Alarmingly, more than 50% of our support had disappeared in nine weeks. Somehow GT had to balance the books on gates already way below the break-even figure but interestingly still more than double that of many Conference sides, including Leigh RMI. About a hundred Herefordians were in a crowd of 535 at RMI's Hilton Park, where Robbo earned his second victory of the week, the paltry crowd illustrating one of the few areas where life in the Conference neatly mirrored the Premiership. Just like its bloated big brother, our little league was also a series of mini competitions within the bigger one. A small group of well-financed, well-supported sides would scrap it out at the top, whilst another, slightly larger group would be aiming merely to survive at the bottom. The rest would sedately plod along in the middle, hoping but not expecting to join the fun above, whilst keeping an eye on events below, just in case. The Bulls, at the moment, found themselves in the middle group and, despite two good victories, still too close to those skirting disaster. It was a brief honeymoon period for Robbo as within a week the Bulls were back in the old routine of conceding soft goals whilst showing nothing at the other end of the pitch. Despite the efforts of Gav, yet again showing ability wildly out of step with his surroundings, Chester and Boston were the grateful recipients of stress-free victories. Which brings us to Scarborough. Here was a match I really shouldn't be watching, and but for a family birthday, no doubt wouldn't have. Bless you, Jacob, for requesting a Bulls shirt and a trip to ES for your seventh birthday. Oh for the carefree outlook of a seven-year-old, someone for whom bankruptcy and insolvency were unheard-of concepts, and who confidently predicted a Bulls victory. He even gave the score, six-nil. I think the four we put past Farnborough had scrambled his senses, as to score six goals before Christmas would be an achievement most Bulls fans would regard as fantasy. 'You should have a fiver on that, stranger things have happened', said my Dad as we strolled past Ladbrokes en route to the ground. 'Waste of money', was my reply. I should have listened, because once in a while strange things do indeed happen. Wrighty nodded home before Baker had touched the ball and with Parry every bit as menacing as Gavin, the Bulls terrorised the visitors. Both added quality finishes which, with a Snapper header, saw United four-up at half-time. Jacob stood firm with his prediction, seeing just two more for the Bulls and he was, of course, spot on. Quiggin and Elmo completed the scoring, the latter providing the best goal celebration ever seen at ES, perhaps anywhere that I could recall. Elmo powered in a trademark header, promptly finding himself locked in a bear-hug by our mascot. Billy the Bull eventually released the school-teaching striker from his clutches, whereupon Elmo, and only he knows why, stole Billy's head and placed it on his own. We now had a Hereford player wearing a bull's head being chased by a mascot minus a significant part of his own costume. By this point even the Scarborough fans were helpless with laughter, as a pantomime scene unfolded in front of them. No doubt Quiggin was still giggling five minutes later when he smashed a penalty into the scoreboard high above the goal.

'I knew he'd miss,' said Jake, his six-nil forecast intact.

That was how it finished, a sadly-scorned prediction that made a seven-year-old believe he could see into the future and a performance that gave 1,500 Bulls fans a reward for standing by their team when many others had turned away. OK, so Scarborough were, on the day, beyond crap, but it was nice to spend a Saturday afternoon with a smile on the face, rather than the haunted grimace that most of the season had seen. I couldn't resist checking what odds had been available for a six-nil home win. The answer was a cruel 80-1, and the fiver would have become a handy £400. As Elton John once sang, I should have listened to my old man. Even if he was only joking.

At the Edge
27/10/2001 Dover Athletic - away. FA Cup 4th qualifying round

At the same time they were ignoring demands for extra promotion, the FA did at least hand out a welcome gift to football's forgotten proletariat. Prize money issued to winning clubs in the final qualifying round of the FA Cup was doubled to £20,000, making the Bulls' trip to Dover yet another, and how many have there been, must-win match. Despite signs that Robbo was getting a little more from the squad, the title had long been conceded, the situation not helped by an injury to the player-coach himself. Robbo was proving difficult to replace, but everyone knew the available budget to find a quality midfielder. It's as true in football as anywhere — if you pay peanuts, you get monkeys. Sadly, Robbo and GT didn't even have peanuts.

Which made the FA Cup and Dover a pivotal point in the season. Whilst the FA had wisely regionalised the early rounds of its showpiece, a trip to Dover was about as regional for Herefordians as Gretna Green, and a two-hour trek from West London. Even so, nearly three hundred supporters made the trip, each of them fully aware of what defeat would mean. The Crabble. Yes, it's the name of a football ground, and you should go and see a game there. Outside of the town, the stadium is cut neatly into the side of a hill, with the luxury, in this league at least, of covered accommodation on all sides, a half-decent playing surface, and a pub fifty yards down the road. With gorgeous countryside above and below, it is the most picturesque ground I've had the pleasure of visiting, although my judgement may have been influenced by the result.

To be fair to GT and his troops, most of the games in this must-win category have indeed been won, including Sittingbourne, just up the road, and today Robbo's lads were worthy winners of a real battle, Dover being in a financial situation little better than our own. The home side had done their homework, as Gavin was policed by two, sometimes more, of Athletic's more physical players. What they found to their cost was that when Gav was in the mood, it didn't make any difference. Having created two chances that should have opened the scoring, he decided that passing to a lesser mortal was too risky an option and scored a solo goal of the highest quality. Even the home supporters applauded, but it was too much for the hard men of Dover. Gav was chased from one end of the Crabble to the other, taking a kicking whenever a disgruntled Doverite could get close enough. Which, whilst it wasn't often, eventually resulted in him limping off, amazingly not accompanied by at least one of the home side heading for an early bath. Thankfully, Gavin did his damage today before being kicked off the park, ironically securing the victory that would probably delay his inevitable departure for a few more weeks. By ten to five, GT was £20,000 richer than at three o'clock. By five fifteen, although he didn't know it at the time, the day had become a whole lot better, courtesy once again of those velvet bags at the FA. Not that long ago, on the same stretch of motorway, BBC radio had given us Brighton in the first round of the Cup, and today it brought another little gem. Again first out of the bag, and when we needed it most, the Bulls were given the plum tie of Wrexham, at ES. Yes I know, but at this level, that's about as plum as it gets. Two teams with a fantastic pedigree of FA Cup upsets was surely the tie that the Beeb would choose for its live coverage, particularly attractive because Wrexham had also fallen on hard times and equally desperate for a lucrative Cup run. Would they be able to resist the allure of an old-fashioned blood and thunder FA Cup tie that might just mean the end of the road for the losing side? We would know by Monday, but I had a feeling that Motty was heading back to ES. Today Hereford United had been perilously close to the cliff edge, both literally and metaphorically, and a foot in the wrong place could have seen potentially disastrous fall-out. Fortunately, the right foot found itself in the right place and belonged to a young man from Wales who I somehow doubt will see the Crabble again.

I wonder if Gavin realised the true value of his goal today.

The Fabulous Baker Boy
18/11/2001 Wrexham - home. FA Cup 1st round proper

Along with confirmation of the BBC returning to ES, a note of caution was also issued. Whilst we all suspected that the victory at Dover was essential, in a frank statement GT revealed just how vital it was. The chances of the football club still operating in the New Year were, he said, minimal, without the win bonus and subsequent TV windfall. Gavin's winner was worth around £140,000 in the short-term, or a month's wages for a half-decent Premiership player. In the longer term, however, if the club could remain ahead of its creditors for long enough to stabilise, it was a goal that might just prove to be priceless.

A stable football club. Here was a concept unfamiliar to supporters of many clubs but totally foreign to Bulls fans, or at least those on the youthful side of their mid-thirties. The rest of us could remember the days of Addison and Miles, but it was an era that seemed to belong to some other club, one not related to the penniless strugglers of today. Whilst no-one can take your memories away from you, if Gav hadn't found a lifeline in Dover it was likely, even probable, that memories would be all that any of us had left. At the same time as GT's worrying words came more news on the future of the Bulls. Firstly, the Bristol Stadium Group had sold their interest in United to Chelverton, who now held all the leases and the £1.3 million debt, still remaining payable in May 2003. GT added that the only way the board could see any kind of long-term future was to work with Chelverton and relocate to a still unidentified site on the fringes of the city. It was news more good than bad. Chelverton didn't have the ruthless history of the BSG and were at least prepared to talk to supporters about moving the club. HUISA conceded that at present the sale of Edgar Street might be the only way to remain viable, but there were more questions than answers. How would the recreation-only clause be dodged? How much was the ES site actually worth, and how did any development fit in with plans to regenerate the whole area? And where would the new Edgar Street actually be? All of which were questions of more concern to GT than to Robbo, a man with more mundane problems to deal with.

Like reminding players to keep off the sauce on Saturday night because there was a game the next day. Whilst the money was more vital than welcome, the downside to the riches offered by the BBC is the licence it gives them to go a little Murdoch and shift your kick-off time. And day. Whilst a Sunday match wouldn't normally present a problem, on this occasion there was a big one. With my daughter's birthday party due to finish at kick-off time some 140 miles from ES, something had to give and for once I didn't put my team first. 'Sorry Lucy, but Robbo's more important than your birthday, I'm off to Hereford. Oh, and have a good party.' How could I? As I've already said, I'm a fan, but not a fanatic.

Which didn't stop me leaving Pizza Express and the debris of a make-your-own-pizza party at 1pm on the dot. My stock of brownie points had taken another hit, but I hadn't made it through the front door before my mobile announced that something had happened at ES. Phone ignored, I was just in time to see a replay of Wrighty tucking the ball into an empty Wrexham net. Gav had hammered a twenty-yarder against the crossbar and Wrighty, showing all the predatory instincts of his Arsenal namesake, was first to the rebound. You beauty, only 81 minutes of torment to endure. And torment it was. Whilst Wrexham didn't look like a side two leagues above Hereford, they were still that bit sharper, their first touch more controlled and, as the match progressed, the Bulls' defending became deeper and more frantic. Somehow the home goal remained intact and the Bulls' 100% record on live television was preserved. Of course Motty was in cliché heaven, aided and abetted by the BBC's A-Team of match day punditry, Lineker, Lawrensen and Hansen. Alan Hansen had his quota of woeful defending, whilst Gary Lineker tried, although not too hard, to conceal his amusement at our agricultural troops and cattle-shed facilities. I doubt, however, that even the uber-cool Mr. Lineker would have managed to suppress his laughter if Rembrandt the Bull hadn't been temporarily confined to barracks by the foot and mouth crisis. As for a spot of ritual root-vegetable worship, I fear that might have rendered Gary and his chums completely helpless. Lads, your careers could have been damaged beyond repair, had HUISA chosen to unleash the swede. The Beeb's finest did, however, agree, and without the gentle piss-taking that accompanied most of their observations, on a Man of the Match. Which, to be honest, was a shoe-in, as Matt Baker played the game of his life. Bakes stopped everything that Wrexham threw at him, and it was plenty, showing the full goalkeeper's repertoire. And when his reflexes weren't enough, his good fortune was, three times saving point-blank efforts with feet, knees and even his head. Our young goalkeeper deserved his 90 minutes of fame, for here was a lad released by Hull who probably wondered whether he had a future in the professional game. Somehow he and GT decided to take a chance on each other, only for Bakes to spend twelve months watching Scott Cooksey become a cult hero. Baker's patience had been rewarded, and whilst he had already shown plenty of promise, today's performance loudly announced that there was another young player at ES who looked destined for a stage bigger than the Nationwide Conference. Whilst not a thing of beauty, Hereford and Wrexham had produced the sort of match that makes the FA Cup what it is. Two teams of modest talent had scrapped and battled for the reward of being a step closer to a crack at one of the big boys. Who would probably field half of their reserves, assuming they had bothered to enter the competition in the first place. Whilst there is undoubtedly still magic in the Cup, I think most of it resides in places like Wrexham, York, Woking and, of course, Hereford, all backwaters that once saw the football world turned briefly upside-down. A quick glance toward the record books however, will tell you that no non-league club has inflicted FA Cup defeat on a Premiership side or even, for that matter, a Premiership reserve side. Sport is supposedly a cyclical phenomenon. Perhaps this is true and one day we may see a British champion at Wimbledon, or England reclaim the Ashes. Whilst both border on fantasy, both are far more plausible than the prospect of Spurs being humbled by Dagenham and Redbridge. More likely, given the similar cyclical nature of fashion, would be the sight of marauding hordes in fur-trimmed coats cavorting over a muddy field. Another Parka Army anyone?

Maybe, but I doubt it would happen at a football match.

Silver Boot Boy
8/12/2001 Swindon Town - away. FA Cup 2nd round

Apologies for again turning to the FA Cup, but the Conference has becoming seriously depressing, hovering two points above the relegation zone following defeats at Northwich, an horrendous performance, and Barnet, somehow even worse. Since the demolition of Scarborough, the Bulls have become an outfit that now couldn't score in the proverbial house of limited morals. With a wheelbarrow full of tenners. Although where we might find even the smallest pocket of loose change at present is an unanswered question. Some light relief was needed, so it was off to Swindon and the unprecedented arrival at a football ground a full two hours before kick-off, and with good reason. We were today obliged to stand in an endless queue, eventually handing over a sum of money sufficient for a season ticket at some clubs, and all for the privilege of joining another terminally slow line of fellow Bulls. The hour spent travelling fifty yards allowed access to a cramped corner of the County Ground, ideally positioned next to seating occupied by two dozen of Wiltshire's more unhinged residents. Late arriving Bulls fans found themselves keeping one eye on the match and another on some locals whose first concern obviously wasn't events on the field of play. Mercifully, the Herefordshire equivalent of this retarded army were either on manoeuvres elsewhere or savvy enough to realise that whilst its football team had long since given up ideas of Premier League status, Swindon's lunatic fringe were still committed to remaining in the big-time. And could anyone explain quite why, in December, twenty-odd grown men feel the urge to display their twelve-packs and tattoos to another crowd from a few miles up the road? Whilst mildly amusing when viewed from a safe distance, I suspect that making us laugh wasn't high on their list of priorities, whereas sending us home in an ambulance possibly was. They certainly told us so enough times.

OK, enough of the freak-show. Time to focus on the Bulls' attempt to rescue something from another ruined season. Amongst the Swindon ranks was Neil 'Razor' Ruddock, until recently a Premiership hard-man of some repute. As the sides lined up, Ruddock seemed preoccupied with Gavin

Williams and his shiny new boots, wondering quite why a park player would consider himself good enough to justify a pair of silver Reeboks. Mind-games from an old pro who no doubt thought that our boy had delusions of grandeur, but Gav apparently gave as good as he got. 'You remind me of Neil Ruddock, only fatter' was his reported response. Ruddock, or at least his team, had the first word on the pitch, when the wonderfully-named Danny Invincible outpaced Wrighty to open the scoring after ten minutes. Oops, this could be a cricket score. But no. Three minutes later the silver boot fired an equaliser. Gavin unleashed a twenty-yarder into the top corner that again had most of the home support applauding along with the visitors. Yes, we'd seen a few specials from Gav in our time, but this one was a jaw-dropping spectacular. We were back in the game and, before half-time, actually in front, as a scandalously unmarked Wrighty nodded home. The same team that had been abject in Conference games were once more turning it on in the Cup and had Swindon rattled. Which begged a question.

Why, if we can match a team like Swindon, were we being embarrassed by the likes of Woking and Northwich? As was to be expected, the second half was one-way traffic and seven minutes in, Swindon were level. Jamer, Wrighty and company stood firm but with fifteen minutes remaining, the pivotal moment of the match arrived. In a rare foray into the home penalty area, Gavin — who else? — was felled for a nailed-on penalty. The referee, knowing full well that we never score from the spot, saved someone's blushes and waved play on. Within thirty seconds Swindon had scored and the game was over. Whilst the Bulls had run themselves to a standstill and given their higher-graded opponents a real fright, Swindon had just enough in the tank, and the better side on the day eventually won the match. The final whistle saw the ugly-crew cheerfully inviting us outside for some bodily re-arrangement, in stark contrast to the bonhomie on the pitch. As the players left the field, Ruddock made a beeline for Gavin. Two footballers at opposite ends of their careers swapped shirts, deep in conversation, heading toward the same tunnel but in very different directions. Neil Ruddock had seen what we already knew. Those silver boots were going places, we just didn't know how soon, or how far. Willie Carson, proper football's smallest chairman, was typically generous with his post-match assessment, praising Hereford's efforts both on and off the pitch, and declaring Gav's strike the goal of the season. Fine words Willie, two hundred grand and he's all yours. As another Conference Christmas arrived with little to cheer, a final word about our small taste of life back in the land we once knew so well. Whilst stone-age ticketing and local cavemen did their best to spoil our day out, they failed, for today was a pleasant reminder of times gone by. A better class of football was served up on a perfect surface, in front of a big and almost universally sporting crowd, and it was played in a proper stadium.

Notwithstanding our current form, I liked the Conference and had almost forgotten what went on just a couple of rungs up the ladder, but there was really no question to be answered. I would take Swindon over Stalybridge every time.

Ye of Little Faith
18/2/2002 Boston United - away

Defeat at Swindon saw the end of the cup revenue, but a few welcome bonuses from elsewhere found their way into the club's bank account. £7,000 was raised at a Sportsman's Dinner, where John Motson and Ricky George royally entertained Bulls fans, neither taking a penny for their efforts. Another £4,000 came from an on-line auction of the shirts worn at Swindon, although the winner of Gavin's shirt might have to ask Razor if he would send it to Hereford. Both contributions were vital, as sub-1,500 crowds were rapidly devouring the television windfall. Although there didn't appear, for the time being at least, to be the threat of closure, niggling injuries were stretching limited resources ever further. Scott Cooksey's broken wrist however, was far from a niggle, having progressed from a setback into a situation that almost cost him everything. What should have been minor surgery resulted in complications requiring two further visits to the operating theatre, with Cooksey at one point in danger of paying the ultimate price for playing the game he loved. Scott Cooksey had played his last football match and, whilst happily recovered from his hospital traumas, is another player who might quibble with Bill Shankly's musings about life, death and football.

Off the field, Chelverton declared that whilst they could see little mileage in demanding their £1.3 million if it resulted in a bankrupt, and therefore deceased, football club, they were still identifying potential sites for the new ES. GT was obliged to support this course, but the local council and HUISA were now robustly in defiance, although nothing was likely to happen until Herefordshire Council decided just what they wanted to do with Edgar Street and the surrounding area. Credit here to

111

HUISA, who continued to ask the right questions, even if straight answers were rarely forthcoming.

As for me, relocation fatigue was becoming an issue. When the club, council and developers stop running around in circles and deliver something solid, then great, I will happily listen, until which, it's back to the football, where Robbo enjoyed a decent few weeks. A six-game unbeaten run delivered twelve points that should have been enough to ensure a stress-free run-in. One more win and it probably would have been, but Leigh RMI had other ideas, leaving the Bulls again casting worried glances downwards. With an ominously tough-looking trip to Boston next up, those meaningless end of season games were looking more attractive, but increasingly less likely. Whilst Boston were vying with Yeovil and Dagenham for the top spot, they didn't appear to be winning many friends, the take-no-prisoners attitude of manager Steve Evans being wholeheartedly adopted by his team. They had both money and ambition, and it appeared, a win-at-all-costs outlook that would quite probably make their stay in the Conference a short one. The fixture had been moved to a Monday evening, not great for Bulls fans who now required a day off work to see their team humbled. That is, until they stopped and gave matters a moment's thought.

For most only a moment was needed, the cancelled supporters' coach testament to the common-sense of all but the handful of diehards who made the trip. They did so in the knowledge that it was going to be a freezing and miserable night and one likely to end pointless in all senses of the word. Given the presence of Sky cameras, there was little excuse for any rational Bulls fan to be at York Street, but the forty or so who travelled were rewarded with the game of the season. With just twelve minutes gone, however, even these brave fools were asking themselves quite why they had bothered. Already two goals down and with a makeshift defence terrorised by Boston's expensive strikers, a good result for the Bulls would be to survive as embarrassed but not humiliated participants in Sky's biggest goal-fest of the season. Which is what it became, but it was Robbo's men who enjoyed their half-time cuppa a little more. Three goals for the Bulls had silenced the home crowd, along with a small handful of disbelieving Herefordians in a near-deserted visitors' enclosure, whilst Steve Evans no doubt suggested that his overpaid charges pull their collective fingers out or risk a P45 or two at the final whistle. When Boston equalised with an hour remaining, the sages of satellite TV could see only one winner and a long journey home to Wales for the plucky losers, but they were oh so wrong, and should perhaps have done their homework properly. Firstly, and despite much of both team and support being proudly Welsh, Hereford is in England, and has been for hundreds of years. Secondly, the Bulls always win on live TV. Don't they have researchers in Murdoch land? Two schoolboy errors that Motty would never have made, but he is of course a professional.

Nonetheless, Sky had struck gold in choosing this match to fill a quiet Monday evening. It was already a six-goal thriller, and Boston were now laying siege to Matt Baker's goal, the cavalry nowhere to be seen. Until from the subs' bench lumbered Elmo, not fit but always willing. Replacing the again wounded Robbo, he found a header worthy of Dodger's perfect cross for a magnificent end to an enthralling game. Bettered only by the post-match interview with the Boston manager. Steve Evans had seen his side beaten at home by a patchwork crew from the wrong end of the table, one which included a debutant centre-half from a local village side and able to name only four substitutes due to yet more injuries within the division's smallest squad. To say that Evans was unhappy would be putting it mildly, although understandable as his side had lost a match they had expected to stroll, but I have never seen a less gracious or more surly manager after a game. Not helping matters was Garry Hill, his Dagenham counterpart and TV expert of the day, struggling to contain his mirth at the misfortune of his chief rival for the Conference title. Two men who probably won't be sharing a friendly beer in the near future. The travelling support were probably half-way home before Mr. Evans had finished his debriefing in the privacy of the home dressing-room and it's a good bet that at least one group of Conference footballers would be in for some early morning training on Tuesday. The Bulls, meanwhile, would no doubt be enjoying a lie-in, or at least those who didn't have a day job. Elmo of course would be back at school, but I didn't have a clue where Jon Hill would be. Jon is the lad who stepped up from minor league football and the Herefordshire town of Kington to make his professional debut against the strongest attack in the Conference. At times he looked out of his depth but as the game progressed so did he, delivering a performance of which Robbo, GT and indeed Jon himself could feel justifiably proud. The final word must surely belong to the forty or so Bulls actually at the game, addressed to those, myself included, who stayed at home in front of the telly.

Oh ye of little faith, the Bulls always win on TV.

Vital games, none of them matter
March and April 2002

The fabulous win at Boston left the Bulls needing perhaps ten points from thirteen games to ensure another year of Conference football, the first of which was Dagenham at ES. Or it should have been. The roof of the Meadow End terrace was blown off in a gale two hours prior to kick-off, knocking out the electrics and therefore the match. GT was busily checking insurance policies while a very small group of Daggers fans were checking train timetables. The solitary win in the next nine games came at Dover, courtesy of the goal-machine, doing little to halt another slide toward the drop-zone. Cynical Bulls supporters figured that Piearce was playing for a contract, but it was too little too late, his eight goals in three years being probably one tenth of the return GT would have hoped for from his investment. Piearce and Hereford United would be parting company in May but not for the first time Steve had shown a glimpse of the quality that was undoubtedly there.

I hope Piearce doesn't end his career asking himself 'What if?', but I suspect he will.

Three much more able bodies, however, would be at ES next season, as Jamer, Parry, and the still-improving Matt Baker agreed new deals. Sadly, our talisman and best hope of another transfer windfall would be moving on. Gavin Williams stated that he felt the need to move away from ES to further his career and he was undoubtedly right.

After another thrashing at Doncaster, the Bulls again found themselves perilously close to the relegation line and points were urgently needed. Whilst his future was clearly not at ES, more magic from Gavin secured a win against Northwich and Conference football for his soon-to-be-former club. Three days later Robbo scored a late winner against the Daggers which did more damage to the visitors' promotion chances than the freak wind which this time failed to rearrange the ES roofing.

The season ended with two all-too-typical performances, when defeats by Hayes and Stevenage left the Bulls in their lowest final placing for more than three decades. In an irony lost on many, the position we had made our own in the Football League was now ours in the Conference. Just two places and eight points separated Hereford United from the Dr. Martens League; we had finished seventeenth. I was glad that that we had escaped the drop, for to fall out of the Conference might have meant falling out of football, but the last eight weeks of the worst season Bulls fans had witnessed passed me by in a blur. The week following victory at Boston saw what I thought would be a routine out-patient appointment for my wife Sarah, at which we were told that a small lump in the breast was in fact a malignant tumour. These simple words, heard by thousands of people every week, in a second alter those lives and many around them. And now they would alter ours.

Breast cancer. Everyone knows someone who has had it, many know people who survive it, whilst others know someone who has fought the battle and lost. Now, it was horribly close to home and after the news come the questions. What type of tumour is it? Will I need surgery, chemotherapy or both? Has it spread?

And will I live? Five minutes before the appointment, my biggest concerns were where my football team would pick up the few points still required to avoid disaster and whether to trade my ageing Peugeot for a Volkswagen or a Volvo. What concerned me now was the fact that my partner of almost twenty years would be undergoing major surgery, with no guarantees given for the days and weeks beyond that. And they wouldn't even begin to discuss years. We are all guilty of taking things, life even, for granted, and then something comes along no bigger than a stud in a football boot, that changes you forever.

Whilst our surgeon told us that until the tumour was removed and more tests were performed we shouldn't fear the worst, the human mind just doesn't work that way. The reality was that Sarah might not be around to see our two girls grow up. And Sarah wasn't just my wife, but my best friend, my soul-mate, and the best part of me from the day we had met. Which is why these vital matches meant nothing to me. As Yeovil, Telford, even Farnborough inflicted defeats on Hereford United, the vile, gnawing ball of tension within me softened slightly as early test results came back. The lungs, liver and skeleton, each a common site of secondary tumours, were all, for the moment, clear. Now for the surgery.

Make no mistake, a mastectomy is a traumatic and unpleasant procedure, but it was presented as our only real option, and Sarah is a strong and brave woman. We both needed every ounce of strength during the week that followed, this being the length of time for the laboratories to deliver their most crucial judgement. If lymph-nodes removed during the operation were clear of malignant tissue, the tumour had not spread. A bad result and the immediate future involves chemotherapy, perhaps radiotherapy as well, along with all the nightmares that come with them.

Again, most of us know someone who has endured the vomiting, the hair loss, the sleepless nights and constant pain that signify one toxin in your body duelling with another, even more odious poison. Here was a result that mattered more than any other. Sarah had just come home when my mobile rang, radiologist Farhad Aref on the line. He was both a work colleague and a friend, but more importantly had the ear of our surgeon, and between them they badgered the lab into fast-tracking Sarah's tests. Farhad was the first and, I would imagine, the last Manchester United supporter to bring a tear to my eye and, believe me, tears of joy taste nothing like tears of despair.

The lymph-nodes were clear and Sarah was going to be alright.

For six weeks normal life had been suspended, but now it could begin again.

Where Do We Go From Here?

The season had been a massive step backwards. Too good to go down, just, but light years behind the teams at the sharp end of the table. Boston took the Conference title from Dagenham on goal difference, demonstrating again that nice guys don't come first, whilst Stalybridge, Dover, and Dynamo Fox and Hounds slipped downwards into the pyramid.

Bouncing back would be Kettering, along with Gravesend and Northfleet, another two-towns-but-one-club outfit and, after several near misses, Burton Albion. Making unwanted history were Halifax, the first club to be relegated to the Conference twice. Which, if your glass is half-full, presented the opportunity to become the first club to be promoted from the Conference twice. Whilst the season past had been depressing, the immediate close-season was unusually lively, and not just in Hereford. Graham Turner enjoyed a brief moment of sanity in late April, only for normal service to be resumed when he withdrew the resignation tendered 24 hours earlier. It was news which brought mixed reactions from Bulls fans, but it seemed that GT wasn't prepared to let the club drift gently towards obscurity, insolvency, relocation or even oblivion without a final dramatic throw of the dice, as Hereford became the team with no players. Two-thirds of the playing staff were shown the door, including to universal surprise, Robbo. With Gavin signing for Yeovil (why them, Gav?), the only bodies remaining at ES were the still-contracted Jamer, Wrighty, Parry, Scott Voice, and the two Matthews, Clarke and Baker. Radical action from a conservative man, GT figured that no change was not an option, and a kill-or-cure approach was required. He now had to assemble a new squad and one considerably stronger than the one just culled. With no money. Whilst it was all action at ES, two pieces of Conference news made the back pages of the nationals, even if it was in the very small print. Firstly, and out of the blue, came the announcement that there would be a second promotion slot from the Conference, perhaps even more surprisingly, from next season. Had a sudden epidemic of altruism persuaded the turkeys to vote for Christmas?

Had it fuck. It was the promise of a generous parachute payment for the relegated clubs that finally shamed the shameless. Great news, albeit several years late, but an even bigger headline loomed. The FA had been quietly looking into the financial affairs of a certain Conference club and, having smelt a rat, appeared to have caught themselves a large one. The manager and a director of said club were alleged to have made illegal payments to several players, the manager also gifting £8,000 to two of his staff for deliberately misleading an FA enquiry. Amazing to think that some Conference clubs barely have two pennies to rub together, whilst at others, brown envelopes stuffed with bank-notes are passed around like after dinner mints. You may not be surprised to hear that Hereford United weren't in the frame for this particular caper, so just who considered it acceptable to defraud not only the league in which they played, but the FA, the taxman and, even more importantly, their own supporters? Put it this way. A lot of Daggers fans were suddenly looking at League Three venues, because, joy of joys, Steve Evans and Boston United had been caught cheating. Red-handed. The good news for the Daggers, of course, was that on the rare occasions a similar miscreant had actually been caught, the punishment was relegation. Couldn't have happened to a nicer chap. Whilst Evans would be spending the close-season awaiting his fate, GT would be shopping for players in bargain warehouses and reject-shops, and not with the bundles of twenties that at least one of his counterparts favoured.

OK, this is going to hurt, but it's time to reflect on a truly dismal year. Despite flashes of genius from Gav, one of which kept the club alive, the fare served up by the Bulls was frequently ordinary and too often utter crap. Whilst there wasn't a huge amount of talent in the squad, any team that included Williams, Parry, Robinson, Clarke, Wright, James and Baker should have finished a lot higher than seventeenth. Apart from the freakish trouncing of Scarborough and the wonderful televised slap delivered to the Boston cheaters, the whole campaign was best forgotten. With the Trophy again a disappointment, it was the FA Cup that delivered a little cheer, along with some much needed cash. Without it, who knows what would have happened. So who do we blame? GT, Robbo, both, or neither? It's a tough one, for once again GT was working under the threat of closure, should the numbers not add up, and we'll probably never know just how 'in charge' of team affairs Robbo was when GT handed over to him. So after a crazy month of May, Graham and his retained half-dozen have some added incentive for next season, where a placing in or near the top five will inject some desperately needed life back into Edgar Street. Whilst matters concerning Herefordshire Council and Chelverton are out of GT's hands, five years has been long enough in the doldrums and I suspect that too many more of the same will see the football club I love quietly disappear.

The final word on the season should be addressed to two people. Gavin Williams, you can do better than Yeovil Town. And Scott Cooksey, too young and talented to be retiring from the game, I wish you well, and hope that we can both stay as far away from the surgeon's knife as is humanly possible.

Because football isn't more important than life and death, not even close.

7   2002-2003 Spineless, Gutless, Chinless Wonders. And a Kid in a Bulls shirt

17/8/2002 Farnborough Town - home

Not only a description of Sven's feeble World Cup effort, but also something closer to home, and an embarrassment to the whole of English football. According to the very people entrusted to uphold the traditions and standing of the game, it's alright to cheat, because Boston United are unbelievably, now a league club. Whilst they and manager Steve Evans were found guilty on multiple charges, a token slap on the wrist was delivered, Boston receiving a paltry fine and four point deduction, effective from the following season. Not such a beautiful game, more a mystery as to where the justice in this fiasco has been delivered. I doubt many Daggers fans could tell you, for it is they who still reside in the Conference, one division but a whole world away from Boston. Steve Evans, for his troubles, is £8,000 poorer, and starting a twenty month ban from football.

So there you have it, the men in suits have clearly shown us the way. It's OK to cheat your way to a title, but beware if, as at Slough, your lease doesn't have all the full-stops in the right places. Even worse, don't expect a sympathetic ear if you're a few days late resolving the carnage left by a sugar daddy grown tired of his toy. Perhaps Barrow should have thrown a roll of bank notes at some vital witnesses.

The whole affair reeks, and brings nothing but shame on the spineless committee that sanctioned this so-called punishment. The cruellest cut of all is the timing of the whole charade, giving Dagenham no time to seek redress in a court of law, the new season kicking-off within days of their supposed justice.

I hope the Pilgrims' new playmates in the Football League send them straight back down, and the Daggers give them a wave as they go

119

in the opposite direction next April. Which, lest we forget, is one month before Chelverton are repaid their £1.3 million loan. Or, as I may already have hinted, they aren't. GT hasn't got 1.3 million pence, and Chelverton know it, but another twist has arrived in this never-ending tale. There is apparently, now funding identified for the city centre rebuild, with ES becoming a state of the art multi-sport arena, and Hereford United playing a leading role. Yahoo, fantastic, we can sit back and relax as ES becomes a West-Country Wembley, whilst the Bulls find the funds and form to match their new home, charging through the Football League as we did in the seventies. Fabulously simple, but where's the catch?

It is, of course, that this project is in the hands of planners and politicians. Believe me when I say that no-one is holding their breath.

But enough of ES. How about this for a pleasant surprise? Dishing out Pimms to the yummy mummies at the children's school fete isn't the worst way of killing a summer afternoon, especially as I was well placed to keep an eye on the penalty competition across the playground. Unsurprisingly in a World Cup year, many England shirts were on display, but amongst the hordes one stood out. Yes, it was white, but bearing, instead of three lions, a Bull's head. Which was how I met seven year-old Ben and his Dad, John, a genuine Bulls fan from the wilds of north Herefordshire, who followed his team wherever and whenever he could. A swift introduction followed, along with the promise to share travelling to a few games in the coming season. Along with Alan there were now three Twickenham Whites, news I shared with Sarah.

'Oh yes', she said, 'he's married to my friend Viv, she said you two should get together.' Almost lost for words, I asked her just how long she had kept this little nugget to herself. 'Ages. Ben is in Lucy's class. I forgot to mention it.' Different priorities or, as I suspect, men really are from Mars and women from Venus. So I had found a new playmate, but had GT found some players to add to the dutiful half-dozen still registered? Of course he had, but started with a first-team coach, Richard O'Kelly, once of the West Brom Youth Academy, but more recently a postman. Not a household name, but word from a couple of Baggies fans suggested that we had found a gem, and one more than able to deliver. Sorry, there I go again. Also signing for the Bulls, amongst others, would be left-back Michael Rose, centre-half Andy Tretton, and midfielders Ben Smith, Rob Purdie, Danny Williams, and Jamie Pitman, the latter for his second spell at ES. Steve Guinan and John Grant would be entrusted with scoring frequently enough to stay in or around the top five. All appear to have a little more quality than the players they had replaced, and all are young enough to have genuine ambitions of playing at a higher level. Time will tell, but it had been the liveliest summer break for years, and a better one for GT than for Sven. A new coach, a dozen new players, and finally, play-offs. Perhaps something to look forward to for Jamie Pitman, renamed Jenny and back in Hereford after seven years, although the truth was that he had never really left. As a part-time fitness instructor at Hereford Leisure Centre, Jenny had covered a few motorway miles in his spells at Yeovil and Woking and, rumour has it, asked GT for a job closer to home. Having lost a schoolteacher and an electrician, we gained, and how tinpot is this, my sister's aerobics instructor. It looked to be a good decision for all parties, as he fired both goals in a 2-1 victory over Farnborough.

It's good to have Jenny back, although somewhere there must be a picture of him ageing with each passing year, because in the flesh he doesn't look a day older than he did when leaving the Bulls seven years ago. Jenny would routinely get stick from opposing players and fans alike, usually advising him to get back to his paper-round, for then as now, Jenny had the cherubic looks of an altar-boy, and a stature to match. Which certainly didn't stop him putting a foot in where others may have baulked, added to a range of Anglo-Saxon vernacular that wouldn't sit well in a house of God. Yes, in Pitman we had a committed and gutsy midfielder who could do a decent job at this level or, as one regular put it, a lad who might be useful when he grows up. I wonder where our very own Dorian Grey is hiding his portrait.

Interestingly, our next opponents also had a player who looked about fifteen. Stone, that is. Our first away trip of the season was also the shortest, to the Gump and their rotund custodian, Steve Perrin. Many Bulls fans had Perrin marked as public-enemy number one, largely due to last season's less than subtle piss-taking, but I quite liked him. Characters like Perrin are rare, even at this level and, in fairness, he could take the stick as well as dishing it out. There were 700 Bulls fans at the Lawn, most of whom were enquiring of Perrin's pie consumption when, in a rare lull in proceedings, one of the Bulls asked him how he became so fat. A bonus of places like The Lawn is their intimacy. Insults can comfortably be traded for an entire match, and Perrin's reply came back loud and clear. 'Because every time I shag your missus, she gives me a cake.' Not original, but it brought the house down. Perrin's grin widened further when a Gump striker latched on to another route one missile and smashed a shot into the roof of the net. It was something we had all seen before, and many times, as thirty-seven year-old Neil Grayson put the Gumpers ahead. GT had put his faith in younger men, but if the limited resources of Forest Green could tempt Grayson to sign, there were more than a few Bulls supporters wondering why he hadn't been offered a run with his former employer. As the match progressed however, Grayson became increasingly isolated as the more controlled play of the Bulls gained a foothold and before half-time, Paul Parry found himself one on one with the home keeper. Whilst rounding Steve Perrin could be equated to kayaking around an oil-tanker, Pazza succeeded to level the scores. 'You're not scoffing any more', was the unusually clever play on words offered to Perrin, who suffered a rare sense of humour failure. I didn't catch the first word of his riposte, but the second was definitely 'off'.

Bad soon became worse, as a Gump defender baulked Perrin to allow a gentle Wrighty header into the net. The Bulls were ahead, and when Parry again raced goalwards, it looked like game over. Pazza's shot flew toward the bottom corner, only for Perrin to pull off a save of quite staggering agility for a man of his physique. I think even the hardest of Bulls hearts felt a little for the home keeper, as Danny Williams tapped the rebound into an empty net. It just wasn't Perrin's day, but he'd had plenty and would no doubt enjoy more in the future. No, today belonged to the Bulls, where another encouraging display, three goals and three points, completed a decent week's work. So, would this be our year?

As we had discovered two seasons ago, no prizes are handed out in August, but GT's newly assembled unit looked to have a little more class, pace, and importantly, desire, and on the evidence so far, a play-off spot didn't look as far away as it had in June, with only six players on the books.

Flag Day
September 2002

GT often says that Edgar Street should be a fortress, no doubt meaning a place where opponents are intimated, perhaps even frightened. One where the Bulls tear into the cowering visitors, sending them home with nothing more than relief at keeping the hiding in single figures.

If, however, a fortress has been redefined as a place where ground is yielded without a whimper, allowing invaders to cruise unchallenged, free to create carnage as they please, then ES qualifies in style. Short of rolling out a red carpet and giving Wrighty a tray of canapés, our home ground couldn't at present be much more welcoming.

Lost, drew, drew (both goalless), lost, and hardly promotion form. Contrast that with our away games over the same period. Won, won, won, won, ten goals scored, fabulous attacking football, and without doubt promotion material. Bash Street Kids on the road, Sesame Street kids at home, the Bulls were becoming predictable. Highlights included another live Sky match and customary victory at a rain-sodden Woking, and a last-minute winner at Kettering, including, already, the goal of the season. Step forward Wayne Duick, who converted a Guinan cross with the sweetest of twenty-yard volleys. Duick would struggle to score a better goal if he played for the next forty years, but he was of course a Kettering player, and had scored an own-goal of rare quality.

And then to Woking, where more surreal entertainment was provided both on and off the pitch. Had the game not been on TV it may not have happened, but to the surprise of many, the pitch was declared playable. To be fair, there was little wrong with the islands of green dotted around the lake that was Kingfield, the problem being the inch-deep water everywhere else. No matter, as the Bulls adapted better than their hosts, the second goal allowing a celebrating Matt Clarke to body-surf from the penalty area to the corner-flag. As the rain continued and the match became ever more farcical, the two sets of fans took it upon themselves to provide alternative second half entertainment. With the away terrace resembling the closing scenes of Moby Dick (no, Steve Perrin hadn't appeared, it was just very wet), the hundred or so Bulls fans took refuge in the home Kop. The Woking faithful welcomed us into their shed, not least because it allowed them a distraction from the water-polo they had paid to watch. What followed was twenty minutes' worth of banter that quickly went from stereotypical to beyond surreal.

'We've got more cash than you, Hereford, Hereford.' True, without being original, as everyone has more cash than us. However, the gauntlet was down, now we needed to sing something. 'Two-nil to the Hereford,' was our reply, a lame effort. And so it continued, with relative salaries (ouch), house prices (worlds apart), beer quality (one for us there), tractors and BMWs all heavily featured. The verbal jousting had gone way beyond the usual sheep-shagger/imitation cockney jibes, but as we were dredging up a witty coup-de-grace, we were undone by a ditty that I can safely say I

123

have never heard before or since. 'If you prospered under Thatcher, clap your hands.' Surreal, and something to which we had no answer. Defeat was conceded to the Woking comedians, but a word to the wise. Don't repeat it when a redundant mineworker from Halifax is within earshot, especially if you like your facial features as they are.

Harmless fun, but something a lot less pleasant had occurred at ES, with another public relations own-goal from the club that scores too many. Club mascot Billy the Bull had organised a display of national flags at our ground, contributed by exiled supporters. It was a good idea from Billy, aka Darren Coates, and certainly ES could do with a little more colour. Unfortunately, a match sponsor at an early season game objected to the Welsh Dragon forming part of the display, and Darren was instructed to remove it. Whilst barely believable that someone was sufficiently offended to complain, in ordering its removal, the club was at best being naive in the extreme, at worst grossly incompetent and offensive. Darren, and credit to him, said that if one went, they all did, and the fourteen national flags that had illuminated ES were gone, and a distasteful row kicked off.

GT and his staff were working tirelessly to keep Hereford United in business, and huge credit is due to each of them, but someone at the club had clearly acted before engaging any semblance of reasoned thought, immediately inviting and receiving an avalanche of criticism. Like all clubs, and indeed communities, Hereford had some bad apples, a few of which were obviously bigoted, and our friends from across the border were their target of choice. It was clear that an overwhelming majority of Bulls fans, many having Welsh blood, were not willing to tolerate this idiocy but, inexcusably, one club official did, and at a time when the Bulls needed every ounce of goodwill, it was a self-inflicted wound that they could have done without. A peace of sorts was restored with a GT apology, so hopefully with flags back in place and at least one suitably contrite club official, we could move on to other matters.

Like more dropped points, and the long-running soap-opera of ES taking yet another, possibly significant twist. Chelverton, like the BSG before them, had run into financial problems, and parts of the business would be sold off to keep the parent company viable. What price another change of landlord in the near future?

Stranger in a Strange Town
23/11/2002 Dagenham and Redbridge - away

I will confess to not having paid much attention to Dagenham last season, due largely to the date on which the match was played, and also because at night most of east London looks the same. Whenever I hear reference to nine-eleven or see crumbling tower blocks, I think of Dagenham, and a strangely subdued one-nil defeat that for once didn't seem to matter. Today was different, a perfect winter afternoon, and with the M25 for once not resembling a car lot, touchdown in Dagenham was a scandalously early 1.15. Time for a leisurely stroll to meet Justin and Woody, and enjoy the splendour that is Dagenham East.

Some observations. Despite the glorious sunshine, everything in Dagenham is grey, from the shop fronts and the windowless factories right down to the cars, every other one of which appeared to be an Escort of the same early eighties vintage. Even the odd patch of surviving grass was grey, and although I've seen worse, it wasn't pretty. A stand-up comic once observed that whilst Dagenham wasn't twinned with a picture-postcard town in the Algarve, it did share a suicide pact with Beirut. Probably unfair, for there was no air of menace about the place, particularly the pub where we had arranged to meet. When so unfashionably early, what was there to do, other than watch the preening slaves to Rupert's millions on the TV? My mistake was sitting close enough to three affable-looking locals also enjoying the match. As you do, we passed the time with musings about overpaid prima donnas, and how the modern game isn't a patch on football's golden era of our youth, knowing full well that the Arsenal side dismantling Bolton on the big screen would have done just that and more to any of our fondly remembered heroes. It was a relatively pleasant twenty minutes, ruined in a second by one casual observation on the match in progress.

'That Thierry Henry, I know he's a coon and all, but you have to admit, he can play.'

It was a comment issued with the same benign lack of emphasis with which you might request sugar in your tea, and came from the sort of chap more than happy to help old ladies across the road. Not an eyebrow was raised by either of his colleagues, although both managed a nod of agreement.

Had I stepped back a generation? Whilst the bar may not have seen any serious redecoration since the days of old-money and brown wallpaper, the plasma screen confirmed that this was indeed the twenty-first century. So, was it just these three, or was I in a right-wing meeting house? A brief glance around showed a universally white clientele, perhaps a little unusual in an ethnically diverse part of the country, but maybe not when remembering that the BNP had a high profile around these parts. In an ideal world I would have asked him to justify garbage like that, but I was a stranger in a strange town, and too old for heroic but utterly pointless gestures. These guys were clearly beyond any re-education that I could offer, added to which I wanted to see the Bulls and the Daggers, not the local casualty department. It certainly left a nasty taste in the mouth, partly remedied by a rearranged pint in the Daggers supporters' bar, where, along with Justin and Woody, a more eclectic clientele applauded another master class from Monsieur Henry.

So what can I tell you about the Daggers and Victoria Road, home of the club who should be enjoying life in the Football League? The ground itself is compact, drab, and has nothing taller than the two-up two-downs boxing it in. The little atmosphere that exists is drowned out by an irritating drummer, joined occasionally by an equally tiresome bugle. If these misguided musicians can't control their compulsion, why don't they do us all a favour and join the Salvation Army? As well as a house-band, the Daggers also have a physiotherapist the size of a house, a ringer for Ricky Tomlinson in his Jim Royle guise, and almost as entertaining as the match, an early goal sending the Bulls to another defeat and a season low of tenth place. The half-time introduction of the injury-prone Smith and Grant was the only bonus of another referee-ruined game, Andy Tretton having received a straight red for what to everyone else in the ground appeared to be a perfectly-timed tackle. It was just one of those days, at the end of one of those months where nothing had gone right, despite several performances that deserved more than a solitary draw gained against Halifax. The travelling Bulls were far from happy, although one cheerful soul did his best to lighten the mood. As the Daggers' rotund sponge-man passed the Bulls fans in the last minute, his attention was called for.

'Oi, Jim', he yelled. 'Physiotherapist my arse.'

'You lot', he replied, 'Play-offs *my* arse.'

Good on you big man, not enough people with a sense of humour these days. Back in the club bar, we found assorted Daggers happy to share a pint and a moan, us about Conference officials, them about the Boston cheaters. We both had a point, and after the lunchtime unpleasantness it was good to sit down with some decent football fans. And also, apparently, at least one decent footballer. Junior McDougald, victim of Tretton's red-card tackle, had spoken to the referee, telling him just how good and fair a challenge it was. Thanks Junior, there may be some belated justice coming Andy Tretton's way. So was big Jim right, and were Hereford looking at another season of mediocrity or worse?

He was, according to a disgruntled majority on the internet forums, with yet more Bulls fans defecting to the New Meadowender camp, insistent that with GT in charge, the club would continue to underachieve, and perhaps even ultimately fade away and die. I disagreed. Many Herefordians had failed to see the bigger picture, showing little or no patience whilst the assembled parts were working towards the whole, but in this OK/Hello/Big Brother age of instant gratification, Hereford United were failing to satisfy.

Fortunately, a resilient minority are standing firm behind what they see. Which is a determined chairman/manager working damned hard with his coach and players to give the supporters what they crave. Having endured a nightmare five years, there are signs that the tide may be turning. The current squad are streets ahead of previous seasons' efforts, and better times may not be far away. Sometime soon the pieces will click into place, and someone is going to take a hiding.

Play-offs my arse? Don't bet against it just yet.

No Chairman, No Players, No Money, No Hope
4/2/2003 Farnborough Town - away

A crap team in a tinpot league, playing in a dilapidated ground a quarter filled by sad losers with nowhere better to go? Close to the truth in many ways, but what we do have is Talking Bull, a fanzine to match anything produced by our rivals from the Conference and beyond.

Regular contributors include The Village Idiot, The Twilight Zone, Talking Billy Bollox, Yokel, and of course, The New Meadowender. Most offer balanced and entertaining insights into life as a Bulls fan, and the editors should be applauded, particularly by exiled Bulls trying to keep up to date with their team. Without Talking Bull, the spark of gallows humour needed to retain both perspective and sanity would be missing. Without doubt the funniest article in the latest issue again came from New Meadowender, although I suspect that humour wasn't the primary motivation, as GT took another verbal pummelling, including likening him to Saddam Hussein. The genius of comedy is supposedly timing which, if true, would place New Meadowender up there with the best. Their article bemoaning our dismal results, clueless manager and invisible strikers was published just before GT received the Manager of the Month award for December. A month when our dismal results were four wins and a draw, a solitary goal conceded, and six for Steve Guinan alone, showing real quality in leading the attack. Twenty/twenty hindsight is a gift possessed by many supporters, but didn't someone say that the Bulls were due to give someone a hiding? Barnet went for four and Woking for five, neither due merely to Guinan at last finding his shooting boots.

GT and O'Kelly finally had the strong, classy spine essential to winning football matches. Matt Baker was becoming an excellent keeper and saving penalties for fun. Tretton was a robust and reliable centre-half, and Jamer now a complete, high quality defender. A fully-fit Ben Smith was our best midfielder in a decade and pulling the strings for Pazza and Guinan to cause havoc amongst Conference defences. A New Years Day victory over Telford saw the Bulls back into a play-off place, and with two 3,000 plus gates in a week, Conference optimism was at an all-time high, as for the first time the season was alive going into the New Year. An indication of better times came with an FA Trophy defeat at Yeovil, most Bulls fans taking the view that we could now concentrate on securing a play-off spot. Yeovil Town it has to be said, albeit through gritted teeth, looked a useful outfit, and it was easy to see why they were running away with the Conference, their blueprint for success simplicity itself. Keep a close eye on any neighbour struggling in a sea of debt and despair, bide your time until another final demand for the VAT/electricity/telephone arrives, and then make an insulting offer for their star player, and repeat until promoted. A strategy working for Yeovil every bit as well as it did for Cheltenham, now adapting comfortably to life in the Football League. It would take a hard-hearted Bulls fan to deny that Gavin and McIndoe deserved a better stage, but it's easy to understand why our rivals were known to Herefordians as Yeovile and Cheltenscum. Jealous? I don't think so. Who wants to watch the cream of non-league talent win promotion in a spanking new stadium in front of 5,000 fans every week?

And so to Farnborough, and a clash with the club described as having no chairman, no manager, no players, no money and no hope. An easy three points for the Bulls then, or so you would have thought, but why has it all gone so suddenly and dramatically wrong for the Hampshire side? Farnborough had recently enjoyed a lucrative FA Cup tie at Highbury and, shamelessly masquerading as proper players, were only days ago enjoying a winter break in the Algarve.

The answer requires just two words: Graham Westley.

A man who until last week was owner, chairman and manager of Farnborough Town and who, whilst not setting the Conference alight, had enjoyed an excellent cup run, along with the biggest match in the clubs history. And then, with club and supporters buoyant and a large cheque in the bank, Mr. Westley resigned. Two days after which, he was manager of Stevenage Borough. Not in itself unheard of, but when you consider that in addition to Westley, Stevenage had in the same week signed half of the Farnborough first team, something smells a little fishy. Incredibly, no rules had been broken, due to some less than conventional contracting arrangements, and the players joined Stevenage on free transfers.

Farnborough were left without a manager or chairman, and a skeleton squad bulked-up with youth team players. All this in addition to a surprisingly bleak financial picture, despite their FA Cup bonus. Farnborough supporters had been shafted by a man who had shown the moral fibre of an alley-cat, and were looking at a nervous couple of months trying to ensure the survival of their club. And what about Stevenage chairman Phil Wallace, joyfully welcoming such a bastion of integrity into the bosom of his club?

Maybe these two characters deserve each other, but whilst Stevenage and Westley would certainly be public-enemy number one in Farnborough, a majority of Conference supporters are lining up squarely behind fans of the Hampshire side. Stevenage are at present embroiled in a battle at the foot of the Conference, but with half a team gone and a transfer embargo in place, what price Farnborough going into freefall, and filling one of the dreaded relegation slots?

And should that happen, who would stand to benefit most? With contracts seemingly worth next to nothing, what is there to stop Mr. Wallace poaching key staff from Leigh or Southport, or anyone else likely to finish above his precious Stevenage? This was footballing sleaze at its worst, neatly demonstrating one of the few areas where the Conference could give the Premiership a run for its money. My feelings on an individual being both manager and chairman of a football club are clear. It's patently wrong, largely because very few people will sack themselves when the job is proving beyond their abilities. It is however, a scandalous abuse of position to betray the very people you purport to represent in the manner Graham Westley has betrayed Farnborough supporters. In a single ruthless act Westley achieved what Peter Hill did with twenty years of neglect, placing his club in a position of such peril that they may never recover. It's that same old question, but why are the men in charge of football clubs so often the type that shouldn't be allowed near a pub team? As for the match, Farnborough's hastily assembled side gave us a first half runaround, and were two goals up at the break. GT's version of the hairdryer obviously galvanised the Bulls, and a more acceptable second 45 minutes and twenty-yard missiles from Jenny Pitman and Danny Williams saw the points shared.

I like Farnborough and their supporters, and genuinely hope they survive this crisis. If they can hold onto their Conference status, even better. This might be a Mickey Mouse League, but what lies beneath is in comparison a wasteland. To be consigned there on the whim of another bored millionaire in search of a new toy would be a fate no genuine football fan should endure.

Not even those in Yeovil.

Down to Margate. No, Dover. No, Margate
11/2/2003 Margate - away

Let me explain. For reasons known only to themselves, Margate are this season ground-sharing with neighbours Dover. Stadium re-development is supposedly why Margate fans are trekking to the Crabble every other week, obviously a smokescreen, as Hereford were last week informed that the fixture would take place in Margate. Only to be told that no, it's in Dover. And then, just a couple of days before the match, sorry chaps, the Crabble's in a bit of a mess, you're going to Margate.

Whilst the M2 and the M20 are much of a cone-plagued muchness, if you're going to an evening match you want to be on the right road, particularly with Justin's time-keeping. There was therefore still a feeling of unease as signs for Margate appeared, until Alan, as usual and courtesy of Network South-East, in situ hours earlier, saved further stress with a timely text-message.

Plyrs coach sptd, def in mgte. c u in mech. elphnt.

Thanks Alan, Margate it is, but what was the rest of that about?

'Perhaps it's a pub', Justin offered. Followed by 'and Alan thinks he's thirteen again'. Knowing Alan, it probably was a pub, but for the next twenty miles we remained in the dark, as north Kent became a cellphone blackspot.

We needn't have worried. On an eerily deserted seafront, there it was, neatly sandwiched between an empty amusement arcade and a closed chip-shop. Yes, there is, in Margate, a pub called the Mechanical Elephant, and it showed the only signs of life for hundreds of yards around. Why anyone would so bizarrely christen a pub is a mystery, unlike the name of the hotel outside of which we were parked. Fatty Towers, would you believe, demonstrating that at least one proprietor in this fading seaside town has a sense of humour. And Alan was, as intimated, ensconced within the Elephant and looking reassuringly like a man in his early forties. One day I might have a crack at this text-speak.

After a quick pie and pint it was back in the car and to Hartsdown Park, a comfortable twenty-five minutes until kick-off, and with floodlights quickly located, things were looking good. Fifteen minutes later, we were still driving around back streets and industrial estates, lights still in view but no closer to the ground. Not only have we actually been here before, last season in fact, but we've been here before metaphorically, and many times. Why do relatively intelligent, reasonably practical adults so often find themselves in a mad rush to beat players on to football pitches, and will we ever learn?

Probably not, but tonight the god of disorganised football fans smiled on us. The ground was located with minutes to spare and, right on cue, a car pulled out of a parking space in front of the Hereford team coach. As omens go this was a cracker, and we agreed that a Bulls win was inevitable. Hartsdown Park, given the alleged re-development, was in remarkably good shape, with perfect playing surface, half-decent facilities, and not a concrete-mixer in sight. Safe enough to remove our tin-hats, we watched some left-footed magic from Rose and Pazza deliver both the points and third place in the Conference.

And Margate itself? A ghost-town, very different from the sunny resort of last season's Bank-Holiday encounter, but in a strangely quiet way, better for it.

And whilst we had expected mechanical diggers, we got a mechanical elephant. How unproper is that?

The Ides of March
22/3/2003 Barnet - away

So not only had the Bulls reached Christmas with something still to play for, but here we are in March, and looking good for a play-off spot.

Sadly, Margate represented the pinnacle of the season, and rather than consolidate a top five finish, the season was thrown away. A brace of draws followed by a thumping at Yeovil left plenty of work needed if an extension to the season was to be enjoyed. A victory over the uber-crap Kettering briefly lifted spirits, but defeat at Scarborough (how? why??) left the Bulls needing perhaps five wins from the last seven games, starting at Barnet.

It was two days before my fortieth birthday, and an early party was planned in the cultural centre of North London. That is, if football, a decent curry and perhaps an ale or two are your definition (as they are mine) of culture. Sorry Barnet, but that really is it.

They say that life begins at forty. Perhaps it does, but all too predictably, the season ended the same weekend. It was an excellent day out, and when Matt Baker saved yet another penalty shortly before Pazza equalised, even the football was looking good. Sadly, the team with nothing to play for edged out the team with everything to play for, the gap to the vital fifth spot now looking insurmountable, and another season of unproper football beckoned.

News, however, wasn't all bad. Chelverton's financial problems were confirmed, and United's leases are now in the hands of a company called Formsole. The Richardson brothers, two ridiculously wealthy Midlands builders, will now have a say in what happens to ES, and the Bulls. And so far so good. The £1.3 million has been deferred to May 2005, giving GT two more years in which to win the lottery.

Yeovil had already won their jackpot in sealing the title, but at the other end of the table, matters were less clear. Kettering looked doomed, but incredibly, no less than thirteen teams were looking nervously at their remaining fixtures, including Farnborough Reserves, still referred to by some as Stevenage Borough. Graham Westley and his relocated mercenaries had failed to reverse the fortunes of the Hertfordshire club, and were sitting above the drop zone on goal-difference. Chairman Wallace decided that drastic action was required, and in the absence of another shameless owner/manger to poach, he changed the rules.

Or at least he tried to. Wallace (and perhaps Gromit) proposed to the 21 other clubs that the Conference next season be expanded to 24 teams, still allowing three teams to be promoted, but vitally, only one relegated.

Brilliant, the man is clearly a genius, realising that thirteen of his fellow chairmen would have to vote against his plan for it to fall. Of course, with thirteen teams still in danger and football club chairmen generally unencumbered with an excess of Corinthian spirit, if indeed any, his plan was approved.

A magnificent seven opposed Wallace, including GT, who confessed his 'surprise' that the motion was passed. It was another turkeys and Christmas debate, so whilst GT's moral fibre is to be commended, for him to confess his surprise was a clear indication that he spends more time on the training-ground than he does in the boardrooms of his Conference colleagues.

The plan was sent to the FA for ratification, where for once the blazers did the right thing. Sorry chaps, but you can't be serious. Changing the rules three parts through a season just isn't cricket, and neither, in this case, is it football. Case dismissed, now toddle off back to your Mickey-Mouse League and relegate three clubs, just as you agreed last summer. And if one of them just happens to be Stevenage, your tinpot competition might perhaps be a better place.

The Ego has Landed. At Edgar Street
26/4/2003 Doncaster Rovers - home

April wasn't much better than March. A feeble performance handed vital points to Leigh's relegation fight, followed two days later by a committed and skilful victory at Southport. A win for the Lancashire side would have ensured Conference safety, but with scores level, a fluked injury-time goal from on-loan striker Albano Correia condemned them to defeat, and ultimately, relegation. And ourselves to sixth place in the Conference, where we would remain, win, lose or draw the season's finale against Doncaster.

Donny Rovers, the team we never beat, came to ES with a play-off place sewn up, unsurprising given the investment enjoyed over the last five years. Investment courtesy of one John Ryan, club chairman, and a man reportedly several million pounds poorer, who in true Max Griggs style has taken his plaything to the verge of the Football League. No doubt he could have bought numerous proper clubs with that sort of cash, but, and credit to him, Donny are his team, and for once, it appears that a fan has actually put his money where his mouth is.

OK, that's more than enough of being nice to Mr. Ryan, time to let him have it. John Ryan, at 52 years of age and probably not in his physical prime, registered himself as a Conference player at the start of the season. Not an unreasonable indulgence I suppose, as to see his name on the back page of the programme as well as the front isn't a lot to ask for his millions. But, and this is where the line between mild self-indulgence and the feeding of an out of control ego is crossed, there is more. Amongst Donny's substitutes was John Ryan, who, if the game wasn't in the balance, would become the oldest player ever to grace the Conference.

Which caused something of a stir. Donny supporters no doubt thought it was harmless fun, a few Hereford fans likewise, and GT apparently had no objections. And straight from the horse's mouth, Ryan himself stated that his appearance would do Hereford a favour by putting another five hundred on the gate.

What? I fear Mr. Ryan has lost contact with reality, for why would anybody pay good money to watch a wobbly old man kick a football around?

Unless of course their name is Robbie Dennison or Jimmy Quinn. But I digress. The reaction from a large majority of Bulls fans was predictable, seeing it as an insult to pretty much everyone, particularly the players of both teams, along with the Conference itself. There was the hope that the match would be too finely poised to indulge Ryan's fantasies, but the sugar daddy got his wish and, with Donny 4-2 up, on he tottered with two minutes to play.

In an ideal world, a trademark Jenny Pitman tackle would have dumped him flat on his back, but Ryan didn't actually touch the ball, or even get near to it. Or, as one website tactfully put it, he failed to make an impact. The Doncaster benefactor, chairman, and once-only substitute had lived the dream, even if it did come with a seven-figure price tag. However, in an irony lost on many observers, his brief moment of fame presented a priceless opportunity for a tabloid punch-line. John Ryan's fortune had been earned through the supply of prosthetics to the medical world, including the enhanced frontage of many a page three wannabee. I have absolutely no problems with entrepreneurs like John Ryan, and if they choose to put their money into football rather than yachts or racehorses, good for them.

Today, however, the implant man made himself look a bit of a tit. Just my opinion of course.

Has the Tide Turned?

Signs were generally positive. The summer cull by GT was drastic but effective, the players coming in appearing better equipped for a challenge at the right end of the table. Tretton and Rose added to Jamer's quality at the back, Guinan a clever striker who should add to his tally of 14 goals given a regular partner, and Ben Smith in half a season showing more class in midfield than we had seen in many years. Pazza is finally adding consistency to his undoubted class, and I wonder just how long GT can hang on to both him and Jamer. Baker, Clarke and Pitman all had a good year, Pitman's strike at Farnborough the goal of the season. Slightly disappointing were the gifted but inconsistent Danny Williams and Wrighty, who found both injury and Andy Tretton limiting his chances.

GT's best signing was, however, universally agreed by Bulls fans. Richard O'Kelly was a huge hit, most importantly with the players, who clearly enjoyed playing for a first-class coach. If he and GT could coax even 5% more out of them next season, the play-offs would be the least they could hope for. HUISA player of the season was Paul Parry, but my vote was for Tony James. It was a joy to watch, as Jamer frustrated one Conference striker after another, usually with indecent ease. His speed of thought was matched by his speed over the ground, and he was man of the match so often it was almost an embarrassment, the only downside being that our best player might develop a taste for the Bollinger he would take home most weeks.

Biggest disappointment of the season was the timidity of our run-in, where a great chance of being in the inaugural tinpot play-offs was thrown away.

Villains of the campaign would be the morally-bankrupt duo from Stevenage, along with the blazers who mishandled the Boston affair, only partially redeeming themselves by throwing out the nonsense proposed by Wallace and Westley. Pantomime villain would have to be John Ryan, relegating the impossibly athletic Steve Perrin into second place in the comedy footballer stakes.

Off the field, we had another new landlord and a new deadline on the loan repayment, welcome, even essential good news. Along with the encouraging increase in attendances, and the prospect of the CVA being removed in the not too distant future, it appeared that there was more optimism around the club than for many years. A little more of GT's close-season bargain hunting and we could, just maybe, have some real fun next season.

Whilst the season ended quietly for the Bulls, Dagenham, Chester, Morecambe and Donny would play-off to join Yeovil in the Football League, replacing Exeter and, much to the delight of Bulls supporters, our neighbours from Shropshire, Shrewsbury Town.

And in an unusual quirk of fate, two more former league clubs were joining the Conference from below. Accrington Stanley and Aldershot Town had risen from the dead, and were now just one step away from where they once, in a previous life, enjoyed their football.

Exiting the Conference downwards would be Southport, Nuneaton, and Kettering, those three drawing the short straws on a final day lottery when any of six teams might have taken the drop. Farnborough survived, one point and one place below the reviled Stevenage Borough, but remain a club in crisis. I hope that next season both sides get exactly what they deserve.

So, who would be the first winners of a Conference play-off final?

It was Donny Rovers, as John Ryan finally saw a return on his investment, in the form of a golden goal and 3-2 extra-time victory, Ryan bravely resisting the temptation to put his boots on again. Whilst Donny were promoted, the Daggers were left with nothing, although this time their defeat at the hands of the men with the cash was legitimate. Perhaps money can't buy you love but, it appears, can buy you a place in the Football League. Rushden and Donny are extreme examples, but every club promoted since Hereford joined this league have spent considerably more in achieving it than that coming through the turnstiles.

Please tell me that's not the only way to escape this sometimes charming, but categorically unproper division.

8   2003-2004 Lambs and Bulls. And a Couple of Pigs

9/8/2003 Tamworth - away

To enjoy rather than endure a summer made a refreshing change, but it's August again, and another Cathedral City is in a world of trouble. New boys Exeter City lost their League status with a reported debt of three million pounds, and three directors arrested over alleged financial irregularities. Surely not someone else doing a Boston? I doubt it, but Exeter join the Conference in both administration and the hands of a Supporters' Trust. Good luck gents, you're going to need it.

Managerial appointments included Jimmy Quinn at Shrewsbury, Colin Addison at the Gump, and a new Chairman at Chester, one Stephen Vaughan.

But wasn't there a Stephen Vaughan at Barrow not so long ago, one who walked away and left the club in a sea of debt and uncertainty? With Barrow still suffering from the fallout, if I were a Chester supporter I wouldn't be having a party to celebrate Mr. Vaughan's arrival. As for the Bulls, a few ins and outs. The athletic but profligate Grant and the less athletic but legendary Wrighty were released, the latter snapped up by Burton. All Bulls fans will wish him well.

More surprising was the departure of Matt Clarke, tempted by a better deal at Telford and another chairman looking to buy a place in the Football League. And perhaps another club whose supporters find that there is no pot of gold at the end of their rainbow. Time will tell, but moving in the opposite direction was striker David Brown, not prolific, but Michael Owen was just out of our budget. And whilst Bulls fan were disappointed not to land an England international, we did catch a Welsh one, amazingly not one on the wrong side of 35 with a flaky cruciate ligament. Quite the opposite, as Ryan Green, the youngest player to win a full Welsh cap joined from Wolves. And only 22. Perhaps another in the talented but wayward bracket, but the type of player GT seems able to bring out the best in.

Another McIndoe? We live in hope.

Pre-Season had been spectacular, especially if you liked your goals in big bunches. Amongst the victims were Ludlow (small town in Shropshire) by 13-1, Bromyard (smaller town in Herefordshire) by 7-0, and HUISA (collection of slightly under-prepared Bulls fans) by 8-1. Whilst all were something of a turkey-shoot, another new signing stood out. Daniel Carey-Bertram was a striker with quite ridiculous pace, who if able to show even a fraction of Stevie G's composure would prove a handful. (That's Guinan, not Gerrard, lest you've not been keeping up.)

And so to the Lamb, home of the Lambs, and also of the Tamworth Two. Pinky and Perky were the porcine pair who decided that a Tamworth abattoir was not the place to spend their last minutes of pre-sausage existence, and made a break for freedom. Having made national headlines with their escape bid you might, like me, have thought that they were smarter than the average pig. But also like me, you've probably never been to Tamworth. Believe me, if Pinky and Perky had been that clever, they would have turned straight around and begged for a swift end in the slaughterhouse.

Why? Because, as far as I could see, Tamworth is a nothing-happening sort of place. Unless you're into butt-ugly pubs, or skiing down a man-made mountain on artificial snow. Yes, the biggest thing in Tamworth is the Snowdome, dwarfing the Lamb, a ground distinctly lacking in Alpine charm. In fact, lacking in charm, period.

As for the ugly pubs, they made a perfect setting for some equally ugly skirmishes between the local Neanderthals and their Herefordshire counterparts. This was always going to be one of those matches. A local derby against a new opponent, easy rail connections, and ample time to fuel up beforehand all pointed toward an opportunity too good to ignore. Added to which it was the hottest day of the year, and fuses already short were trimmed to a point where confrontation was inevitable. Whilst on the pitch the Bulls delivered a convincing victory, the terracing was not a comfortable place. You might think that on such an oppressively hot day a water-fight would be the perfect way to cool down, a concept heartily embraced by the warring factions who continued battles started in the town centre. The problem today was that these lads forgot to take the water out of the bottles before launching it at the enemy. The ongoing skirmish was curiously handled by stewards and police, the former appearing out of their depth, the latter content merely to record events on a camcorder.

You've Been Framed, anyone?

Despite all of which, it had been a good day for GT, with three points in the bag, and sitting nicely on top of the Conference. Which begged the obvious question.

How long could we hold that coveted top spot for this time?

We would soon see, as two former Bulls brought their sides to ES. The Gump were dismissed in similar style to our other recent village opponents, with Colin Addison fulsome in his praise of his former club. Steve Perrin's comments are sadly not on record, but a five goal thumping would shut almost anybody up.

A strong Morecambe side went the same way four days later, this time 3-0, and manager Jimmy Harvey had few complaints, for here was a man who knew good football when he saw it. For most of the nineteen eighties, Harvey stood head and shoulders above the rest of the fourth division, and he remains a Bulls legend to this day. When GT has had enough, Harvey would be top of my list and, I suspect, that of many others, as replacement. If this level of performance is maintained, the play-offs this season might just be something for others to worry about.

Yes, the start to the season really had been that good.

Best Player in the Conference?
30/8/2003 Stevenage Borough - away

A scrappy point gained at Barnet was followed by the game of the season, when Aldershot visited ES for the first time in twelve years.

It was worth the wait, as second entertained the leaders in the year's first six-pointer, and a match with seven goals, 11 yellow cards, one red, and a 93rd minute winner in front of a near 5,000 crowd, comfortably our unproper best. It was unmissable drama, all of which I unfortunately, well, missed, having used up the weekend's allowance of Brownie points at Barnet two days earlier.

Never mind, the joy of teletext when David Brown notched his first Bulls goal made up for being elsewhere when events were unfolding at Edgar Street. Which is, of course, bullshit.

I was delighted to see my team at the top of the league, but less than chuffed that they'd done it without me. That said, I should have been anything but surprised that the Bull's finest hour and a half of Conference football took place whilst I was battling with an evil piece of Ikea furniture. Whilst both wardrobe and Bulls were looking good right now, would one, or perhaps both, have fallen apart by Christmas?

Of more immediate concern was a trip to a revitalised Stevenage, and the opportunity to shut, even if temporarily, the biggest mouth in the Conference belonging, in the absence of Steve Evans, to Graham Westley. I travelled to Stevenage determined not to like it, a mission accomplished with ridiculous ease. A mercifully brief tour gives the impression of a community obsessed with those two bastions of Home Counties culture, DIY and fast-food, the conclusion being that behind every fence is a spotty chubber erecting a garden shed. Hertfordshire is supposedly a haven for real-ale drinkers, something categorically not true of Stevenage. The ground-hopper's bible, the Good Beer Guide, lists the town's best pub as being in Old Knebworth, a picture-postcard village a ten minute drive and a million miles away from what passed for civilisation just up the road. The Lytton Arms would run a close second as the best watering hole in the Conference to Farnborough's Prince of Wales, which by happy chance we would be revisiting in just seven days. That is, if Stevenage didn't steal the rest of the Farnborough squad in the interim.

Suitably refreshed, it was time for the B&Q McHomebase Hut, aka Broadhall Way, where the £2.50 invested in a match day programme was money gloriously well spent, firstly in confirming that Graham Westley is indeed worthy of the abuse he so frequently elicits. His notes use the word 'we' on no less than 22 occasions, with more than a few 'I's and 'ours' thrown in for good measure.

Compare that to the number of name-checks afforded to his opponents. That's right, none. Not even to wish the travelling supporters a safe, if pointless, journey home. Stevenage could have been playing the local Scout pack, not the team currently sitting on top of the Conference. I have no problem with focussing on your own side, but in most people's eyes it takes two teams to make a football match, and it appeared that basic courtesy and Graham Westley are entities yet to be introduced to each other.

Westley's bravado, however, was a mere appetiser when compared to the staggering ego displayed in the Player Profile section, featuring one Anthony Elding. Try this for a self-portrait of someone just a little in love with himself.

Nickname? - Eldinho. (Obviously Brazilian flair in abundance.)

Best Player in the Conference? - Anthony Elding. (Only 500 others, must be special.)

Who would you most like to meet? - Alan Shearer. Maybe I could learn something I don't already know. (Clearly not going to learn anything from Graham Westley.)

And least like to meet? - David Beckham, because he's nearly as good-looking as me. (Brazilian football genius *and* drop-dead gorgeous.)

Was Elding just a modest lad with an overdeveloped sense of irony, or the runaway ego suggested by the gratuitously topless photo opposite his musings? Allowing him the benefit of the doubt, I asked a steward his opinion of the self-proclaimed finest player in the league.

'Oh, he's a good striker at this level, bit of a handful really.' Which, quite honestly, wasn't what I wanted to hear. 'But he's an arrogant twat with it.'

That's better. Time to see if he could get the better of the league's second best player, and another Anthony, our very own Jamer. The short answer was no. Eldinho was indeed a useful if petulant, player, but was getting little out of Jamer and Tretton, whilst further upfield Ben Smith orchestrated waves of magnificent attacking football. It was a joy to watch, as the Bulls pummelled what purported to be one of the strongest sides in the Conference, and we waited for the inevitable goals to come. Until Elding took a theatrical dive, conning a penalty out of yet another clueless official. Eldinho no doubt assumed he was about to be on the score sheet for the fifth successive match, until Matt Baker saved his spot-kick. Unfortunately for the prostrate Bakes, the rebound fell straight back to Elding, with an undefended goal at his mercy. It was a tap-in, but the Brazilian in Eldinho obviously couldn't resist a little showboating, and delivered a volley that nearly decapitated a Bulls fan sitting in row F of the Buildbase Stand. (No really, it *is* called the Buildbase Stand.) Cue the priceless sight of the best player in the Conference with head held in embarrassed hands.

Such a shame that no-one knew the Brazilian (or is it Portuguese?) for wanker. Salt was rubbed swiftly into the wound as Smithy gave the Bulls a half-time lead. Guinan added a second, a safety net enabling Smith and Parry to perform a little showboating of their own. It was men against boys, and the more Stevenage chased and harried, the more inept they were made to look by a team at the very top of their game. Although

141

ending at an unspectacular 2-0, this was comfortably the best 90 minutes I had seen from a Hereford team in a Conference fixture and, bless 'em all, they'd produced it in Wallace and Westley's own little kingdom of hot air and dubious morality.

It was a small but buoyant troop of Bulls fans heading south that evening, for whilst we had all wanted out of the Conference since the day we joined, we knew that the talent present in each of GT's squads made promotion a long shot, if not an impossibility. Until today, for this an immaculate performance from a team that looked equipped, for the first time in seven years, to go all the way. Today, the Bulls were that good, and Smithy in particular on a different plane, confirmation coming from a surprising source. No less an authority than Graham Westley told Three Counties Radio that he had no complaints, and that the better side had won. Whether his verdict was delivered through gritted teeth is unknown but he had, if belatedly, conceded that Stevenage weren't the only team on show today. Which doesn't mean I'll be enrolling in his fan-club.

Likewise anyone I spoke to at Farnborough seven days later, many of whom were as thrilled as us with the result at Stevenage. My second favourite team were still alive but struggling and pointless at the bottom of the Conference, bereft of quality and confidence, and surely set up for another Bulls goal-fest. Which is invariably when the hot favourite is turned over. Today however, I just couldn't see that happening, and so confident was I of big victory that I broke the habit of a lifetime and had a bet on my team. Sporting Index were offering up a one goal start for the home side, not enough in my mind, and I went with the Bulls in a big way, at least by my own usually modest standards. It was of course taking a chance, particularly as GT had been cursed as Manager of the Month, but when Guinan nodded a third just before half-time, it was money in the bank.

As Jamer made it four, Justin voiced his disappointment at the one-sided game, admitting to feeling sorry for Farnborough. At which point I confessed my tryst with the bookmaker. A brief lesson on spread-betting, and the knowledge that every goal the Bulls scored put another wad of cash in my pocket placed his usually Corinthian outlook temporarily to one side.

'Come on Hereford, bury this fucking pub-team, we want five.'

Whilst said with tongue slightly in cheek, he got his wish, and as well as a thumping away win and a decent pint in the Prince of Wales,

I'd banked enough for a weekend in Barcelona with Mrs S. And, lest we forget, the Bulls were top of the league.

Without question, it was another new entry into the top ten of great days out at the football.

Of course, if we had lost the match five-nil.........

Making Plans, is Nigel
19/9/2003 Burton Albion - away

A more mundane victory over Scarborough followed the slaughter at Farnborough, witnessed by a crowd just twenty short of 5,000. If Scarborough had brought more than a taxi full, we might have broken our recently set record, but it's a long way to come for a hiding. Let's not forget we had put six past the Seadogs when we were, quite frankly, crap.

So, before Burton, where do we stand? Played eight, won seven, drawn one. Goals for, 25, goals against, seven. And sitting happily on top of the Conference, playing proper football that absolutely warranted our lofty position. Not to put too fine a point on it, we were fucking great.

More good news came from off the field, where a scandalous rumour hinted that the club was trading at a profit. Perhaps true, given that an insulting bid for Paul Parry had recently been rejected. Yes, Yeovil were again sniffing around for a bargain, but for the first time in seven years, GT could hold onto his prize assets. Sorry, but this once moribund football club is reviving, if not yet fully recovered, so take your cheapskate offers somewhere else.

Yes, the Bulls' finances were stabilising, if still far from healthy, and yes, we now had another new landlord. The million pound ticket was confirmed to be in the hands of a company called Formsole and the Richardson brothers. They had reportedly acquired said ticket for considerably less than the £1.3 million owed, and might just be in a position to sit tight for a little longer than Chelverton.

We can only wait and see. And so to Nigel Clough's Burton Albion and a Friday fixture, moved because Burton share their stewards with Derby County, also at home the following day. With the reputation of our mindless minority at an all-time low, the Friday night option was considered the best way to deal with potential problems. Predictably, our cast of idiots took the day off to enjoy the fare on offer in Burton, where it's no coincidence that the local club are nicknamed the Brewers. Suitably prepared, it was a re-run of the Tamworth experience, with a small but telling difference. Burton, it would appear, are a club lacking a moronic minority to occupy the invaders, meaning an evening where anyone in the wrong place was in trouble. Although small in number, they create havoc massively disproportionate to their size, tonight culminating in a half-time invasion of the home terrace. Where most of the stewards were at this point is a good question, perhaps already in Derby, but the resulting carnage was amongst the nastiest I had seen for many years. The Hereford substitutes became reluctant and only partially effective peace-makers, again filmed by the police. As at Tamworth, however, this was where any involvement from the Constabulary began and ended. In a match highlighted and rescheduled as potentially troublesome, both police and club seemed significantly under-prepared when it actually happened. Although unlikely to be of concern to the perpetrators, entering into a CVA is not the only way to lose points around a table at Conference HQ, and if this continues, Hereford United will be facing sanctions which could at a stroke put us out of the title-race. Whilst clearly not responsible for or encouraging this small section of its following, the club will have to get rid of them or face the consequences that would inevitably follow. Whilst no restaurant would invite rats into the kitchen, it would quickly be out of business if it continually turned a blind eye.

As a sideshow to the main event, a football match did take place, in which Nigel's men attempted to end the Bulls' unbeaten run at the ninth time of asking. Burton were a decent and well-organised outfit, happy to concede possession whilst calmly snuffing out any danger at their own end of the pitch. It appeared, however, to be a matter of when and not if the visitors turned possession into a goal, and Danny Williams duly obliged with twenty minutes remaining. And onwards rolled the Bulls bandwagon, another tricky encounter behind them. Or not.

Burton, as well as being solid at the back, showed on the night a faultless exhibition of scoring on the break. Four times they turned defence into attack, stretching the Bulls as they broke up field, each time converting the opportunity, and they ran out winners by 4-1. Whilst not the better side, Burton deserved their victory, no-one more so than the newly qualified electrician marshalling their defence. It was another man-of-the-match display from Wrighty, who had found a part-time home to wind down his first career. Good luck to you Ian, if anyone deserves a stress-free if not exactly lucrative final season or two, it's you. It was a memorable night in Burton for all the wrong reasons, but such is the way of the Conference fixture-list that the opportunity to put things back on track would come just a few days later.

And back we were, with a 2-1 win over Telford at ES, where two Bulls old boys gave their previous club a welcome boost. John Grant blazed characteristically over an open goal, shortly after which Pazza left his friend Matt Clarke chasing shadows, before crossing for Guinan to head home. Lee Mills, not so long ago a Premiership striker, equalised only for Ryan Green to notch his first Bulls goal in the 93rd minute. Telford could count themselves unlucky to leave with nothing, but here was another sign that this might just be our year. Telford's wage bill is reportedly three times that of the Bulls, much of which no doubt tempted Mills away from early retirement, but served only to illustrate that a goal scored by a player on a couple of grand a week was worth nothing if two lads on less than half that between them popped them in at the other end.

My Sister's Little Boy
13/10/2003 Dagenham and Redbridge - home

The Bulls followed up the victory at Telford with a draw against Gravesend, a gritty win at Woking, and a goal-fest at Northwich, where a 5-1 victory brought a petulant outburst from another Conference manager. We were according to him an ordinary side riding our luck and heading for a fall. Furthermore, 5-1 was a flattering scoreline, and such results wouldn't continue when injury and suspension hit our small squad. There are two points to make here. Firstly, Tretton and Purdie were missing, injured. Secondly, and more pertinently, these comments came not from the mouth of Northwich manager Alvin McDonald but, according to the Bullsnews website, the larger although less well informed orifice belonging to Jimmy Quinn, manager of Shrewsbury Town. Quite why Quinn should see fit to bad-mouth his rivals is a mystery, particularly when his own side were ten points behind us and hardly setting the Conference alight in the manner of the 'lucky' and 'ordinary' Hereford. Perhaps GT's worst ever loan signing couldn't forgive the reception he received after his mercifully short stint at ES. Or was it simply envy that his local rivals were receiving the plaudits that his more expensively assembled side weren't? Of course, Quinn isn't the only Conference manager who should think before speaking, no names mentioned, of course. And certainly not Daggers manager Garry Hill, who, whilst not short of a comment or two, seems a decent enough sort, and one who arrived in Hereford hoping to find a stadium with its roofing

145

in place, particularly as the match presented another chance to show the world just how entertaining Conference football could be.

Or at least those in possesion of a satellite dish. Yes, once again we were on TV, along with my nephew Jacob. It's a long story, but here goes. As the Bulls were finally rediscovering the beautiful game, Conference football was losing its appeal for Jake, skateboarding having that little extra street-cred so important to a nine year-old. Or even worse, when he was so to speak bored with his board, watching the Premiership, and especially Arsenal, would keep him happy. Here was an emergency calling for desperate measures. A quick call to ES revealed that the Dagenham fixture required a match day mascot. Duly booked, it was the last chance to steer a wayward youth back toward the path of righteousness. And then something which doesn't happen every day, in the form of another telephone call.

'Hello Mr. Stansbury, Hereford United here, do you have a moment?'

Of course I did, I had all week if required, but what did they want? Had I hurled foul abuse toward a clueless official once too often, and they wanted my season ticket back? Had my thirty-year-old crime of selling a complimentary ticket to a mate been discovered? Or had Matt Baker sprained his wrist washing up, and a goal-keeping emergency left little option but to recall a lad once selected (though I never played) for the club's youth team?

No such luck for me, but Jake had hit the motherlode.

'The Dagenham game has been moved to the Monday night for live TV coverage. Is Jacob still available to be mascot?'

Has Jimmy Quinn got a big mouth? Of course he's available, bring it on. My objections to Rupert Murdoch's march toward global domination were again brushed away, a small price to pay as the birthday present of a lifetime landed at Jacob's feet. And of course he needed an escort inside the inner sanctum of what was my second home.

We both had a memorable evening, starting with the presentation of a full away strip, just too small for me but perfect for a nine-year-old, an autographed football, and a matchday programme with Jake on the back page. Jamer then took him onto the hallowed turf for a warm-up, followed by a quick hello from GT and a name-check over the stadium PA. He and Jamer then led the team onto the pitch for more handshakes, a few photographs, and a final wave to four thousand Bulls fans inside ES, and probably hundreds more at home who preferred crap football over Coronation Street.

As for me and my first visit to the parts of ES that had been off-limits for thirty years, a few items stick in the memory. Footballers are all smaller when you stand next to them, Jamie Pitman really does look twelve years old, and Ryan Green should spend less time on a sun-bed. And the match itself? It started modestly, and went slowly downhill until Smithy hit a screamer on the hour. The Daggers equalised with a goal as scruffy as Smith's was sweet, but far more in keeping with a game unlikely to keep the casual satellite viewer on the edge of his seat. Or even awake.

The point gained left the Bulls still sitting pretty on top of the Conference, although Chester were closing, making next Saturday's trip to the Deva Stadium a little more spicy than it might have been, as a win for Steven Vaughan's side would see Hereford knocked off the top of the league.

World Champions
22/11/2003 Shrewsbury Town - away

It's a pity when at ten o'clock on a Saturday morning you suspect that the weekend has peaked, and it's downhill from there on. You would also suspect that it's not just any Saturday, when at the same time you find yourself walking out of, not into your local pub.

Before which, an update. The Bulls had exchanged uninhibited attacking football for parsimonious defence, as a comfortable goalless draw kept Chester in second place. An FA Cup exit at Peterborough and grim defeats by Leigh (not a-bloody-gain) RMI and Accrington Stanley followed, and the Bulls found themselves in something of a slump, and a disappointing fourth place, below Chester, Barnet, and Aldershot, with today's opponents Shrewsbury close behind.

There, at the fabulously named Gay Meadow, two thousand travelling fans endured a miserable day. A last minute strike from the excellent on-loan Baggie Tamika Mkandawire was merely consolation, although it was the fiftieth goal scored by a Bull this season. The Salopians, or as we prefer, the Slops, gave us a lesson, 4-1 fairly reflecting their dominance and leaving GT and Richard O'Kelly with a rebuilding job on their hands. Interesting to note that GT resisted the temptation to rubbish Jimmy Quinn's side in the way Quinn himself had the Bulls a few short weeks ago, and after a similarly convincing result. But then GT is a gentleman in both victory and defeat.

Something that sadly can't be said of the small number of Bulls fans unable to resist an after-match punch-up in the Town centre. Four Herefordians were arrested on this occasion, complementing the dozen recently awakened from their slumbers in a dawn raid by Staffordshire police. It appears that the low-profile film-making at Tamworth and Burton was being put to good use, and each of these characters is now banned from all football grounds until a judge dispenses his wisdom later in the year.

So, rewind to ten o'clock, and a couple of slightly pissed Bulls fans walking out of their local pub. The reason for this outrageously early session was the small matter of the Rugby World Cup Final, and a goal machine in gloriously full working order. Johnny Wilkinson's extra-time drop-goal sealed a fabulous victory, the final act of what had been a perfect example of peaking at precisely the right moment. Clive Woodward and Martin Johnson had produced from their men performances that had improved as the competition progressed, always doing just enough, and saving their best for when needed most. It was a lesson that should be heeded by any number of managers, particularly the other national coaches, Ericsson and Fletcher. I would be surprised, as well as ecstatic, if either brings success on the same scale, but at present the cricketers look decidedly more upwardly mobile than Sven's strugglers. Time will reveal all, but the rugby lads gave us a weekend only slightly soured by Jimmy Quinn and the Slops.

We Can See You Sneaking Off - Again
1/1/2004 Exeter City - away
So how long would it take for Turner and O'Kelly to restore the Bulls to their former free-scoring selves?

Three days was the answer, as Halifax took a first minute lead at ES. Big mistake, chaps. Again prompted by Parry and Smith, the Bulls tore into their opponents and delivered a stunning 7-1 victory, Stevie G grabbing his second hat-trick in a month. It was irresistible attacking football, and exactly what was required after the disappointment of Shrewsbury, although witnessed by the lowest ES crowd of the season. The fickle nature of football fans can seldom have been better demonstrated, as incredibly, fewer fans turned up at ES than had travelled to Gay Meadow four days previously. Three weeks later the faithful were again rewarded, as those who made the Friday night journey to Nailsworth witnessed an identical scoreline, the Gump on the wrong end of another thrashing.

This time it was Paul Parry who claimed the match-ball with a clinically taken hat-trick deserving of a setting more refined than The Lawn.

Our last game of 2003 was a Boxing Day clash with Exeter, or more accurately put, a Boxing Night clash. Again Murdoch and his dark legions were involved, this time excelling themselves with an 8pm kick-off. Do they not understand that the public appetite for football is finite, and the appetite for crap football on Boxing evening is nil? Perhaps even less. Whilst Rob Purdie's goal was out of the very top drawer, it was only enough to earn a point, despite the dismissal of James Bittner. The Grecians' keeper made the same mistake as many before, fatally under-estimating just how swift Pazza can be, leaving our winger in an undignified heap, although with little time to make the extra man count.

We would enter the New Year in second place, but very much in touch with Chester, who appear a team ominously efficient at grinding out victories when not on top of their game. It's a good habit to have, but of all the teams we could be chasing, it had to be them. Why not someone harmless, like Margate, or even someone nice, like Farnborough? But then how often do nice guys come first?

So, New Year's Day in Exeter, and another kick-off adjusted to cause maximum inconvenience. This time, the local police were the villains, if I'm allowed to say such things, insisting the match would be easier to manage if played at lunch-time. Great. If that's the case, what's wrong with breakfast time, or three in the morning? And why stop there? Lock the ground, close the roads and shut down the railways, that might just guarantee a trouble-free afternoon. Admittedly our lunatic fringe have been more active this season, but hadn't most if not all of them been banned from going anywhere near a football match? Whilst it was a ridiculously early start for two hundred hungover Bulls fans, Mr. Righteously Indignant of Twickenham enjoyed a twenty minute drive to St. James Park, less of a journey than many of the home supporters.

'How so?' you may ask, and my good lady is the answer. Without so much as a glance at the fixture list, Sarah had booked a New Year break just ten miles from Exeter. Which is known as a result. I was happily munching through a late breakfast, observing that the only time football ground catering even remotely resembles food is when it is used as a hangover cure. Having said which, there are one or two places where the most nuclear of hangovers wouldn't tempt me to eat, one of them being Edgar Street. There was also a result out on the pitch, where for

44 minutes, the Bulls were struggling against the far livelier home side. That was, until James Bittner collected a through-ball on the edge of the penalty box. Cue a frenzied bout of semaphore from the assistant referee, a prolonged chat with his boss, and a growing suspicion that Bittner was heading for his second early bath of the week. Almost reluctantly the red-card was produced, to a mixture of outrage on one side and hilarity on the other. Poor old Bittner must have been no more than inches outside the box, but rules as they say is rules, and as Exeter fans know just as well as us, there is not a more pedantic species on this planet than Conference officials. Inevitably the first job undertaken by Bittner's replacement was to retrieve the hitherto anonymous Danny William's free-kick from the back of his net, whilst the away terrace was still singing a farewell ditty to Mr. Bittner.

'We can see you sneaking off, we can see you sneaking off again.'

Cruel, but it had to be said, followed by a goalless second half in which Hereford played like the side with ten men. As away days go this was up there with the best, partly because of a result more jammy than a bag of doughnuts, but largely because I was home by the time the Hereford coaches left Exeter. And happily, but to no-one's surprise, there was no hint of trouble, the most arduous task befalling the Devon Constabulary being that of collecting their considerable overtime.

It had been an undeserved win, and was swiftly followed by another. The Wallace and Westley show rolled into Hereford just two days after the trip to Devon, and both sides looked tired. So tired, in fact, that the most eccentric player in the Conference was time-wasting long before the half-time whistle. Former Premiership stopper Lionel Perez had somehow ended up in Stevenage, but today was taking huge pleasure from winding up the Meadow End, as he and his colleagues appeared more than happy to settle for a point. That was until Paul Parry collected the ball in his own half and suddenly remembered that every other seat in the main stand was occupied by a scout. A blistering run was aimed straight toward Perez, and as defenders retreated, Pazza found himself one-on-one with the Stevenage keeper, and then the back of net for a last-minute winner. It was a magnificent goal, but one which the game didn't deserve. Whilst it had been a dire match, to send Westley home with nothing had made the journey worthwhile, and as once again the Bulls recorded a squeaky win against one of the league's bigger sides, I couldn't help but think that just maybe, this would be our year.

150

As a footnote to the day, the 2,800 Bulls fans inside ES that afternoon witnessed Pazza's last game in a Bulls shirt, his final touch as a Hereford player earning three vital points. Whilst it was no surprise to hear two days later that Paul had finally moved on, it was something of a shock to learn that Yeovil had been beaten to his signature by Championship side Cardiff City. A six-figure fee and talk of a place in the Welsh squad proved too much temptation for the club and player to resist, and whilst we would miss him, Pazza had been good for the Bulls, and was clearly too good to stay in the Conference.

Without Pazza, another trip to Exeter saw a 3-2 Trophy defeat, but as last year, we could smugly say that it was now possible to concentrate on the league. And this time James Bittner wasn't sent off as, hiding in the stand, he was safe from the clutches of the referee. Even one of the Conference variety.

Invaded by Mexicans
27/2/2004 Dagenham and Redbridge - away

Revealed. The real reason for the Bulls' conceding three at Exeter. Keeper Matt Baker didn't get much sleep the night before, along with room-mate Jenny Pitman. The pair were snoozing when Bakes sensed a presence in their hotel room, one which then tried to jump into his bed. Whilst Jenny is both petite and blonde, he probably isn't Bakers's type, but with Pitman safely in his own bed, the pair were unwittingly involved in one of those 'football stars in hotel threesome' shockers so beloved by the tabloids. Whether the uninvited guest was a stalker, a groupie, or merely lost is unrecorded, but for the two players, it was West Country hospitality gone too far. The pair resisted the temptation to go Premiership, and suggested that the young and naked lady look for another room, as they had a match in a few hours time. What price a different ending, had the hotel been in Chelsea or Newcastle. The manager, apparently, wasn't unduly concerned, but how could he be? After all, he was sleeping with the chairman's wife.

And so, back onto the pitch, and a quite staggering night in Dagenham, where the Bulls badly needed a victory. The previous five games had seen two draws away from ES and a pair of horrible home defeats, when Woking and Burton took the spoils. A pyrrhic victory at Gravesend saw a second dislocated shoulder for Ben Smith, and with Parry gone, there was a resigned air amongst Bulls fans, each wondering how the creativity offered by this talented pair could be replaced. Perhaps we would find out

151

at Dagenham, where the assembled wisdom of Sky television pondered the same question. Yes, once again the Bulls and the Daggers were going out live to the nation, which, given the fare served up on Jacob's birthday, was something of a mystery. Recent mixed form had left the Bulls eight points behind Chester, and with eleven matches remaining, a win was essential. Home win, by the way, was the 'expert' Sky verdict.

As was now traditional, John and I drove across London, collecting Justin en route, whilst Alan opted for the safer bet of London Transport, and for once got it wrong, as his call 15 minutes into the game testified. 'Bloody District Line is down, how are we doing?' I was happy to talk him through Jamer's penalty, despatched after Ryan Green had been upended. One up, and against ten men, I urged Alan to get his skates on, lest he miss something spectacular, including a small group of Herefordians dressed as Mexican bandits. He very nearly did, but a helpful taxi deposited him in Victoria Road in time to witness David Brown double the lead. Shortly after which, Guinan made it three, and a half-time talk that would make interesting listening in Garry Hill's 200th match as Daggers manager. Only a select few will know quite what Mr. Hill said to his depleted troops, but let's just say, it didn't work.

Put yourself in Garry's shoes. It's half-time, you're a man down and three goals adrift of the best counter-attacking side in the division. It's a fair bet that he didn't suggest throwing the kitchen sink at the Bulls, and damn the consequences. Incredibly however, that's what happened. Unless Dagenham had lost a couple more players whilst no-one was looking, the second-half began with what seemed like eleven against nine, or sometimes eight. Such was the space available that every time Hereford were in possesion a goal looked likely, the Daggers chasing shadows and getting nowhere near them. Brown and Guinan added two more, Danny Williams two screamers of his own, and as Brown completed his hat-trick with fifteen minutes remaining, the chant of 'We want ten' was heard, for probably the only time without a hint of irony. When Mark Beesley added a ninth, it was looking more likely than not, but two stunning saves from Tony Roberts kept the score in single figures. The Bulls had dismantled the Daggers on live TV, in the process equalling the record for a winning margin at this level. It was an evening when every option chosen by a Bulls player was the right one, and once chosen, perfectly executed. Ever imagined having a page of teletext all of your own? Tonight, Hereford had precisely that, along with a mention on Radio Harriers and Worcester, just after an in-depth report on the recent service to the Aggborough groundsman's mower.

The home supporters, and immense credit is due to them, endured a post-match beer with a handful of Bulls fans with nothing more malicious than an ironic 'We was robbed.' The normally verbose Garry Hill was shell-shocked, and in his post-match interview, barely able to speak. He was however not lacking courage. As for the 'expert' who predicted a home win, well, I hope he had a substantial bet on it.

As Sky TV replayed each goal, we were able to appreciate fully just how special an evening it had been. A Daggers fan observed as the seventh goal hit the net that this was the exact point in the season he would remember for a long, long time. When asked why, he took a deep breath and replied thus.

'Because that, mate, was the first time in two years that our fackin' drummer stopped banging his fackin' drum.'

Concise, funny, and hard to follow, but as we dragged ourselves toward the car park an hour later, a few Bulls fans had a go. Our departure coincided with that of the team coach, with GT and ROK in the front seats. As it pulled away, a handful of supporters dropped to the ground on hands and knees, bowing with huge reverence to the bus.

'We are not worthy' was their offering, and whilst a gesture fuelled by adrenaline and a couple of pints, it raised an interesting point. Whilst all too often our team, in fact most teams, are not themselves worthy of the dedication shown by their fans, today came close to being an exception. It was a near-perfect performance and a once in a lifetime goal-fest, but every one of the Bulls fans that travelled to Dagenham, Mexicans included, was more than worthy. They deserved every second of every minute they witnessed, because for every Dagenham there was a Billericay, a Hitchin Town, or a Newport Isle of Wight.

In seven years of Conference football, we had suffered more than most, if not all of our counterparts, but there is a truism that holds more in football than almost anywhere. Success tastes all the sweeter to those who have suffered failure. Even in a crappy league.

O'Kelly's Heroes
24/4/2004 Chester City - home
So, after the Lord Mayor's Show, relocated for one year only to Dagenham, came eight points from ten matches. Yes, eight miserable points from our

final ten games of the season, and no, it doesn't sound much, not if you're hoping to nail that elusive top spot hogged by Chester since November.

Oh ye of little faith. Eight points is simply the gap between ourselves and Steven Vaughan's team, with ten games remaining. Assuming that we win them all, Chester would need to drop five points, as we would surely beat them at ES in the final game of the season, and take the title on goal difference. Yes, another Edgar Street showdown was looming, in the unlikely event that Chester wobbled and the Bulls broke another Conference record.

The first of the ten was at Telford, where the curse of the old boy struck twice, via David Brown's right boot. However, a pointless evening was not the most pressing of Telford's troubles. Rumours floating around the new and very impressive Buck's Head ground suggested that the club could no longer rely on benefactor Andy Shaw, his companies apparently not in good health. Another CVA was looming.

Boardrooms and fans across the country should be warned. The value of your sugar daddy can go down as well as up, and any or all of your assets are at risk in case of changes of heart or circumstance.

OK, move on, and a few more off-field snippets. Thieves broke into the ES dressing-rooms, stealing the usual array of wallets, phones and car-keys. And an Armani watch. Yes, Armani, raising the frightening thought that GT is paying these lads considerably more than any of us thought, and way more than the club actually has. The owner was not identified, but I suspect that it was one of the few full Internationals in our squad of superstars, and one with an unseasonably deep tan.

On the subject of International superstars from Hereford, two more items, one being good news, the other a sad loss. John Charles, who as player-manager assembled the first pieces of the famous giant-killing side of the seventies, died this week. As well as being Hereford's most famous and without doubt best ever player, he was also regarded as the greatest Welsh International of all time. I can barely remember seeing him play, but those who did and those who knew him record that his footballing ability was matched by his modest good nature, and if playing today, he would have commanded transfer-fees way beyond anything so far seen. King John would often come on as a substitute at ES, usually stubbing out a cigarette as he entered the fray, and once reportedly hit the bar with such force that the rebound fell outside the penalty area. With a header. He will be missed not only in Hereford but in Wales, Leeds, Turin, in fact

154

anywhere he may briefly have travelled, and without a trace of hyperbole could be described as a legend.

And as one Welsh cap departs, another is born. Paul Parry, just two months after sampling the delights of the Lawn, played his first game for his country. Quite a step up for Pazza, but good luck to him. A welcome bonus found its way into GT's promotion kitty, as Pazza's International debut activated a clause sending another chunk of Cardiff's money to ES, some of which was immediately spent on two loan signings.

Tam Mkandawire was back from the Baggies, and Scott Willis joined from Lincoln, both of them adding a little class and steel to the side. Willis also added a couple of vital goals, the first of which came at the little known resort of Margate-on-Dover, where the Mexican branch of the Hereford supporters club were once again centre-stage. In a monsoon that had everyone else scurrying for cover, a dozen saturated Central Americans showed us that whilst a sombrero and poncho were no match for an English winter, a few Tequilas could keep the spirit warm. These lads didn't let up for the full 90 minutes, and had been equally vocal in the preceding victories over Northwich and Accrington, assuming, in a few short weeks, cult status. What started as a bit of fun at Dagenham had snowballed into a movement that witnessed five straight wins, a 17-2 goal tally, and a growing conviction that they were a lucky charm essential to the Bulls' success. With six games remaining, a gap of three points now separated the Bulls from Chester, although a game more had been played, and more Mexican magic was needed. It was a scenario the polar opposite of previous years of meaningless matches, and one in which results elsewhere were every bit as important as those involving the Bulls.

The first of these was at home to the Slop, where sweet revenge was exacted in front of almost six thousand fans, whilst Chester also won. We then beat Halifax, and again, Chester won. Victories over play-off contenders Barnet and Aldershot were matched by six Chester points, from play-off contenders Aldershot and Exeter, and you may see a pattern developing. Nine straight victories had seen us claw back a meagre two points from the leaders, and more were needed. We were now in the uncomfortable position of willing Shrewsbury Town to win a football match, for this was Chester's game in hand. Of course, the dream result would be for both sides to end the match pointless, or better still, in breach of some obscure ruling that levied an immediate twelve point deduction. It didn't happen, although the Slop almost granted our wish, earning a goalless draw at the Deva stadium. Chester had stumbled, although not as badly as we would have liked, leaving a situation where the Bulls had to win at relegated Leigh, and Scarborough needed to take something home from the Deva.

Both matches were bankers, and short of a miracle, we were looking at a play-off, with any three from Barnet, Aldershot, the Slop, and Exeter to join us. First to Hilton Park, where home supporters were outnumbered two to one, and five goals saw the Bulls take their tally past three figures for the season. A small ground a few miles south of Leigh was now the focus, and there the news was not good. As Danny Carey-Bertram slotted home Hereford's fifth goal of the afternoon, confirmation that Chester had edged past Scarborough filtered through.

Whilst the table showed that Chester City had won the Conference, the way I looked at it, Steven Vaughan had bought it. Sour grapes?

Perhaps a little, but with Chester reportedly losing a small fortune each month, the Max Griggs/John Ryan blueprint for Conference glory had triumphed once more, but this time with a crucial difference. Griggs and Ryan hadn't flirted with and then abandoned another club before their success at Rushden and Doncaster.

All of which leaves a 7,000 sell-out at ES, where pride, and the chance to break a few more records, were the only spoils that remained. An eleventh consecutive win would equal the Conference record, three goals would beat Barnet's 103, and a victory would confirm most people's opinion that the best side in the Conference had finished second. As it turned out, the match with nothing at stake was an excellent advert for unproper football, the good guys achieving a deserved 2-1 win and inflicting only the fourth defeat of the season on the Champions, and as the game drew to a close, attention turned to the issue of where we would be travelling in five days' time. The answer was Aldershot, who relegated Exeter to sixth place, whilst Barnet and the Slop would contest the other semi-final.

So, the season was over, and there was now a knockout competition, where four teams would endure a nail-biting few days. The fact that we had finished a massive 16, 20, and 21 points ahead of the teams below us counted for nothing, our goal-difference of 59, against 25, 14 and 13 the same. The four teams competing for that coveted place in the Football League would do so with the same chance of success, and the incredible record-breaking journey we had taken to reach this shoot-out would be forgotten, at least temporarily.

It was a lottery, but at least we had a ticket.

Beaten by a Bull
29/4/2004 and 3/5/2004 Aldershot Town -
Conference Play-off semi-final

In 1997, Peter Hill almost did for Hereford United what Aldershot FC actually achieved five years previously, when in March 1992 they ceased to exist as a football club. In the days before CVAs were de rigeur, the sea of debt engulfing the club finally swallowed it, and all matches that season were expunged from the records. Crucially, however, they hadn't given their home away to a property developer, and were able to start again. The Phoenix and Flames on the crest of Aldershot Town represent a new club born from the ashes of the old, a fabulous achievement by the supporters and directors of our opponents. Rising through leagues whose names mean nothing outside of Hampshire, the Shots last season won the Ryman League by 18 points, and now sit just three games away from a return to proper football, an incredible story of almost continual success. Here were two clubs with much in common, principally the fact that enough people had both the desire and the energy to keep them alive. Both also had managers who played football the proper way, both had grounds which could benevolently be described as characterful, and both had a decent number of loyal, vocal supporters.

The game of four halves against a side we had already beaten twice, started perfectly as David Brown slammed home a seventh minute opener at the Rec, silencing the biggest terrace in the Conference. The Bulls took the game to the hosts and, despite missing the injured Guinan, created far more than their opponents. Unfortunately, they came up against a goalkeeper at the very top of his game, as Nikki Bull stopped everything that came his way. The Shots eased back into the game, and after being denied a cast-iron penalty that would have seen Ryan Green dismissed, were awarded a spot-kick for reasons apparent only to the referee. Roscoe D'Sane smashed it past Matt Baker, and despite chances at both ends, the game finished level, Nikki Bull earning the man of the match award, and the two sides not looking anything like 21 points apart. Four days to wait until we did it all again at ES, but more immediately, something to calm those frayed nerves.

I'm not sure what passes for a decent Thursday night out in Aldershot, but most of the options appeared to include flashing lights and sirens, so it was again the short hop to The Prince of Wales, where we found a couple of Farnborough supporters with even more to cheer about than ourselves. Having failed to crawl out of the bottom three, they were handed a reprieve by virtue of Hucknall Town's ground being unacceptable to the Conference. I've never seen it and hopefully never will, but if it's worse than Cherrywood Road, fond though I am of it, then it must be a tip. The Borough fans, a restrained and mellow bunch until Aldershot or Stevenage are mentioned, felt that we were home and dry, and would of course be right behind us in the second leg. Whilst the Shots' demise would be a little more icing on their celebration cake, we knew our club a lot better than they did. The tie was far from over, and it would be a long 90 minutes on Monday.

Little did we know quite how long it would eventually be.

Is there a better way to spend a Bank-Holiday Monday than watching your team progress serenely to a play-off final? At ten to three on a perfect afternoon, with Guinan back and ES packed and expectant, Hereford was surely the place to be. A mere thirty minutes later, on the whim of a man in black, the mood had become one of depression and rage. Andy Tretton tangled with Shots striker Aaron McLean, certainly impeding him, but more clumsy than cynical, and categorically not denying him a goal-scoring opportunity. McLean, as any footballer would, made the most of Tretton's challenge, earning himself a free-kick and Tretts a lecture. Andy Woolmer was the man in charge, and came with the reputation of a fussy, card-happy official, but nothing we hadn't seen a hundred times before. The lecture continued, giving McLean an extended cameo as a man gravely wounded and unlikely to leave the pitch unless carried on a stretcher. Still, amidst much waving of arms and pointing of fingers, Woolmer talked, and still McLean lay motionless, surely breathing his last. The longer nothing happened, the stronger the feeling grew that something would. Eventually Woolmer reached for a card, and scandalously, it was red. For a foul that was at worst a debatable booking, Tretton had been dismissed, and if the Bulls were to extend the season, they would have to do so with ten men. In a season packed full of special moments, something extraordinary was needed, and I, and I think most Bulls fans, had that sinking feeling that this just wasn't going to be our day.

Half-time arrived with little further to report, apart from a medical miracle. Aaron McLean was back, and enjoying the extra space afforded by his partner in black, gambolling about the pitch with speed quite remarkable for a man so recently recovered from a coma.

Someone cancel the air-ambulance.

A further 45 minutes, perhaps more, awaited, and it would be a time when courage would be every bit as important as ability. The latter was undeniably present in each of the ten players out on the park, the former obvious in just three. Pitman, James and Travis would fight until they dropped, Tretton also, but he was elsewhere. The remaining seven had yet to convince me that they possessed the mental strength now so desperately required, and if even one of them were to go missing, we would be playing Conference football in August.

Each of them stood up, putting in the extra 10 per cent, and in a surprisingly open and even second half, it was Hereford who created more chances. Danny Williams somehow missed from four yards, Guinan headed wide the type of chance that he had routinely despatched all season, and the game remained goalless. Extra-time belonged more to Aldershot, but the deadlock remained, and as the final minutes ticked away, it was the Bulls who appeared happier to play out time. On a savagely hot day, the ten men of Hereford had matched their opponents and had done so with enormous heart, and huge credit is due to each of them. As a group, and as individuals, the players looked utterly drained, yet somehow had to pick themselves up one more time, for the purgatory of a penalty shoot-out.

Consider this. The pressure on any player placing the ball on the penalty-spot must be huge, more so if he isn't a regular taker of spot-kicks, and increased again if, say, a place in the next round of the FA Cup is on the line. Now factor in the rewards at stake here, and you're probably beyond the place where pressure becomes sheer terror.

All of which highlights the biggest fallacy in football, the one insisting that you have to be mad to be a goalkeeper. Nikki Bull and Matt Baker were surely the only professionals out there even remotely in touch with their sanity, and certainly the envy of every one of their team-mates. And they both knew with stone cold certainty, that before long, one of them would be a hero.

I'm usually a glass half-full type, but I didn't feel good about the spot-kicks, even after D'Sane had crashed the first against the bar and away to safety. It was advantage Bulls, but not for long, as Brown and then Beesley had their shots saved. Both were weak efforts, and although Jamer and Tom Smith scored emphatically, Bakes, who had been saving penalties for fun all season, was unable to get near any of the next three. If Tim Sills converted, it was all over.

As more than 7,000 people held their breath, he did, and it was. How did I feel?

Hard to say really, but not surprised (for this is Hereford) would be a start. Whilst there were shades of May 1997, there is a world of difference between losing something you almost took for granted and failing to win something you really want, and there was really no comparison.

This time, however, there was a lot more anger, a little of which was directed toward Aaron McLean, the rest toward an incompetent little gnome on a power-trip. There was no guarantee that the match would have been won with eleven players, but in the eyes of all Bulls supporters, and the vast majority of neutrals, a diabolical piece of refereeing had ruined a season's hard work. As the players dragged themselves around the pitch to say their good-byes, Justin raised another, even more depressing thought.

'Half of those lads won't be here next season. We'll be starting from scratch in August.' Just when we needed cheering up, he's got that to offer, but sadly, he was almost certainly right. He then redeemed himself.

'Fuck it, we've lost a football match, nobody has died, let's have a pint.' That was more like it, but technically he was wrong. We had drawn a football match and been robbed by a referee.

A once-in-a-lifetime season was over, and yes, it was time for a beer.

To say that we had enjoyed a memorable season would be an enormous understatement, and to say that it had ended in disappointment would be another.

GT and the ROK had assembled a squad on a pitifully small budget, coaxing enough out of them to send records tumbling.

91 points, 103 goals, an incredible 61 of which were scored away from ES, a goal difference of 59, and five or more scored on nine separate and magnificent occasions. The team had routinely shown attacking football of such pace and quality that even opposition fans were applauding, and the Bulls were hailed as the best footballing team the division had seen for many years.

It was a season when it had been a privelige to watch my team, the sort of campaign that most fans don't see in a lifetime, and whatever happens in the future, a season that will never be forgotten. We had seen, with the occasional blip, something scarily close to proper football.

Pundits would have us believe that football is part of the entertainment business, whilst managers, equally forcefully, insist that theirs is a business where results are paramount. Occasionally a team will deliver both, and this season Hereford had done just that. Sadly, it wasn't enough, and the spoils went to a side displaying a fraction of the flair shown by Hereford. Whilst the Bulls were defeated four times by a single goal, Chester recorded an incredible 14 victories by the same margin, demonstrating clearly that what they lacked in style, they compensated for with efficiency and grit. I would concede, albeit grudgingly, that they deserved their success, and that over 42 games the only number that really matters is that of points collected. To withstand the Bulls' run of 11 straight victories was some achievement, and to the players, and especially the supporters of Chester City, I would say well done, and enjoy the Football League. Whereas to the Slop, who edged past Aldershot in the play-off final, I would say this. Fifteen points doesn't even begin to demonstrate just how much better than you we were, and if there is any justice, we'll swap places this time next year. Does that sound bitter? Good, it was supposed to. OK Mitch, move on, and think about the good, the bad, and the ugly of the season past.

The good being the frequently staggering quality of attacking football on display, the goals of Guinan and Brown, the artistry of Ben Smith, the class of Jamer and Parry, and the contributions of each and every member of the squad.

Performance of the season in my opinion, was not at Dagenham but Stevenage, a near-perfect display of controlled, beautiful football.

Goal of the season, amongst many contenders, would be Rob Purdie's at home to Exeter, and player of the year, the immaculate and consistent Tony James.

All of this was watched by crowds more than 80% higher than last year, at 3,704 the second highest average in the Conference, and for this and everything else in this incredible season GT and the ROK should take a bow.

The bad would be headed by the small but massively disruptive group of moronic idiots determined to cause havoc whenever and wherever they travelled. We can but hope that the Camcorder Cops have done their job, and that these misfits find themselves in a position where a Saturday afternoon at the match isn't an option for many years to come.

And the ugly, or at least the villains of the piece. The usual suspects, Westley, Wallace, Vaughan, and Sky TV, were joined by Eldinho and Jimmy Quinn, both of whom might do well to realise that occasionally, especially when reporters are within earshot, less is more.

And not forgetting Aaron McLean, whose Oscar-Winning performance in the play-offs might just have cost us a place in the Football League. I wonder what sort of reception he'll get at ES next season.

Chester and Shrewsbury weren't the only team to make it into the Football League. A squad of Conference referees was also promoted, including ironically, the man who denied us our chance to go to the same place. Avoiding Mr. Woolmer next season might just be one of the few reasons to appreciate remaining exactly where we are.

Finally, a word for Garry Hill. The televised damage inflicted on the Daggers ultimately proved to be fatal, and two years after having the title stolen from them, the parties have gone their separate ways.

Keep your chin up Garry, you'll be back. Right, where are my golf clubs?

9 2004-2005 Bob's not your Uncle — he's your Dad

14/8/2004 Farnborough Town - home

More about Bob and his son in a moment, before which, and to cut a long story mercifully short (which having got this far is the least you deserve), a condensed account of another busy summer. Gone were Guinan (to Cheltenham, boo hiss), Rose (to Yeovil, no, not another), Baker (to Wrexham, shame), Smithy (to the Slops, way too good for them), and the ROK (Bournemouth, good luck Richard). Better news came from Brown, Tretton, Carey-Bertram, Travis and Purdie, who joined the already contracted Jamer, Jenny, Danny Williams, and Ryan Green. Inbound were Tam (Baggies loss, our gain), Adam Stansfield (Bulls in shock signing of Yeovil player!), and three once-useful thirty-somethings.

The first was Graham Hyde (nickname crab, sideways movement), Lee Mills (see journeyman in any football dictionary), and Jonathan Gould (International goalkeeper, great, for Scotland, oh crap, but only on loan, could be worse). Margate wisely, if belatedly, decided that financing two grounds was no way to remain solvent, and will no longer lodge at the Crabble, relinquishing their Conference status along with their tenancy, as Hartsdown Park isn't up to scratch. Good news for Leigh RMI, the latest in an ever-growing band of relegated clubs to be reprieved. Less good news from Telford, they of the impoverished benefactor, who sacked their entire squad shortly before going out of business, the unfortunate Matt Clarke learning the hard way that sometimes when money talks, it doesn't necessarily tell the truth. (Also see Lee Mills above.) Bad news, except in Northwich, the Vics earning a reprieve from the joys of the Unibond League.

A dubious dozen with Herefordshire addresses earned themselves some of Her Majesty's hospitality, as guilty pleas were entered in the face of overwhelming video evidence. Apologies to the Camcorder Cops, I

163

take it all back. Hopefully, our off-the-field reputation can now climb to somewhere near the level of our on-field activities.

And Andy Woolmer sent a note to GT. Surprisingly, not an apology for his criminally inept officiating, but an invoice for some minor damage allegedly manifested on his car whilst parked at ES. I suspect that if any Bulls fan actually knew which car belonged to Mr. Woolmer, charred ruin would have been a more accurate description of the vehicle.

And more trouble for dear old Steven Vaughan, who became embroiled in a fight with the editor of the Non-League Paper at a celebration dinner. Only in the Conference.

We also have a new coach. John 'Tucka' Trewick, tempted away from the Wolves youth squad, and recommended by the ROK. Amongst his attributes will need to be a thick skin, unless he has the immediate Midas touch we all hope.

And so to the new season, and Farnborough, still in the Conference but at the centre of a fractious ownership dispute. Hard to believe that not one but two parties are desperate to sit in the big chair at Cherrywood Road, I wonder if either has ever even been near Farnborough? Good luck to both them and their psychiatrists, they'll need it, particularly as any luck Farnborough were to enjoy ran out at twenty past three, when a penalty was athletically saved by Johnny Gould. The former Celtic and current Preston keeper had immediately begun earning the small fraction of a very large wage that the Bulls were paying. Within seconds the Scottish International had his own tribute from the Meadow End choir.

'Scotland Scotland's Number Three' was their tongue-in-cheek reference to the number of times Jon had made the Scottish squad without actually making the team, but already Gould had shown some of his International quality. Jamer, Travis, and Mills sealed a convincing victory, leaving a contented home crowd, and what would be a long season for Farnborough.

So, to the question of Bob, and just whose Dad he is. Jonathan Gould is the answer, someone not a stranger to Edgar Street. When Johnnie Gould was barely in his teens, he would often be found at ES watching his Dad Bobby, for a season in the late seventies the Bulls' player-coach. My abiding memory of Gould senior is one of baffled amusement at how a player quite as slow as he was could make a living out of football. But he did, and many more like him, including at least one newly promoted League Two manager.

Stevenage in Disguise?
17/8/2004 Crawley Town - away

Crawley, the identical sibling of Stevenage, and towns so similar, it's scary. Both invite you to leave the motorway and admire cheerless housing estates and superstores, negotiating identikit roundabouts and teenage push-bike gangs before braving a dodgy underpass on your way to the stadium. The grounds, despite the admittedly impressive new visitors' stand at Stevenage, also share an uncanny likeness, both claiming origins in the same batch of Meccano. Whilst the Broadfield Stadium, like Broadhall Way, is compact, neat, and sort of functional, it has no soul. Rather like Phil Collins. This plague of charmless edge-of-town grounds shows no sign of abating, each with the same obvious bias toward cost over character, but it's worth remembering that we at ES came horribly close to suffering a similar, perhaps even worse fate under Peter Hill. And what exactly would Bulls fans have lost?

Nothing like Broadfield, that's for sure. A decaying hotch-potch of a ground, complete with inedible food and unusable toilet facilities is what. You think I'm joking? Edgar Street is not a pretty sight, with massive work needed to take it to a place even remotely near Football League standard, and undeniably a mess.

But a beautiful mess full of character, and it's ours. It is more a part of the club's history than any trophy won, or any player or manager or coach who may have passed through, no matter how heroic. Vitally, it is also the only constant in the lives of Bulls supporters, and the place where battles have been fought, tears have been shed, friendships made and memories formed. Thanks Crawley, but you can keep your soap-dispensers, your electric hand-dryers, and your polished floors that you genuinely could eat your Egon Ronay pie and chips from. I'll stay with the mayhem at ES.

And you can keep your Ryman League winning team as well. In a match dominated by the Bulls, there was a sense that Adam 'Lisa' Stansfield's goal might not be enough to secure a thirteenth consecutive Conference victory, and it wasn't. In added time, an own-goal by Gould junior saw the points shared, although to be fair to Scotland's number three, he didn't know a lot about it, nodding home a goal-line clearance by Simon Travis.

And not one reporter described it as a Travisty. Shame on them all, and five out of ten for the Crawley experience.

And at least a nine four days later, when the five hundred or so Bulls who travelled to York would have had to look pretty hard to find fault with their day's entertainment. Trouble-free motorways, friendly landlords, a perfect summer day, and a three goal victory for the Bulls that could have been many more. York City were given a lesson, much as Welling had given to us seven years ago, clear notice to a newly relegated side that the Conference would be more difficult to get out of than it was to get into. Most encouraging performances came from recently signed midfielder Craig Stanley and left-back Mark Robinson, the latter looking accomplished in a defensive unit that barely gave the home side a kick.

As the Bulls hit second spot in the Conference, the week ended with the news that our CVA was no more, and in the short term at least, the club was safe. We had come a long way since losing to Welling, on a long and difficult road, but for the first time in years, Bulls fans could enjoy some relatively stress-free football. We now had a side capable of a serious title challenge, and were soon to announce a trading profit for the previous year.

Let me say it again. Profit. And not only that, but a half-decent team out there on the pitch.

Proper football, coming soon to a ground near you. So didn't say the Hereford Times, but love him or, as many still did, loathe him, Graham Turner had slowly transformed a wretched, bankrupt basket-case into a viable and dynamic football club unquestionably heading in the right direction, and the Turner-Out brigade were strangely silent. Of course, GT hadn't done it on his own, and without the dedication of its hard-core of support, particularly HUISA, the club would almost certainly have died, and their contribution should never be undervalued. Also deserving of mention are another small but vital group of people who also refused to walk away when it looked like the only sane option. GT has been blessed with a backroom staff who have supported him all the way, often apparently without pay, amongst them Joan Fennessy. Joan was club secretary long before GT arrived, dealing with one crisis after another, doubtless wondering why she put herself through almost daily torment. If, as it appears, the good times are back, there is one person who deserves to enjoy them every bit as much as GT, and that's Joan.

There are still problems, not least of which are Formsole, the local council, and what is still some dreadful PR, but given last year's near-miss and the current form of the squad, it's a good time to be a Bulls fan.

Which is of course the moment that someone turns up to piss all over your candles. That it was Graham Westley made it all the more difficult to bear, but his, let's call them robust, Stevenage side came to ES for a point, only for an injury-time mugging to give them all three. Whilst the Bulls failed to deal with the physical approach of the visitors, it was an ugly match, and easy to see why the Stevenage DoItAll was busier than Broadhall Way. The solitary bright spot in a dark day was that Eldinho's only contribution was to miss another open goal shortly before being subbed. Best player in the Conference? I don't think so.

Hereford had been unbeaten since the 21st February, a league run of thirteen wins and a draw, with the previous defeat being followed by the savaging of Dagenham. There was a backlash of sorts, although two days later Northwich could justifiably claim that 4-1 flattered Hereford. Suddenly incapable of putting two similar results together, a home defeat at the hands of Halifax was perhaps not surprising, nor the 2-1 victory that followed in Gravesend.

Tucka Trewick, let's see what you're made of.

Pride of Lancashire
11/10/04 Accrington Stanley - away

Sixteen matches and eleven months had passed since Bulls fans saw their side beaten away from ES, thirteen of which were won, often by obscene margins, so you could say that the travelling supporters have had good value for their time and money. Which is why the almost forgotten experience of an away defeat got the biggest ovation a beaten team has had in a long time.

Despite finally losing at, oh the irony, Dagenham, the applause was not for a heroic display that deserved better, but for the many successes, and indeed excesses of the previous year. On the night the Daggers were full value for their win, and given the frequently quirky nature of the game, it shouldn't have been that much of a surprise when our run ended at the site of a record-breaking triumph earlier in the year. Almost as predictable was that Accrington Stanley made it two from two the following Tuesday, and Carlisle completed a month to forget with a 3-1 defeat at Brunton Park. Two home draws saw our sole victory in October — the FA Cup defeat of Radcliffe Borough. Nope, never heard of them.

But back to Accrington 'who are they' Stanley, and a club which more than most, has history. Stanley resigned from the Football League in March 1962 under a mountain of debt, entering a side in the Lancashire Combination. Déjà vu quickly struck, as a Stanley-less Accrington FC resigned mid-season from the Combination, at which point you might reasonably have thought that this Lancashire town just didn't want a football club. Maybe not, but in 1968 Stanley were reborn, and despite Blackburn and Burnley being almost walking distance away, battled through local leagues to join the Conference in 2003. It's a great story, and a credit to the people of Accrington, who, like Aldershot, have taken a club from extinction to the verge of the Football League, a feat achieved despite some heavy duty ridicule from the milk-marketing board. Yes, this is the club where you might have endured a career if you hadn't drunk your daily pinta.

Oh, the shame of it, but who's laughing now?

Stanley are, for here is a club that could teach a lesson in self-promotion to Victoria Beckham. Amongst the hard-core of 1,200 fans are the Stanley Ultras, one of whose mother must own a textile factory, such is the number and variety of flags they possess. A recent coup was the trailing of a banner behind a light aeroplane, proclaiming Stanley to be the Pride of Lancashire, captured on live television as Blackburn and Burnley fought out an FA Cup tie. Marketing genius from the self-proclaimed 'Club that Wouldn't Die', although what their local rivals made of it is unrecorded.

And hats off today to the Stanley Ultras, whose greeting to the Hereford faithful was a large banner declaring 'We see Welsh People'. Unacceptable regional stereotyping, or a sense of humour amongst the whippet-racing, flat-capped black-pudding munchers? Definitely the latter, and whilst a few overly sensitive knickers became a little twisted, it was simply banter, and if the Ultras wanted to spend their money on oversized visual gags, then fair play to them. When occasionally entertainment on the field slips below the very highest levels (which is nearly all the time), can't we enjoy a little verbal sparring without calling in the PC Police?

Just two observations however, to the club perhaps a little more in love with itself than most. The Interlink Express Stadium is a pretentious name for a few strips of concrete terrace and two tin sheds. And the eighteen stone gentleman who kindly advised departing Bulls fans to 'fuck off home, you soft Southern twats' perhaps shouldn't be employed as a matchday steward.

The Ultras had a good day, and so did their team, and on current form, Accy look the more likely to occupy a play-off spot in April, although this year's pacemakers were Barnet, sweeping all before them, and already a convincing candidate for the title with a third of the season gone. More worrying than the seven point gap between the Bulls and the Bees, however, is the loss of confidence apparent in recent performances. If a challenge is to be mounted, some serious work is needed.

Ghost Town
20/11/2004 Canvey Island - away

You're going to Canvey Island, aren't you.

More of a statement than a question from Woody, who of course was, Canvey being a short hop from his Dulwich home, but was I about to head off to yet another version of Wherethehellisthisville?

Seven games without a win, out of the play-offs, and Son of Bob back at Preston counselled against the idea, but it was hard to resist a trip to what is the low point of British Football. Or certainly the lowest, with Canvey's sub sea-level ground protected from the Thames estuary by a sea-wall.

Which had to be seen, along with, according to Woody, a beach-front greasy-spoon sharing a designer with the Sydney Opera House. The Labworth Café is apparently the masterpiece of Art Deco craftsmanship featured on the cover of an album by the Island's only celebrities, Dr. Feelgood, and believe me, this is the sort of Operatic Pub-Rock crap that Woody knows better than anyone.

The first of too many scary features about Canvey is the residents, or lack of them. There are apparently 45,000 souls on this small patch of land, but none of them appeared to be around this Saturday lunchtime, and the place was a ghost town. It being too early for football, the Essex Opera House was calling, so it was along another (deserted) street, past an (empty) car-park, ending with a short walk over a beach (not even a seagull) and to the Labworth Café. A huge white building stood in splendid isolation, a monument of elongated windows, soft curves and sharp angles, and a surreal sight on this strange Island.

Maybe the missing thousands were tucked cosily inside, the Café perhaps a culinary Tardis where each and every Islander enjoyed his Saturday lunch. Not so, although a handful of, and this may be an oxymoron, culture-seeking Bulls fans had beaten us to the hottest spot in this part of Essex, and were tucking into some decent-looking fare. Empty stomach and curiosity satisfied, it was time for some culture of a different but more traditional Saturday afternoon variety, and to Park Lane.

To be critical of another's home is bad manners, although it's never stopped me before, but here's a quote lifted from a website where the local population offer insights on the best and worst of their home town.

169

'Park Lane, like the rest of this blighted place, is a job that will never be finished. It is as though a child has been let loose with a Lego set, and got bored half-way through. A dump.' Certainly harsh and probably fair, but many grounds possess dumpish qualities, ES included. The 921 fans present were doing little to generate atmosphere, and Park Lane at three o'clock was, like the Island, flat. Within half an hour, however, the visitors were jigging around the few slabs of concrete which passed for a terrace, as Mills and Williams placed the Bulls in control. Oh, what a little confidence can do, as the stuttering performances of recent weeks were replaced by the rampant attacking football seen so often last season. Canvey had no answer to the pace of Travis and Lisa, something with which our own Mr. Mills could sympathise. Whilst Lee was undoubtedly the class-act on display, his laboured efforts to keep pace with our high-speed forays into Canvey territory would end with hands on hips and an expression begging for an oxygen tent. The second half saw little change, other than Justin spending more time studying his watch than the match.

And why? Lee Mills, of course, who was now on the clock each time he began his laboured stroll back to the half-way line as another attack broke down. Millsey is one of Justin's heroes, but my best mate is always looking for alternative entertainment in these one-sided games, and today he'd found some.

'Current record thirty seconds', he informed us.

'Reckon he'll manage fifty by the final whistle', offered Woody. Predictions flooded in, the longest an outrageous two minutes twenty. Millsey was now being counted back to half-way by his own supporters, ironic cheers erupting each time he crossed the line. The one-time Premiership striker must have wondered quite how he found himself in a place which almost no-one realised had a professional football team, and even fewer who actually cared. That said, he was enjoying himself more than the home players, as two late strikes from Lisa completed the rout. The Bulls were back in the top five, and had delivered a lesson in quality attacking football, a fact graciously conceded by Canvey manager and owner, Jeff King.

Yes, Canvey Island has its very own version of GT, although Mr. King was reportedly subsidising his club to an extent which would lead to some fairly large headaches should he suddenly be afflicted with a dose of common-sense. On today's showing, his team will continue to find the Conference a place where life is a struggle, the easy pickings of the Ryman League a distant memory.

And the Island itself? In a strange and difficult-to-pin-down sort of way, I liked its austere, silent flatness, and I liked the few surviving locals, with their phlegmatic approach to both life and a four-nil hiding. Rather like Belgium, but without the range of beer.

OK, I'll say it. Canvey Island was an entertaining and very different away trip. Which doesn't mean I'll be looking for a seaside retreat there.

The Sons of Eric Redrobe
27/11/2004 Tamworth - home

5,000-1 is the price offered for the Bulls to win the FA Cup, but having eliminated Southport, we were much shorter odds to beat Boston United, standing in the way of a potential giant (or Leicester City) in the third round. Boston had smashed five goals past Hornchurch in round one, prompting a quote in the NLP from manager Garry Hill, formerly of the Daggers, indicating his 'intense dislike' for the Boston manager. Who else could he be referring to but his former sparring-partner and eventual nemesis, Steve Evans?

It was true. Scandalously, Evans and his Boston Cheaters had been reunited, and with indecent haste, particularly if you were of the view that never would be too soon for Evans and any football club to be reacquainted. More evidence (not that much is needed) that people in football club boardrooms shouldn't be allowed to run a whelk-stall, just as there are blazers at the FA who should check a dictionary for the definitions of crime and punishment.

But before Boston came Tamworth, and the Sons of Eric Redrobe. Let me tell you about Big Eric. Eric was a porter at Hereford County Hospital in my student days there, and a man I had the pleasure of playing both with and against on a few occasions. The pleasure being significantly greater when playing with, due to the dramatically improved chances of walking off the pitch unaided. Eric had the habit of playing with a binliner under his shirt in an attempt to shed a couple of pounds, but he was wasting his time. Some people are just meant to be big, and Eric was one of them, even in his days of leading the Bulls' attack in the seventies.

Yes, Eric is a Bulls legend, despite his modest goal-scoring record at the Street, because with Big Eric, you got more than your average brick outhouse. You got an archetypal old-school centre-forward, a hard case with attitude who defenders would, to paraphrase Garry Hill, intensely dislike playing against. And if defenders didn't much fancy Eric, goalkeepers were reduced to nervous wrecks by his enthusiastic approach to the physical side of the game. Colin Addison had tempted Eric away from a career in Rugby League, and he had found a player who occasionally forgot which code he was actually involved with. Whilst he wouldn't last more than five minutes with today's referees, we always got great value from Eric, which is why, when a dozen exiled Bulls decided to sponsor a match, Woody christened us The Sons of Eric Redrobe. Much to the ire of his two daughters in the party, but hey, football's not really a game for girls is it? — even in today's world, where being politically correct seems more important than being simply correct.

So, what exactly did Eric's offspring get for £35 each? We were greeted by the genial Chris and shown to a small, very small, pitch-side lounge, where refreshments awaited. And when I say refreshments, I mean a can of warm beer and a pork pie. An on-pitch photo-call was followed by another swift half, and then to our seats, excellent viewing, if a little close to the Directors' box. Tam and Millsey supplied bullet headers to place the Bulls in control, until a piece of Beckham-esque genius by Bob Taylor halved the deficit. He might be comfortably the wrong side of thirty, but Super Bob showed all of his Premiership class in chipping our new keeper Craig Mawson from the half-way line. It was the Lamb's only attempt on goal, but opinion was that we had already got our thirty-five quids' worth, and seen the goal of the season. Second half, and what should have been a stroll became an almost edge-of-the-seat affair, and all the fault of the club secretary. Joan had popped in to say hello, observing that the only thing that might deny us three points would be a piece of typical Conference refereeing. Spooky really, as within minutes of the restart Jamer was on his way to the dressing-room, his tackle adjudged worthy of a straight red card. We, of course, all saw it as an outrageous decision by yet another clueless official, whilst at the same time marvelling at the predictive powers of Mrs. Fennessey. Must ask her later about tonight's lottery numbers.

So here's the thing about playing with ten men. The lads remaining on the pitch usually find that extra 10% needed to cover for their missing colleague, but today was different, as the Bulls calmly went about their business much as they had in the first half. No extra commitment was needed because we had Tam Mkandawire, who made the work of two men appear as easy as that of one, a footballing Andrew Flintoff, if you like.

Whilst Tamworth enjoyed the majority of possession, they failed to trouble Mawson, prompting another of Woody's highly individual and often surreal quips.

'Our Tam's worth more than your Tamworth' was an offering closer to the truth than the small handful of Lambs supporters would like to admit. Without the once million-pound-rated Taylor, the entire Tamworth squad would be unlikely to raise a penny on the transfer market, whereas our Tam could before long be commanding a six-figure sum from a much bigger club than Hereford. He was a shoe-in for the champagne, and much as I would like to say that Tamika was a preening, egotistic Billy Big Time, he was in fact a real gent. As was GT, who also said hello after the match, although our adopted father did come in for a broadside from the one time Fourth Division centre-half.

'Eric Redrobe kicked me all over the park. Why did you choose him?' I think, Graham, you've answered your own question there. The match day sponsorship experience was one we vowed to repeat, excellent value at a price that wouldn't secure the worst seat in Stamford Bridge. The inner sanctum of ES is quite frankly poky, the food barely passable, the beer appalling, but at Chelsea I doubt that you would chat with Mourinho, shake the hand of Lampard, enjoy a stroll on the pitch, or choose millionaire of the match. Or, for that matter, get much change out of £400. I know which I prefer.

And a final word on what had been an excellent day.

Ladies, I was of course only joking. The more of you seen at football, the better, and whether or not you know the offside law doesn't really matter, because most of the chaps inside ES obviously don't. Including more than one referee's assistant. And with a line-up that includes Tammy, Jenny and Lisa, Edgar Street is surely a place where gender is irrelevant, especially if you're having a good time.

Today, the Sons and Daughters of Big Eric had a ball.

I Can See Us Sneaking Out
26/12/2004 Exeter City - away
Hands up if you think this sounds like fun. Get up at seven with a hangover, sit on a coach for three hours, and against one of your main rivals, watch your team disappear without trace.

Thought not. Especially on Boxing Day, when there must be a hundred more attractive options with which to occupy yourself. Yes, even The Sound of Music. St. James Park really was that much fun, before which I give you the most outrageous quote ever to pass the lips of a football club manager. Until you consider who they belonged to. Here it is, fresh from the BullsNews website.

'Hereford are a bigger club than us, and are working with a bigger budget.' Stand-up Steve Evans, comedy genius. Or do I mean a laughing stock? Whilst the bigger club issue is debatable, a bigger budget? Unless Mr. Evans is referring only to the undeclared element of his finances, he is either delusional or attempting to take the pressure off his team prior to the Cup tie at ES. I suspect the latter, but his players left Edgar Street in a better state of mind than when the clubs last met, the Pilgrims enjoying a 3-2 victory more comfortable than it sounds. Although it was horrible route-one stuff, Boston were that bit bigger, sharper, and more motivated than the Bulls, and another side reflecting the man in charge.

They knew how to win ugly.

So, without the distraction of a trip to Anfield, it was back to the Conference, and a run of six matches unbeaten, including a Perrin-free Gump, despatched by an embarrassingly modest 2-1. I wonder if Steve Perrin misses us as much as we miss him? There was also a hefty early Christmas present for GT, from, of all places, Upton Park. West Ham had enticed Gavin (Welsh International now, see) Williams away from Yeovil, activating the sell-on clause and a fifty grand windfall for the Bulls. Didn't I say he was too good for them?

OK, back to why Boxing Day in Exeter was such a disaster. Of course, we lost, and badly, putting in the worst 90 minutes I'd seen in perhaps eighteen months, but that wasn't all. On police advice (can you ignore police advice?), the match again kicked off at lunch-time, and was made all-ticket for Bulls fans. A late and quite frankly rubbish decision to drive down from the Bristol in-laws' meant a view from the main stand, and once again I was a stranger in a strange town, wondering quite how I would contain myself when Lisa scored against his home-town club. A quick glance around revealed no obvious threat of physical damage, although given the quality of witticism being hurled toward the small group of Bulls fans, there were clearly a few villages in Devon temporarily missing an idiot, and eerily similar to B-Block back at ES. The question of my non-celebration, however, proved to be hypothetical.

To score a goal, you need to shoot, and to shoot, you need to be at least in the vicinity (unless you're Bob Taylor) of your opponents' goal, which entails possession of the football in your opponents' half of the pitch. You can see where I'm heading. As the home side's third goal hit the net just after half-time, a dozen Bulls fans decided that they'd seen enough and walked out, provoking huge merriment amongst my new friends. With forty minutes still to play, it must have been a new record in the sneaking-out-early stakes, and I was embarrassed.

But why? Each of those voting with their feet had paid the same as those who had stayed, and if an extra pint appealed more than the sub-standard fare offered by their team, then why not ?

For better and for worse, that's why not. It was one of those days when everything Hereford tried failed, and everything Exeter tried succeeded, and anybody who has played a sport, no matter how well or badly, will know days just like this one. Something underlined when the usually faultless Tam completely missed a routine clearance, allowing a tap-in fourth for the home side. A signal for another twenty or so Bulls fans to make their way to the exit gates, a chorus of cheerios echoing around the ground. The final whistle couldn't come quickly enough, at which point the remaining travelling fans could, with absolute justification, have grounds for complaint.

Most of the players were away to the dressing-room with barely a glance toward the visitors' terrace, unforgivable even when compared to the desertion of Bulls fans some forty minutes earlier. With the exception of Travis and a couple of others, our players should be ashamed, not of their performance but of their failure to acknowledge the fans who had given up a day to support their team.

Don't mind us, we're only the shit on your shoe that pay your wages. We don't ask a lot for our efforts, and expect even less, but do deserve a small acknowledgement of the sacrifices we make. The same players who lapped it up at Canvey had let themselves down, and here is where the captain could and should step in. Because it works both ways, chaps, for better and for worse. Of course I was pissed off, as much with myself for even going to the bloody match, but as usual, the trials and tribulations of supporting Hereford United would find some perspective.

Which today came immediately, and brutally. The car radio brought news of a tsunami in the Indian Ocean, where countless lives had already been lost. Merry Christmas India, Sri Lanka, Thailand and a hundred other places that would never be the same again. Some days, football appears to be more than just a game, but occasionally, like today, it really is only that.

A Bus-Stop near Farnborough
30/1/2005 Aldershot - away

If the Manager of the Month award is, as widely believed, a curse sure to bring a good run crashing to an abrupt end, then GT would be untroubled by worries in that area, as January had seen a dismal start to the year. Defeat at Exeter was followed by a hiding at Burton, which once again was a horrible place to be. Clinically beaten on the pitch, belligerent and embarrassing off it, where the anti-GT brigade called for the return of the ROK, and were ready to fight anyone who disagreed. This time properly secure and stewarded (how thoughtful of Burton to make us our very own cage), Eton Park was once again the centre of an utterly crap day out at the football. This was compounded by the Daggers stealing a one-goal victory at ES with their only shot of the match. And whilst the milkmen of Accrington were despatched in the FA Trophy, Wrexham proved to be one League scalp too far in the debatably unproper LDV Vans Trophy.

Points were urgently required, but with the next two fixtures being at Aldershot and Barnet, where they would come from looked a problem. First up were Aldershot, also chasing a play-off spot, making the game a mustn't-lose more than a must-win. Not for the first time the two sides produced a cracker, with chances spurned at both ends, until Danny 'DCB' Carey-Bertram fired the Bulls ahead late in the second half.

Cue bedlam in the away stand, anger in the home, resorting to some almost original farm-related ethno-centric abuse (and there's a concept).

'You're from a cowshed in Wales' was their best effort, but credit to our lads, who realised that sharply honed wit can be every bit as wounding as a swiftly delivered size-ten.

'You're just a bus-stop near Farnborough' came the reply. Given the reaction of the Shots' small but nasty squad of hoodies, I think they may have touched a nerve. But back to the match, and injury-time. David Brown was introduced to waste a few seconds, prompting Justin to offer the first of two staggeringly apposite observations.

'I like Browner, but he misses too many sitters.' Within seconds, Brown had missed a sitter.

'Mind you, when he does score, they're usually special' was his next, as David picked up a loose ball and turned toward the home goal, finding himself and Danny Williams two-on-one with a home defender. Williams was the better placed and screaming for the ball, along with four hundred Bulls fans, Justin included.

'Give it to Danny, give it to Danny, give it to.......... fuck-me what a goal.' Brown had sealed the victory with a thirty-yard strike that Nikki Bull probably didn't see. Within seconds, the same players who couldn't manage an embarrassed wave at Exeter were almost in the crowd, and you could tell just how much it meant to all of them.

Once again, the Bulls and the Shots had produced arguably the best match, and certainly Hereford's finest 90 minutes, of the season. Until a week later, where a repeat scoreline at Barnet and a display conceded by Bees manager Paul Fairclough as the best he had seen at Underhill, outshone the Aldershot performance with something to spare. It was Championship form which with a little luck, might see us safely into the play-offs. That, fellas, is much more like it.

A Pub Team. And then another
25/3/2005 Farnborough - away

In a league where crowds can be a little disappointing, two men and a dog was frankly, well, disappointing, although by half-time it had grown to a more respectable two dozen. Despite twice leading, the Bulls went down to a 3-2 defeat, hindered by an injury to their debutant goalkeeper, who by the final whistle was playing almost on one leg. Also unhelpful was the team coach arriving forty minutes after the scheduled kick-off, and several players nursing a hangover. Nonetheless, an improvement over their previous excursion, where Barnet romped to a 12-1, yes twelve-one victory, hence the need for a new keeper.

I am, of course, talking about the Bulls Supporters team, and the new keeper was me. Despite an old injury returning before half-time, it was a lot of fun, even though most of the players were young enough to justifiably call me Dad, if not Granddad. Whilst waiting for the Hereford-based Bulls, a chat with the home side revealed two little snippets worth sharing. Firstly, Farney supporters were not only resigned to a spell in Conference South, but looking forward to it. Their club was in disarray, and they felt a period of consolidation and reduced overheads was the best long-term option. Added to which, they were fed up with being slaughtered every other week.

The second was, I thought, a wind-up, but is apparently absolutely true. I asked one of the Farnborough players who was their danger man. 'Don't worry, he's not allowed to play.'

I enquired why. 'He's in the first-team squad now', came the reply. I was suitably impressed. A Conference side with a supporters' team, *and* a reserve supporters' team. I sensed we might be up against it when we finally got underway. 'But he might not make the bench this afternoon, he's carrying a knock.' Whoa, hold on a moment, did he mean this afternoon *out there on Cherrywood Road, against the Bulls?*

Now I was seriously impressed. The gap between park football and the Conference was a vast canyon compared even to that between the Conference and the Premiership. Unless, of course, Farnborough had become a pub team since we met back in August. Twenty minutes into the other Match of the Day, it was beginning to look that way, when loanee Leroy Williams chipped a debut goal barely reflecting the Bulls' dominance. Which he promptly followed by bizarrely attempting to head-butt a home defender a good eight inches taller than he, under what appeared to be minimal provocation. Leroy's throat-butt, whilst comical, didn't amuse the referee sufficiently to avoid a red-card. 'I'll bring you a fucking box next time Leroy, do the job properly', was the parting shot from a travelling Bull, but Leroy's moment of madness left the Bulls a goal up but a man down with an hour to play. After Leroy's red mist and card, one side so dominated proceedings that had it been a boxing match, it would have been stopped. Unusually, the five goals which followed were all scored by the side with ten men, as Farnborough disintegrated.

This time, and without involving a bookmaker, I felt genuinely sorry for them, for this was closer to a bullfight than a football match. As one party strolled and strutted, the other charged and blundered, pierced again and again by an opponent from a different plane. Farney were looking every inch a pub team, and a fairly crap one at that.

With the slaughter concluded, it was back to the clubhouse for a pint that didn't really have a celebratory feel, especially when observing the team photograph behind the bar. Farnborough FC 2004/2005, a typical pre-season shot with twenty odd professionals in view, all obviously hoping for a decent campaign. This one, however, was different. More than half of the players' faces were covered by a small sticking-plaster, no longer part of the set-up. It was a pitiful sight, and one this time achieved without pillaging from Westley and Wallace.

And as an image of pure pathos, it was followed by a scene of the highest comedy. A lady presumably connected to the football club entered the bar with a face like thunder. Locals shuffled feet and averted eyes, sensing that an explosion was imminent, and they were right, for this was one extremely upset supporter.

'I hope you lot agree that that was a fucking disgrace.' There followed an embarrassed silence, until a little fellow in the corner piped up, 'Actually, I thought it was fucking brilliant.' He was wearing a slightly pissed, very silly grin, and a Bulls shirt.

Another lifetime of glorious silence was broken by a snigger, and then another. And then of course, the whole room was convulsed, with some reduced to tears, and even our irate lady friend unable to resist.

Football. It means so much to so many people, but it is still only a game.

The Lottery Ticket
19/4/2005 Woking - away

With eight games remaining, the top of the table had an M25 look about it. Congested, tense, and a lot of people wondering if they would reach their destination. Nine teams were covered by just six points, and only four would be claiming a lottery ticket, and the chance to join the irritatingly consistent Barnet. Five of these League Two wannabees featured in the Bulls' remaining fixtures, and the toughest run-in was ours. No problem for GT's men, who collected five wins and a draw from their next six games, including victories at Stevenage, Halifax, and Forest Green, condemning the Gump to almost certain relegation. Since the disastrous trilogy of January defeats, the Bulls had lost only once, and that to a suspect penalty at Morecambe. There had been no more half-time walkouts, and no more calls to bring back Richard O'Kelly.

And whilst the team had often been entertaining and always resilient, the supporters had been magnificent. At a time when they were needed most, Bulls fans assembled behind their team in fabulous numbers, and particularly away from home, gave a level of support rarely seen in this league. The half-time exodus in Exeter seemed a long time ago, and another 500 of the faithful were gathered at Kingfield. Four, however, were missing.

Four days previously, a car taking Bulls supporters to Halifax was still in Herefordshire when it overturned, and four men are now in intensive care, two still in a critical condition. Once again, I refer you to the words of Mr. Shankly. Not even close, Bill, especially for these four. Hang on in there, chaps.

So it was Woking again, where DCB, looking more and more like a player who might go on to better things, put the Bulls ahead with five minutes remaining, and the ticket was secured. In contrast to last season, when a play-off place had been sealed in March, this year had seen a lot of nervous Bulls fans, and their celebrations were more of relief than joy.

So on a final Saturday of bitten fingernails, who missed out on a shot at the Holy Grail of proper football? Aldershot comfortably beat

Scarborough and claimed fourth place. Stevenage struggled past the remnants of Leigh RMI, rendering Exeter's win over Carlisle meaningless. Which left Morecambe needing a victory at Tamworth, one that they failed to secure, despite a 90 minute battering of the home goal. Which, for the Bulls, added up to a two-legged shoot-out with Stevenage, having once again finished in the runner's-up spot, twelve points behind Barnet. Four points separated the four sides, a reflection of how closely matched they appeared to be, and in stark contrast to the 21 point spread of last year.

And we know what happened then. If the history of play-offs tells us one thing, it is that current form counts for little, and that the team finishing highest rarely wins through. Yes, that's two things, but as Bulls fans know all too well, both are true.

Groundhog Days
2/5/2005 and 6/5/2005 Stevenage Borough - away and home
Play-Off Semi-Final

Back to the land of roundabouts and retail parks, with 1,400 all-ticket Bulls housed in the least ugly building in Stevenage, the Buildbase stand. Ironic that Hereford should sell out their allocation whilst sizeable gaps were seen around the remaining three sides of Broadhall Way. A small consolation for ticketless Herefordians was that Sky TV were covering the match, and unlike most Bulls fans at the game, they could enjoy a pint with their afternoon viewing.

Have I mentioned that there are no decent pubs in Stevenage? Well, there are hardly any crap ones either. As if there wasn't already enough deprivation in this corner of Hertfordshire, the majority of travelling support would have to enjoy, if you can say that about a semi-final, proceedings without a little refresher to calm the nerves. None of us were confident about either the day or the tie, forseeing a struggle to contain the physical threat offered by a side with less flair but more brute force. And importantly, the memory of last season's failure was still fresh in our minds, and almost certainly in that of the players as well. Could they put Aldershot and Andy Woolmer behind them?

Doubtful, and it was certain that Westley would have his players whispering sweet-nothings in the ears of our boys, heavily featuring the word bottle. Get past that, and we were in with a chance.

With twenty minutes remaining, those chances improved dramatically. DCB had just replaced a tiring Millsey when he picked up the ball in

180

midfield. Having earned himself a little space, he unleashed a shot worthy of winning any tie and a thirty-yard strike that matched Ronnie Radford's effort of thirty years ago. In what was a physical, attritional game, it was a goal that none of us had seen coming, but enjoyed all the more for it. And that should really have been that, but with two minutes remaining, Brady located Maamria, both players in a scandalously large amount of space, the latter duly equalising in the last act of the match.

Or should that be the half. Act two would see someone progress to Stoke, and another reflect on a season's hard work, with assurances that they would bounce back bigger and stronger next season. Stoke for us, please.

The following Friday saw a serious case of déjà vu, for there we were, the same dozen or so characters in the same corner of the same pub, counting down the minutes until we could wander to the same corner of the same ground, hoping our players could improve upon the drawn first leg. Common opinion is that the Bulls failed to show up for the second leg, but I don't agree. For 45 minutes we took the game to Stevenage, missing several half-chances, and had a good shout for a penalty denied. The second 45, however, was another story. Westley obviously instructed his players to get into the face of their opponents, play an even more physical game, and hope that the passive refereeing continued.

It worked, and all too well, and as an attacking force, the Bulls became invisible. The midfield was surrendered, and the inevitable goal came once again courtesy of Maamria.

Stevenage had made sure that size was important. They were bigger, stronger, and seemed to want it just a little more, and grudging, very grudging respect is due to their manager, who got it absolutely right on the night.

Full-time arrived with the ghastly sight of Westley and Elding cavorting around *our* ground in front of *our* supporters, most of whom were too stunned to issue the abuse they so richly deserved. I felt sick, for whilst our second half showing deserved exactly what it got, to see two of the biggest egos in non-league football rubbing our noses in it was a sight to give any decent supporter nightmares.

Amidst all the joy and despair however, came a touch of humanity from the victors. Or at least from two of them. Stand up Jason Goodliffe and Jon Brady, honest and decent pros both. They alone came to the Meadow End to acknowledge the home support, in what was a genuine gesture of sympathy. Which served to show that nowhere, not even Stevenage, was all bad.

Pain supposedly becomes more bearable with exposure, and we had been here before, so did it hurt as much second time around?

No and yes, I suppose. No because we still had a little residue of the Aldershot defeat in our system, but yes because of both the nature of the defeat and the identity of the victor. Graham Westley got his tactics right, and his players delivered. If it had been Morecambe jigging around ES, I would have found it within me somewhere to wish them well. As it was Westley, I hope that Carlisle wipe the floor with his team in two weeks' time.

In comparison to the previous season, given the identical finishing position and ultimate demise, this had been a far less dramatic campaign, although O'Kelly's Heroes were a hard act to follow. Whilst the Bulls were less spectacular, apart from a couple of frustrating spells there was a solidity about the side often missing previously, perhaps reflecting a contrasting attitude shown by the two coaches. And whilst without Smithy and Pazza there was less flair, the Bulls still possessed more artistry than most sides in the division.

Which in many cases wasn't much.

Barnet's ultimate cushion of twelve points fairly reflected their dominance, and Carlisle, who thankfully overcame Stevenage in the play-off final, were certainly the biggest and probably the strongest of the rest. Leigh RMI were undoubtedly the worst side seen in eight years of Conference football, and Farnborough, by the end of the season, not much better. Joining them on the way out of the Conference would be not Forest Green but Northwich Victoria, who finished one place but nine points ahead of the Gump.

How so? The Vics began the season in a CVA and consequently with a ten-point deduction, despite which they battled away to comfortably survive relegation. Or so they thought. The Conference, in their uniquely caring way, decided in April that they didn't like the look of either the Vic's finances, or their ground leases, or something else unconnected with football, and threw them out of the division. Was this another joke decision by the body that had cast both Barrow and Slough into the wilderness? There may have been a small degree of merit in their argument, until you consider that the Vics were relegated to Conference North. That is the Conference North, feeder league to the Conference, and categorically under the same umbrella as the division in which they were deemed unworthy to compete. I'm yet to hear why one division is suitable for a club with supposedly questionable viability when another is not. Mike Connett and his Northwich side had survived against huge odds, only to be rewarded with another scandalous committee-room relegation, their efforts over the season declared a waste of time.

In an irony perhaps lost on a few, the three teams ultimately relegated were the same three who occupied the relegation slots last year, all of whom for various reasons retained their Conference status. Funny old game, or perhaps just a little perverse?

As for the Gump, well, they aren't the first and I suspect they won't be the last club to be handed a get out of jail free card. It's clearly wrong, but the god of football had taken a liking to Nailsworth, and if it were the Bulls, I suspect we would be keeping a grateful, if embarrassed, silence.

It was far from an embarrassed silence which greeted the news from the League Two trapdoor, for falling through were Cambridge and Kidderminster. Yes, our carpet-making neighbours were back where Bulls fans felt they had always belonged.

Stick that in your pipe, Radio Harriers and Worcester.

Joining in the opposite direction were Southport, Altrincham, and Grays Athletic, the latter a side who had won Conference South with ridiculous ease and, it appeared, without anyone bothering to watch them. Already tipped to be the next Telford, Grays would be an interesting day out next season, if we could find it.

An end of term report on the Bulls' season would give credit to GT, Tucka, and all of the players for again giving us something to shout about until May, and achieved whilst returning a six-figure profit. There remain, and probably always will, supporters out there unhappy with GT, but without him the club wouldn't be where they are today, if indeed anywhere at all.

Falling again at the last hurdle was a bitter disappointment, the inevitable consequence of which would be the Bulls being labelled as a nearly team. Many, including some of our own support, went as far as to suggest that the players lacked the necessary bottle to escape the Conference, and that the millstone of two successive failures would drag them down should they find themselves in the same place next season. The only way we'll find out is by getting there.

End of Season Oscars?

Why not? Whilst we again picked up the award for best team in a supporting role, the truth was that we were little better or worse than at least six other sides, all of whom would be in the frame next year.

As for the rest, Player of the Season, and by a street, was Tamika, with DCB picking up both most promising newcomer and goal of the season, at Stevenage.

Performance of the year was the near-faultless display at Barnet, almost compensating for the no-shows at Exeter and Burton, both new entries into the top ten crappy days at the football.

Best away-day would be Canvey Island, a place so surreal I'm still not certain that I didn't just dream it, whilst the Sons of Eric and Bob Taylor's wonder-goal made the Tamworth match the highlight at Edgar Street.

The biggest disappointments would include the Exeter walk-out and the patchy form of Jamer, looking surprisingly human after several hundred games where he barely put a foot wrong.

As for this season's villains, no surprises or indeed prizes for correct identification. If you need a clue, let's just say that all have been previous winners, and they include two managers, one player, and several men in a committee room.

Enough of heroes and villains — time for some more perspective. Whilst the Bulls were cementing a play-off spot at Woking, Paul Sykes of Dover Athletic collapsed on their Crabble pitch and died whilst simply doing his job. I hope his two sons can forgive the game that took away their father, but if they do play football, they more than anyone will know that it is, and I say it yet again, only a game.

A few weeks after the tragedy at Dover, the last of the four injured fans was allowed out of intensive care. All will apparently be scarred for life, but all will be watching football sooner or later. Good luck to you lads.

Final words. Whilst the Bulls are now one of the biggest fish in this small pool, competitive on the field, financially viable, and with, at last, improving facilities at ES, there is an enormous job still to be done. To finish runners-up twice and be rewarded with nothing is hard to take, but you don't always get what you deserve.

Where the play-offs were once something to be fought for, they may next year be something we might dread, and many Bulls fans are now of the opinion that to leave this league, we'll have to win it.

They may be right.

10   2005-2006 Seven Nation Army

13/8/2005 Scarborough - home

Six new faces lined up for the season opener against, to borrow a cricketing insult, our very own rabbits, Scarborough. Like the batsmen who never scores against you, the Seadogs must despise playing the Bulls. But before the ritual demolition of our favourite Yorkshiremen, some departures and some new faces. Millsey, Danny Williams and Graham Hyde were released, whilst Brown and Tretton were lured away by Accrington, the latter leaving with the frankly incredible line that he had always wanted to play for a club in red.

As opposed to a club merely in the red. But hey, that isn't the Bulls, not any more if, as some seem to have done, you've forgotten the £1.3 million still owed to the Richardson brothers.

Tretton was replaced by Dean (any colour is fine) Beckwith, and joining him were Alex Jeannin and Jon Brady, unsurprisingly finding Hereford a more attractive option than Exeter and Stevenage respectively. Stacy Caldicott and Andy Ferrell joined from Grimsby and Watford, along with Guy Ipoua, from Athletico Madrid.

And one or two places in between. Including Doncaster Rovers, Ipoua's last employer, one of whose fans was sufficiently underwhelmed as to offer the 'useless, overweight lump' the train fare to Hereford or anywhere else that offered him a job. Sounds like a player with both ability and baggage. Here's hoping that Guy enjoys Hereford more than Doncaster. GT's final signing was Wayne Brown, a more than useful keeper in Chester's Conference winning side who would push Mawson for the number one spot on the evidence of a few pre-season friendlies.

And so to the League of Nations that is Hereford United. With the possible exception of the Gump, Hereford is the least cosmopolitan place in this league, perhaps in the professional game, and a city that because of its isolation has traditionally seen most of its residents as born and bred Herefordians. Whilst the times they are a-changing, they are doing so more slowly in our part of the world, except on the Edgar Street pitch, where the starting eleven against Scarborough featured no less than seven different nationalities. Joining two Englishmen and two Welshmen would be Australian Brady, Frenchman Jeannin, Cameroonian Ipoua, and Tam from Malawi. The seventh, and apparently most patriotic, was Andy Ferrell, part of the Geordie nation and a huge Newcastle fan, fortunately born twelve years after Radford and George humiliated his beloved home-town team.

We'll soon enlighten him, but there wasn't however, much talk of Newcastle, as Scarborough came to ES with a game-plan built entirely on taking home an ugly and boring point. And it was working, until Dean Beckwith marked his debut with a well-timed strike, enabling a more traditional Bulls versus Seadogs encounter to follow. Ipoua joined Becks on the score sheet, along with Ryan Green and substitute DCB in a second-half master class orchestrated by the Cameroonian. Whilst obviously short of fitness, Guy showed wonderfully quick feet and enough class to suggest that Conference defences might find their hands full in the coming months. We can but hope.

Broadway Farce
10/9/2005 Stevenage Borough - away

Not a Broadway farce, more of a Broadhall Way comedy, with pantomime villains, shamefully poor acting, and the best one-liner heard at a football match. Ever.

Worth waiting for, I promise, but first, the ups and downs of the first month of the Bulls' ninth, oh how time flies, season in what some call the wilderness. Our reign at the top lasted just three days, as sloppy and uncharacteristic defending by Jamer tossed away the points at Cambridge, followed by a scrappy win at Crawley, and a lesson which Guy Ipoua may or may not learn about life in a small town. There are many places where a tall and debonair black man might not stand out from the crowd, but Hereford city centre on a Saturday night isn't one of them.

Ipoua chose to celebrate his third goal in as many games at Saxtys wine-bar, but apparently overdid things a little. Guy was spotted on hands and knees and, to put it delicately, reverse-sampling some of the refreshments no doubt forced upon him by grateful Bulls fans. Eye-witness reports of which were all over the internet before Sunday Mass, and whilst there was the predictable outrage of Colonel Bufton-Tufton and the like, it was nothing in comparison to the hero-worship of the more proletariat of Bulls support. Anyone capable of scoring for the Bulls on a Saturday afternoon and being legless within an hour of returning to Hereford the same night deserved some credit, and Ipoua was on his way to becoming a legend.

No such celebrations the following Saturday, as Grays Athletic visited ES for the first time, playing us off the park, and themselves to the top of the Conference, worryingly assisted by another howler from Jamer. Also a worry was the failure of Stacy Caldicott to last the 90 minutes for the third game in succession. Rumours of a career-ending back problem surfaced, and whilst terrace gossip is rarely completely reliable, there is often something in it. Shades of Steve Piearce? I hope not, and having had his fingers badly burned by the permanently out of order goal-machine and his three-year contract, GT was wise enough to avoid this nightmare with Caldicott.

Just a two-year deal for Stacy.

And so to the theatre, not of dreams but of high comedy, and Broadhall Way, where a depleted Bulls side took on Stevenage, boasting a perfect home record and fourth spot in the Conference. Missing were Green, Lisa, Guy, and Caldicott, with Tamika and Pitman fit enough only for the bench. Not ideal when visiting the side you want not just to beat but to humiliate, but happily, the Jamer of old was back. For thirty minutes Stevenage laid siege to the Bulls' goal, but Beckwith and Jamer were magnificent, along with Wayne Brown, proving to be the excellent acquisition we all hoped he would be. Of course, Westley and Eldinho received constant abuse from the travelling Bulls fans, but just before half-time, the best player in the Conference found himself at the centre of a storm. Brown collected a through ball comfortably enough, but Elding, as is his wont, made little effort to avoid bundling both keeper and ball into the back of the net. Clearly a foul, and one to have Big Eric Redrobe cooing with delight, but words were exchanged as both players got to their feet, eyeball to eyeball. Browner then did exactly what he shouldn't have, and raised a hand.

It was a gentle, far from Redrobe-esque brush on the chin, but Elding, being both Elding and (according to at least one local) a twat of the highest order, fell to the floor as if, and here is some seriously wishful thinking, he'd been shot by a sniper.

There was bedlam in the away end as the referee reached toward his pocket. Brown was a goner, and we knew it, as did Craig Mawson, tracksuit already off. Our only hope was that Elding would go the same way. It was to him that judgement was first issued, and it was a colour to match the referee's courage, or lack of. Yellow.

Eldinho trotted off, job done, or so he thought. Now Brown was lectured, with GT pondering which outfield player to sacrifice in exchange, and Bulls fans behind the goal forming a lynch mob.

I'm sure Browner was half-way to the dressing-room before he realised that for once, some woeful Conference officiating had actually been kind to the Bulls, as more yellow was flourished.

Oh joy. Whilst the laws of the game had been ignored, natural justice had prevailed, as one Herefordian forcibly pointed out whilst standing on the perimeter wall.

Sorry, but you can't do that. Cue a disgruntled chief-steward, homing in on our over-excited supporter. Focus switched immediately to the two now on centre stage, and a hush descended as the steward barked at the miscreant. 'You on the wall, what's your name?'

Within a second, a voice bellowed out from the ranks of visiting fans. 'Don't tell him, Pike.'

The lynch mob was disbanded in tears, the only person not laughing being Eldinho.

Apologies if you haven't a clue what I'm talking about, but those of you who do, and you'll be in the majority, will know just how priceless a line it was. And to the Bulls fan who delivered it, hats-off to you sir, for your quick wit and impeccable timing.

Hats-off also to the diminutive Jenny Pitman, who, as the players left the pitch at half-time, confronted Eldinho with what appeared to be an offer along the lines of an after-school meeting behind the bike-sheds. Good on you Jenny, living proof that size maybe isn't always important.

The second half was a more sedate affair, the sides sharing a decent nil-nil, although it was now more than four hours since the Bulls had found the net. The defence was solid, midfield OK, but something was missing in attack. Like a striker who knew where the goal was.

Lisa and his double hernia would be out for a while yet, and Ipoua, for all of his ability, just wasn't fit. GT was apparently looking for a loaner, but perhaps it was time for DCB to step up. Watch this space.

Late Again
27/9/2005 Prince of Wales - away

Although some still regard the Conference as a Pub League, we weren't actually playing the Prince of Wales, merely ensconced within it. With the only decent pub in Aldershot being in Farnborough, that's where we found ourselves on a crisp Tuesday night, hoping that despite our current form, we would as usual find the Shots happy to hand over the points. In the nine matches since the Scarborough goal-fest, the Bulls had scored seven and conceded the same, obviously not good enough for GT, who had finally found a striker willing to give a month of his time to Hereford's floundering promotion challenge. Matt Bailey from Crewe Alexandra would play tonight, the only information to hand being that he was very tall and surprisingly enough, hadn't scored thirty goals in the Championship last season.

A couple tonight would be nice, but a question more immediate than the qualities of our new striker was whether we had time for another pint of Hampshire's finest real-ale. Having missed too many kick-offs to remember, my inclination was to leave, not even slightly influenced by the fact that I was driving, and would enjoy nothing more than a cup of tea. Unsurprisingly out-voted, the recurring nightmare of finding somewhere to park as the players strolled out was again a reality. Miraculously, a space was found with four minutes to spare, and with the walk to the ground no more than two, we were safe.

Or so we thought. The visitors' entrance at the Rec was for some reason closed, leaving a mad dash around three sides of the ground to join our fellow Bulls. We were perhaps half-way as the match kicked-off, and no more than three-quarters done when a roar erupted from the stadium. Obviously a goal, but who for?

On we jogged, desperately trying to figure whether the celebrations were by two thousand fans, obviously bad news, or two hundred, clearly great. Above the wheezing of four pairs of forty-something lungs, the PA man was muttering, but one word stood out. Bertram.

'Did you guys hear that?'

Nobody had. 'It's us, DCB, I'm sure it is. Probably a screamer.'

Much scepticism bounced back, but I was confident. Finally inside the ground, there was Alan, along with a couple of hundred very chirpy football fans. Clearly the news was good, but who, how, and when?

DCB, twenty-five yards, twenty-six seconds, were the answers.

And as predicted, a screamer. 'Surely not again', he said, hopelessly failing to keep a smug grin off his face. 'Will you guys ever learn?' Don't push it mate, remember that you want a lift home. The following 89 minutes failed to live up to the flying start, but the Shots were comfortably held, and there were no more goals. Our new striker was indeed very tall, but fell over a lot. Jury out, but given time to settle, he might prove a useful asset.

'Fancy another cup of tea?' asked the lads, as full-time was called. Matt, a great friend despite his allegiance to Chelsea, had tagged along for his first taste of unproper football, and was, to say the least, bemused.

'So let me get this right', he said. 'You pick up your mates, watch them sup gallons of more than decent ale whilst you have a cuppa. We then almost kill ourselves running around the back streets of a crap-hole town, only to find that some kid with three names has already scored the goal of the season. We then listen to 90 minutes of sheep-shagger songs whilst trying to avoid the conkers whistling over our heads, all the while sniggering at a circus act who clowns around like Bambi on roller-skates. And *then* you celebrate by watching yet more Old Embalmer being quaffed with another cup of tea. Madness. When can I come again?'

Yes, there really is a conker tree inside the Rec, and yes, Matt, I think you're right. Absolute madness, and only in the Conference. Someone should write a book about this stuff. Somebody may even believe it.

Family Fortunes
25/10/2005 Alfreton Town - away. FA Cup 4th Qualifying Round, Replay

Bambi scored on his home debut, sadly only enough to prise a solitary point from Canvey Island, but was soon cast as the villain when missing an open goal at Accrington, where defeat saw the Bulls fall nine points behind Grays. Points were urgently required, and three were stolen from Burton in a match memorable for more Bambi disasters, and he found himself replaced by local teenager Andy Williams. Fans will always allow more leeway to a local lad than to an outsider, and with a rookie striker from within the county straining for a game, Matt Bailey was on a hiding to nothing. And a hiding he took, at least in the verbal sense, but in all honesty he rarely looked the answer to our goal-scoring deficiencies, and any confidence he may have had was soon gone.

In stark contrast to Andy 'Willo' Williams, who appeared chock full of the stuff, and like his namesake Gavin, more than willing to embarrass

Conference defenders with a little show-boating. Whilst livening up a dull afternoon, cameos from Willo and a half-fit Ipoua failed to beat an inspired Alfreton keeper, meaning a trip to Derbyshire and another crack at FA Cup glory. And another opportunity for one Mark Turner to put one over his father, before which some worrying news from Morecambe, where manager Jimmy Harvey was rushed to hospital with a suspected heart-attack. Get well soon, Jim.

Also before which, another sighting of Guy Ipoua, again spotted in his favourite wine-bar, although this time displaying his talents on the dance-floor, as opposed to the pavement outside. It seems that Guy, like Steve Perrin, won't let his day job interfere with living life to the full. No doubt GT is tearing his hair out, and tempted to do likewise with Guy's contract, but football is full of talent that never quite realises its potential. If Ipoua chooses the work hard, play harder option, so be it, for I would rather watch Guy for an hour a month than Matt Bailey for six.

But I digress, so it's back to Alfreton Town, and Turner Junior's sixth opportunity to better his father's team. None from five is the current score, but Mark, with another family meal to be paid for by the loser, opened the scoring for his side on thirty minutes. Adam Legzdins was again proving difficult to beat in the home goal, taking a rare Craig Stanley header to earn the Bulls a penalty shoot-out. Mark Turner, under threat of a paternal clip round the ear, missed, leaving Ipoua to secure a first round visit to Cambridge City. GT selected a restaurant, whilst Alfreton were left to contemplate trips to Vauxhall Motors and Farsley Celtic.

Lucky them.

Tears for Souvenirs
29/10/2005 Kidderminster Harriers - away

Bambi's last game in a Hereford shirt saw a wonder strike from Jenny Pitman and backs-to-the-wall defence from the Bulls, but all the headlines surrounded events an hour after the final whistle. Given that the match was a local derby, with over a thousand Bulls fans making the trip to Worcestershire it had been a surprisingly quiet afternoon, with little hint of trouble from either set of supporters. Until, that is, West Mercia Police closed Worcester railway station whilst 200 Hereford supporters waited for a connecting train. The group included many families, and given that the worst of our hard-core fringe were banned from travelling, the potential for disorder was low. An hour of waiting on a cramped platform was, to most people's minds, unnecessary, and a small number of Bulls fans made their feelings known. This was, according to police statements, 'deplorable hooliganism' by 'a small minority' which gave the officers cause for concern, and their actions were justified 'in the interest of public safety'.

Well why else would CS gas be sprayed into a contained crowd including women and children, if not to keep them safe? Accounts given by those present were unanimous in their condemnation of the police, including many who had nothing to do with Hereford United. I was under the impression that CS gas was a riot-control measure, a last resort when events were spiralling out of control, not a sledgehammer used to crack the nut of a small handful of vocal but hardly bellicose football fans.

Somewhere between these polarised accounts lies the truth of Foregate Street station, but consider this. If the behaviour of the fans was sufficiently extreme to warrant measures more in keeping with the West Bank than the West Midlands, then you might expect to see a Magistrate's Court the following morning overflowing with these 'deplorable hooligans'. But the number of arrests made that afternoon?

None. Whilst policing football supporters isn't always a walk in the park, something went badly wrong in Worcester station that afternoon, and I would suspect that many supporters, along with their friends and families, won't be rushing to ES or for that matter any football match in the near future. Memories of the afternoon should have been of a slightly fortunate point. Instead, they were of being penned like cattle, struggling for breath and taking home nothing but tears for souvenirs. A small reminder of the seventies and eighties, an era of almost constant conflict, and one when football was allowed to batter itself almost to death.

I hope, sincerely, that this was an aberration, a freakish throwback to days that most of us old enough to remember are still trying to forget.

Cup Fever, and Two Supermen
Winter 2005-2006 Bognor, Scunthorpe, and a few places in between
Of the 20 games played between mid-October and the end of January, ten were in the cup, or more accurately cups, available to the Bulls. Of course, the only defeat came in the one we most wanted to win, as a tame surrender to Stockport saw the FA Cup dream fall at the hurdle before the really big ones came into range. The FA Trophy offered morale-boosting wins at Bognor (yes, we have a football team) Regis by an O'Kelly-like 7-1, and at Halifax, a Trewick-esque 1-0.

Or so many Bulls fans would have you believe. It's never as black and white as that, despite a small number of voices still demanding the return of the flair-to-spare days enjoyed under the previous coach. If GT ever stumbles across a formula to realise the best of both of these worlds, he'd have a team that would take the Conference by storm.

Which, folks, is a very big if. The third of the prizes on offer was the LDV Trophy, a crumb thrown from the big boys' table to the best eight Conference sides of the previous season. Should we be grateful for the opportunity to challenge the hybrid first XI/fringe/youth teams offered by the League sides, or, as appears to be the option elsewhere, give the squad a shuffle and see what falls out of the pack?

Whilst hardly giant-killings, LDV victories over Mansfield, Port Vale and Scunthorpe saw the Bulls again reach a point two matches away from the Millennium Stadium, and again fail, this time bowing out to Macclesfield. With Grays to visit ES in the next chapter of the Trophy, it may be time to re-focus on the small matter of getting out of this League, so what of the ten Conference games played in this period?

Bad news first. Browner broke a wrist in training, although in Maws we have a pretty good stand-in. DCB looks a shadow of the man he was in August, and is going backwards at an alarming rate, whilst Jon Brady has gone eastwards, to Cambridge United. Joining him, if only for a month, will be the invisible man, one Stacy Coldicott, in an attempt to get match-fit. Losing Stacy for a month was more than compensated by the return of Lisa Stansfield, quickly making up for lost time by notching five goals in his first seven games. Whether or not Lisa's return was the catalyst, there was a noticeable upturn in the Bulls' form, with only one defeat in the ten matches concerned. Depressingly, it was Exeter who once again plundered ES for three easy points, although televised revenge was extracted at St. James Park, where the return of Ipoua inspired the Bulls to a magnificent ten-man victory. This despite Guy, now allegedly sponsored by Saxtys wine bar, being sent off for inciting the home supporters. His crime was to point to the name on the back of Alex Jeanin's shirt after the full-back curled a gorgeous left-footer into the net of his former employers. In a category packed with high-quality offerings, this was an award-winning piece of pedantry from yet another clueless official, the small mercy in this case being that the man was in charge of a football match and not the West Mercia police.

There would have been a blood-bath at Foregate Street.

So where did all of this leave us?

Back in a play-off slot, but twelve points behind the Milkmen of Accrington, a team in the habit of winning matches without always playing well, irritatingly similar to the Chester side of two years ago. Damn, I hate that. Whilst I am at heart an optimist, it looks as though if this is to be our year, it will be via the play-offs, and already there is the recurring nightmare of finishing second, only for Exeter to repeat the Aldershot and Stevenage heartbreak of previous years. Another black armband may or may not be waiting for Bulls fans come May, but to give a little perspective, some genuinely sad news. A few weeks before Christmas, football lost a man who could truly be described as a genius, when George Best died. Few sportsmen are so far ahead of their contemporaries as to be almost out of sight, but George was one, matched perhaps only by Bradman, Ali and Pele. Federer, Woods and Warne may one day join this small band, but there will never be another Best. Gone, George, but never forgotten.

Oh yes, the two supermen. George of course was one, the other being our very own Wayne Brown. A group of Bulls fans found themselves at Turf-Moor after a late postponement at Morecambe, and returned to ES with a song stolen from Reading supporters. Royals fans had christened their favourite son Superman, with a song for their hero.

Whilst his powers didn't extend to the instant healing of a broken bone, his goalkeeping was of a quality so far above that of mere mortals that our net-man became the chosen one, and the song was adopted for Wayne.

Wayne Brown is Superman, Wayne Brown is Superman, and so on. Although if Tam didn't possess a name with sixteen syllables, it might have been him.

Dead Bull on the Pitch
28/1/2006 Grays Athletic - away

Don't be alarmed, everyone at ES is very much alive, it's just a little piece of theatre, courtesy of a player who you could safely say isn't well-loved in Hereford.

No not Jimmy Quinn, but I'm getting ahead of myself, so to Grays, battling with Accy at the top of the Conference, and possibly the biggest town you've never heard of.

And why would you have? Another of those Thames estuary settlements that have dominated the Ryman League in recent times, Grays is a place with few redeeming features even to the most avid of ground-hoppers, and whilst unfair to describe it as the middle of nowhere, it's pretty damn near.

About eight miles to be precise — coincidentally, the exact distance to Canvey Island. But I digress. Without the intervention of Chairman Mick Woodward, Grays Athletic would probably still be a footballing backwater, but last season they won the Conference South and the FA Trophy with embarrassing ease, and on evidence so far seen are the best side in the Conference. In Mark Stimpson Grays have one of the brightest managers outside the Football League, in addition to a good-sized squad of professionals, most of whom would walk into proper sides. So the real question is, how are they paying for such quality on gates often failing to reach four figures? Maybe Mr. Woodward has the answer, but the first thing you notice about Grays is how it almost perfectly lives up to its name, even on a flawless winter afternoon, and had it been named Colourless, nobody could have argued. The town centre car park sits above what must be the world's most depressing shopping mall, one where the walkways were full but the shops empty, and where every item in almost every other shop would cost you a pound. The solitary plus-point is that the Recreation ground is a short walk away, and one which takes you to the only football club bar featured in the Good Beer Guide.

Initially you wonder why, for seldom have I seen a bar with less character than this one, but after sampling one of the many fine ales on offer served by quick and friendly staff, and taking in some pre-match banter with some welcoming locals, you think again. When said locals point out that the visitors' seats are filling quickly, best get over there if you actually want to see the game, you realise that first impressions aren't always correct.

Great little boozer, and without doubt the highlight of a trip to Grays. Bar one. Time for the Dying Bull.

Leading the home attack was one Aaron McLean, he of the play-off red-card tussle with Andy Tretton. Football fans love a villain, and today McLean was it. A constant stream of abuse, some amusing, some nasty, was directed toward the man who denied us a play-off final appearance, of course inspiring him to even greater efforts on the pitch.

When Grays took a deserved first half lead, you can guess whose mis-hit shot fell into Superman's net, and right in front of the visiting support. Now there must be some theatrical blood in Aaron, because the accepted finger to lips 'Shush', or hand to ears 'Can't hear you', were to him the gesture of the amateur, and bigger things were called for. Bigger even than a miraculous recovery from a Tretton tackle. McLean placed upturned index fingers on the forehead, and charged bull-like toward the Hereford enclosure. A menacing scrape of the hoof followed, along with another charge, before a dramatic collapse to the turf, hand now on heart, body motionless.

I think our friend was trying to tell us that the bull was dead.

Here was without doubt the most original goal celebration since Elmo stole a mascot's head, and whether planned or instinctive, to Aaron McLean I doff my cap. That, sir, was genius.

Which wasn't how most of the travelling support saw it, as several half-eaten burgers hurtled toward the deceased bull. Fortunately, no damage was done, and staggeringly, McLean escaped even a lecture from the referee. The clueless official who recently sent Guy packing for incitement would have had him in the Tower. But back to the match, where another howler saw the Bulls two down, and bereft of ideas. We needed a big second half performance, and thankfully, we got it. Several opportunities were spurned before a Tam header almost broke the net, shortly followed by a less powerful, but every bit as much appreciated effort from Dean Beckwith. A draw was a fair result, but more important than the point earned was the confidence gained from the second half display. As last year, too many teams were fighting over the precious play-off slots, but if the Bulls took forward the attitude shown after the break today, they wouldn't be far away come May.

The final word on what had been a surprisingly good day out in pound-stretcher hell came from Justin, reflecting on the antics of the bovine impersonator.

'That Aaron McLean,' he mused. 'Do you think he's their dead-bull specialist?'

A soulful bell chimed, as tumbleweed blew down Grays High-Street.

Yokel Hero
7/3/2006 Gravesend and Northfleet - away
Three days after Grays saw the rarity, for me at least, of seeing an evening match at ES, along with our new floodlights, the recent upgrade essential if ES is to be fit for a return to the Football League. That is, if we scrape into a play-off and then win the damned thing. Some pretty big ifs there,

but the new lights illuminated a brace of high-quality goals from Willo, and Cambridge were despatched with ease. Up to third for the Bulls, and a week later it was second, as Stansfield yet again found the net, this enough to see off Halifax. Which served to make us wonder just how much closer to Accy we might be if Lisa hadn't missed half the season through injury. Or if, instead of sending for Bambi, GT had looked closer to home when our strikers were struggling. After a dozen Conference matches, it was clear that Willo was more than comfortable at this level, and if you're good enough, you're old enough. Looks like you dropped one there, Graham, but better late than never for Andy, who returned to the score sheet against both Aldershot and Stevenage, satisfying home wins serving only to make second place a little more secure.

But even further away from the top. Watching Hereford this season has been a groundhog day experience, as whilst once again the Bulls left their winter inconsistencies behind them, another outfit have embarked on a run better than ours. Yes, it's now ten straight wins for the milkmen, and realistically, nothing short of a bomb at the Interlink Express Stadium will stop Stanley from claiming the title. Whilst a small explosion would without doubt smarten the place up, it's not going to happen. The job now was to finish in the top five, although preferably not second. Having lost two points at Canvey (Middle of Nowhere) Island, but collected a depressed fracture to Lisa's cheekbone, the next stop on our soiree around the bleak terrain of the Thames estuary was Gravesend.

Just like Grays, here is a place which comfortably lives up to its name, but unlike Grays, it was sampled on a foul evening which reduced the Bulls' support to a season low of a little over a hundred. Like the Daggers goal-fest of two years ago, there were many good reasons to stay at home, high on the list being a side so decimated by injury that a Colchester academy player was drafted in. And exactly like the Daggers match, those who made the trip enjoyed one of those nights that live long in the memory for all the right reasons. After 45 minutes, however, not even the most optimistic of Bulls fans could see anything other than a fruitless, pointless, and very wet evening. This is the call I made to my father at half-time.

Me. Hello Dad, it's not looking good, one-nil down, and playing with ten men.

Dad. Oh dear. Who got the red?

Me. Daryl Taylor, tiny winger on loan from Walsall.

Dad. Oh, him. Must have been dissent, what happened?

Me. Dangerous tackle.

Dad. You're kidding, he couldn't tackle a rice-pudding.

Me. I know, but this is a Conference ref.

Dad. Any way back?

Me. No, can't see it, but I'll call you if we score.

Dad. OK, speak to you tomorrow then.

And that was it, game over, or so we thought.

But we were wrong, as the extra ten per cent needed in these situations was found by each of the Bulls, including Stuart Fleetwood, recently signed after being released by Cardiff City. Another one of those problem youngsters that GT likes to adopt, Fleetwood ran himself to a standstill, stretching the home defence with pace and intelligence that didn't belong in this league. It was two other teenagers, however, who stole the glory. Local youngster Rob King showed the watching coaches from Colchester's academy what a good pupil he was, curling in a beauty from twenty yards. This was followed by a Willo special. Finding himself isolated, and with three home defenders in close attention, a more mature player might have headed for the corner and wasted a few seconds, but with a flash of genius inspired equally by Maradona and Houdini, Willo left his markers for dead and smashed home a winning goal of breathtaking quality. A borrowed local hero, and our very own yokel hero had secured a gutsy away win despite losing a player before half-time, on this occasion with a patched-up side missing at least five regulars. Nothing wrong with the spirit in the club, something looking ever more likely to be required in the play-offs, as Accy won yet again.

As for Gravesend, I'm trying, but genuinely can't find anything positive to say about the place. Sure, the ground is fine, in a scruffy and unloved sort of way, and the locals didn't bite, although a few looked as though they wouldn't need much of an excuse to have a nibble. It's just that Gravesend is somehow more depressing and grey than Grays, an opinion shared not merely by a few Bulls but another high-profile member of the wildlife community.

Remember Free Willy, the whale with the faulty sonar who two weeks previously had found himself sight-seeing in Westminster? You may then also remember that Willy was coaxed back down-river and had almost made it to open water, on the way bravely surviving both Dagenham and Grays. Sadly for this poor but perceptive creature, Gravesend proved one dump too far, and it was within view of Stonebridge Road that Willy breathed his last. I can see why. If the lost leviathan had somehow struggled past Gravesend, waiting just a few miles downstream was Canvey Island. There's only so much a whale can take, and Willy, it appeared, could take no more of the Thames Estuary. A season in the Conference may be many things, but a Year in Provence it definitely is not.

Man Behaving Badly
11/3/2005 Accrington Stanley - home

With a win at ES, Stanley would claim the Conference record for consecutive victories, held of course by Hereford. Plenty to play for then, even though Accy were nailed-on for the title and the Bulls a decent bet for a play-off slot. With twenty minutes remaining and John Coleman's side two-up, the twelfth straight victory appeared secure, but to their manager's dismay Stuart Fleetwood and then emergency signing Nicky Nicolau pegged the visitors back to earn a draw. When I say dismay, I may have slightly downplayed Mr Coleman's reaction to being denied his round dozen of victories, for to say that Coleman was a little annoyed would be akin to observing that Bill Gates is comfortably off. Whether it was the inexplicable red-card issued to Danny Ventre or the six minutes of added time, the last of which saw Nicolau's equaliser, that upset the Accrington manager I'm not sure, but John Coleman was in full meltdown and a sight to behold. Imagine John McEnroe's worst tantrum delivered by a scouse Bob Hoskins, then double it, and you're somewhere near John Coleman at five to five that afternoon.

After which he really lost it. The stragglers leaving the main stand were treated to a toys-out-of-pram display of quite breathtaking quality, and one which took a small army of Accy's backroom staff to contain. Coleman was escorted by his colleagues from bench to pitch, presumably the safest place to cool down. It served only to allow Coleman to sail past Graham Westley in the unloved manager stakes, as the storm found fresh energy, perhaps fuelled by a few well-chosen comments from the B-Block regulars. As a spectacle it comfortably outdid the previous 96 minutes, erupting again in the boardroom, where more than a few ears were treated to a display of vocabulary rarely associated with a schoolteacher. Yes, Coleman, in a previous incarnation, was a teacher, and one that I doubt would have tolerated such a display from his charges. On a day when the milkmen of Accrington failed to deliver a Conference record to their boss, Coleman produced a rant of such sustained fury that to call it non-league would be an insult, as this was dummy-spitting of Premiership class by the manager of the little club that wouldn't die.

Spectacular though Coleman's fit of pique was, in comparison to some of the off-field antics occurring since Christmas it was small beer. Steve Evans, another less than angelic character, found himself in front of a Magistrate, entering a plea of not guilty of conspiracy to cheat the Public Revenue, and will appear before Southwark Crown Court to defend himself. No mention of the charges of cheating Dagenham, the Nationwide Conference, English football, and sport in general. I hope, Steve, that you get exactly what you deserve. Also on the wrong side of the Magistrates was a goalkeeping coach soon to be enjoying a hundred hours of community service. Whilst all keepers are by definition madder than a bag of cats, Lionel Perez of Stevenage pushed the envelope a little further, along with a finger into the eye of Northampton's Dave Watson. Ouch. Lionel's insanity plea apparently fell on deaf ears, so it's cleaning duty on the graffiti-ridden wasteland of Stevenage for Monsieur Perez. And from community service to secret service, and the startling news that Exeter have a mole in their midst. Grays manager Mark Stimpson confessed to having received information from a West Country insider, revealing details of the Grecians selection and tactics for the imminent matches between the sides. Whether a disgruntled player or a tea-lady on the take who knows, but the intelligence was apparently of the highest quality. Good of Mr. Stimpson to blow the lid on this outrageous affront to decency and fair play. Even better that he did so shortly after Grays had completed the second of their two victories over the Grecians. Beat that, you would-be spooks of the Premier League.

Whilst the Bulls were rightly concerned with the sharp end of Conference life, just a brief look downward, where events off the pitch appear more significant than those on it. Of the sides battling relegation, only Southport and the Gump appear to have merely football matches on which to focus. Try this lot for an administrator's nightmare. Tamworth have been docked a point for fielding an ineligible player, whilst Crawley have lost three due to their exceeding of the salary cap. Altrincham, meanwhile, have also played an undesirable, at least in the eyes of the men in suits, and are looking at the loss of a yet-to-be-decided number of points, whilst Scarborough have just weeks to extricate themselves from their CVA or face automatic relegation. There is at the moment a fabulously vitriolic debate taking place on the Confguide message-board, where the hunt is on for the whistle-blower who flagged up Altrincham's oversight concerning the registration of one James Robinson. Most fingers are pointing at Forest Green, unsurprisingly placed to benefit most if Alty are hit with a big penalty. There are also rumours that the Canvey dream may be over for Jeff King, apparently close to walking away from the Island. With him would go the financial safety-blanket keeping the club immune from the reality of a population that appears barely to have noticed the progress made in a few short years. Jeff probably didn't expect the level of overwhelming indifference shown to his efforts, but if the locals can't be bothered to get out of their armchairs on a Saturday afternoon, he could hardly expect them to squeeze into Park Lane and support his pet project.

Keep an eye on this end of the table, there's plenty more to come, but for now, back to life at the top, and fast-forward to the second week of April, and four matches remaining. Because this is when the club that wouldn't die won their place in the Football League, two generations after surrendering it. There was a media nostalgia-fest as Stanley celebrated their return to the relative big-time, and whilst John Coleman had probably won a few less friends than the small-in-number-but-big-on-flags Ultras, time for another grudging pat on the back. To achieve what Stanley had was, to be fair, a magnificent effort. On gates of less than two thousand they had won the Conference, and whilst not always easy on the eye, the table doesn't lie. And although they may have had a little help from a benevolent Chairman, if they did, it wasn't on the scale of Rushden, or Doncaster, or Chester. I wonder if Tretts and Browner paused for a moment to offer a quiet wish of good luck toward their former team-mates?

We would certainly need it, although as Accy were celebrating in style, the Bulls confirmed that once again, they had a lottery ticket. Third time lucky?

I hope so, because next season would be our tenth year of Non-League football.

Hand of a Legend
7/5/2006 and 11/5/2006 Morecambe - away and home. Play-off Semi-Final

So where would we finish, and who would we play?

Second, again, and Morecambe were the answers, as ten points from twelve secured yet another runners-up spot. Grays and Halifax completed the line-up, as both Exeter and Stevenage tragically missed out on the end of season ritual that would leave three clubs planning trips to Weymouth and Stafford whilst the other would look forward to spending the £300,000 sponsorship money offered by Coca-Cola. At the same time as which, supporters of Oxford and Rushden would be planning trips to, well, Weymouth and Stafford, along with fellow new boys St. Albans and, bless 'em, Northwich, bouncing straight back after their scandalous demotion last season. Oxford and Rushden were the unfortunates to fall through the trap-door, both good examples of how quickly this game can turn on you. Rushden have been here before, but to Oxford United, life in the Conference isn't the disaster you may be anticipating, but is a division much harder to get out of than it is to enter.

So before looking up, another look downwards, and the shambolic end to the story of which two clubs will be leaving the Conference in the wrong direction.

Follow this if you can. The Gump again survived on goal difference, as Tamworth and Scarborough were relegated. But of course they weren't, because Altrincham collected a massive 18 point penalty over the James Robinson affair. Robinson forgot to mention his brief spell in Iceland before signing for Accrington, and the required International clearance was never obtained. Playing only for the reserves at Stanley, he then signed for Alty, where he did make the first team, collecting 18 points with him in the side. Against the letter of the law maybe, but surely an oversight with no case to answer for either club. Wrong, case to answer, said the Conference board. Hence, relegation for Alty, and a slap on the wrist for the original sinners at Accrington. Here was a group of men in suits who had, in the opinion of just about anybody outside of Tamworth, completely lost the plot. A clear message had been delivered, and it was that it was a lesser crime to cheat your way to promotion than to trust the efficiency of another club's secretary. Cue untold amounts of vitriol toward the Conference board, and also toward Tamworth, now safe, and the newly christened Forest Green Grassers. So now Scarborough and Alty would take the drop.

Wrong again. Enter Canvey Island, and exit Jeff King, who, as hinted, walked away. The remaining three men and a dog who actually gave a monkey's wisely decided that Conference football was unsustainable, and relegated themselves to a point in the Ryman League better reflecting their circumstances. Hurrah then for Scarborough, reportedly out of their CVA in the nick of time, and a Yorkshire club saved by Essex Man. I hope you're keeping up, because there's more.

Enter Crawley Town, still spending more money than they had. With one of the club's owners facing bankruptcy, it seems that they might not be able to guarantee their fixtures next season. Remember Barrow? If the board showed any consistency, it was goodbye Crawley, after just two seasons of Conference football.

Fat chance. Barrow remained a forgotten team, Crawley were safe, Alty still doomed, and yes, this does take a little effort, but stick with it, just one more twist in the tail.

To recap, Canvey were gone, falling on their own sword. Altrincham had been scandalously thrown out due to an oversight by Accrington, and Crawley's indiscretions had been all but ignored, leaving Tamworth and Scarborough, the two worst teams in the division, safe. Until, that is, someone decided that there hadn't been quite enough meddling, and another, longer look was taken at Scarborough's delicate finances. Not a pretty sight apparently, so it was a case of 'Get yourselves down to Conference North, and here, take this ten point penalty with you for next season while you're about it.' Which left Altrincham and their grand, if adjusted, total of 23 points, still in the division. Justice for Alty, but at what price for the reputation of the Nationwide Conference? Unproper football at its very best, and if we ever get out of this tinpot division, I'm going to miss it.

Enough of the madness. Forward now to the crazy world of the play-offs, and a Sunday afternoon in Morecambe, a 5pm kick-off and a past midnight return for the travelling Bulls, all because of Sky Television. Or, alternatively, a five minute stroll to the Turks Head, home by seven, and a whole evening to contemplate the second leg in four days' time. All because of Sky television. Yes, hands-up time, we were in the pub, with the honourable exception of Mark and Alan, real supporters putting the fairweathers to shame. Whilst we're patently more cursed than blessed by Murdoch-vision, this was one occasion when we were grateful for live TV, easing the demands of work, family, and more than a little weariness in the knowledge that we had a good idea of what was coming. Second versus fifth again, following one-all draws at Aldershot and Stevenage, you could say that a score draw was on the cards, and to nobody's surprise, that is again what we got. Morecambe struck first, as Superman failed to fly at an unwisely claimed corner, giving Jim Bentley a free header. Brown, who had more than lived up to his nickname for the previous nine months, chose the wrong time to become a mere mortal, and Morecambe were in control. This Bulls side however has plenty of spirit, and driven on by Ferrell and Stanley, created as many half-chances as the hosts. Something more was needed, and it arrived from an unlikely source, when with nothing of note happening around either penalty box or ball, Mr. Graham pointed to the spot, penalty to Hereford.

They say that to err is human, a saying coined I'm certain with Conference officials in mind, but what a time to get a freebie. With Jamer out of the side, frail little Rob Purdie assumed the job that no-one in their right mind would want. Of all the Bulls squad, Purds is the one who least relishes the physical battle, and thus frequently cops huge amounts of stick. Which annoys the hell out of me, because at all levels, particularly this one, the complete footballer simply doesn't exist. If Purds had Andy Ferrell's tenacity, he categorically wouldn't be a Conference player. Likewise if Ryan Green possessed Trav's attitude, or Superman Craig Mawson's stature, all would be at least two divisions higher. The ultimate example would of course be Ipoua. Given even a fraction of Lisa's energy, Guy would be a player who would have never heard of the Conference.

But back to Purdie. The purest striker of a ball we have demonstrated that he also had that vital ingredient, bottle. A perfect spot-kick was despatched, we were level, and looking the side more likely to snatch the win. And then came the moment that made a few thousand Herefordians think that this might just be our year. The ever-impressive Michael Twiss had a legitimate goal disallowed for offside, and the second key decision of the day incorrectly went our way. Whilst on the balance of play a draw was the right result, had the match taken place in Italy, the bank accounts of at least two of the men in black might have been under a little scrutiny. So, all-square, and back to the Street in four days. Sounds familiar, doesn't it?

Or as a Times reporter noted, 'The Hereford fans returning to their bus bore the haunted look of those who had seen it all before.' Too bloody right mate, because we all know what happened after the two previous away legs, don't we?

So, would it be third time lucky?

The squad were fit, apart from Ipoua, who clearly never had been, although he wasn't injured, and would join DCB and Fleetwood on the bench. Plenty of firepower there if Lisa and Willo are not on their game, and with the Bulls again boasting the meanest defence in the Conference, just maybe we would get a little more of the good fortune enjoyed at Morecambe. Added to which, with the final being played at Wembley from next season, Sod's Law will guarantee we make the big day in Leicester's new Walkers Stadium.

Given the obvious pressure, the first leg had been a cracking game, but the second was even better. Two decent sides kept the ball on the floor and produced something alarmingly close to proper football, and a clear reflection of the men in charge. Within twelve minutes, the Bulls found themselves 2-1 up, Purdie providing the service for Tamika and Willo, either side of a Curtis penalty. It was end to end stuff, but as the game progressed it was the visitors who looked stronger, and on 52 minutes scored through Twiss. Morecambe were in control, Hereford increasingly struggling, at least as an attacking force, but, and I still can't put my finger on the reason why, I felt with absolute confidence that we would come through.

Full-time came, along with Ipoua, languid, smiling, overweight, rumoured to be older than admitted, but still possessed of the weapons to destroy defences considerably better than our visitors. We just had to hope that today they were in working order. Justin had no doubts, asserting that Guy would do the job. And he was right. Guy Ipoua doesn't just score in Saxtys

With twelve minutes remaining, the ball fell to him twenty-five yards from goal, closely marshalled by two defenders. Which is when Guy showed perhaps a second and a half of the magic that has captivated fans in arenas much bigger than ours. A combination of speed and strength saw him brush aside his markers and advance forward, before burying the ball in the top corner of the Morecambe net. It was a strike of the highest quality, and one to which Morecambe had no answer, and the clock ticked down with no real alarm on the pitch.

As the final whistle blew, ES erupted, as much with relief as with joy, as for every Bulls supporter in the ground the memory of those heart-breaking days against Aldershot and Stevenage was brushed away.

We were on our way to Not Wembley.

It was close to eleven as I left my seat, and to my left was a chap of about my age wearing a Morecambe blazer, a man who had given the last ten years of his life to his club, something which almost certainly contributed to his recent spell in a coronary-care unit. Jimmy Harvey was

205

back, and whilst not ready or perhaps not allowed to return to the bench, had overseen his side's bid for promotion, his friend Sammy McIlroy assisting whilst he convalesced. Hurt but still smiling, here was a Bulls legend, and my personal favourite player to have worn a Hereford shirt, just inches away. I offered a hand, but what to say? 'Jimmy, you're still the best player I've seen on that pitch. Good luck to you.' Gracious in defeat, Jim shook my hand, and those of a dozen other Bulls fans. Whilst perhaps not the best ever seen, Jimmy was pretty close to it, and a true gentleman, wishing us all the best for the final. Little did he know what was waiting around the corner for him.

Now here's the thing about following a crappy little team like Hereford, in a tinpot little league like the Conference. For this very reason, people remember you, and the fact that Arsenal, Chelsea or Liverpool are not your team sets you apart from the crowd. My mobile was soon full of messages from work colleagues, old acquaintances, friends both good and distant, and another very special one, as I breezed home along the M4.

'At last your stupid team have done it, congratulations, this is the year.'

Only one person can call them my stupid team and get away with it, but I hope she's right. Thanks Mum, I have a feeling that it will be.

Welcome Back
20/5/2006 Halifax Town - The Walkers Stadium
Conference Play-Off Final
We now had a nine day wait for the day we had waited nine years for. Standing between us and the Football League were Halifax Town, surprising many merely by reaching the play-offs, and quite a few more by despatching Grays, 5-4 over the two legs. Well done to Chris Wilder and his side, for they, like the Bulls, had reached Leicester from a position of almost terminal chaos and financial ruin a few short years ago.

Cast your mind back to the Bulls' first Conference season in which they earned sixth position, twenty points behind champions Halifax. Four years later the Shaymen returned, haemorrhaging both support and money, wondering if there was any way back. They, like us, were nearly there.

The nine day wait saw two contrasting stories, one cruel and another to warm the heart. The cruel came from Morecambe Football Club, who three days after their defeat at ES disgracefully sacked the architect of their success. Jim Harvey had taken the Shrimpers from nowhere to two play-off semi-finals and a reputation as one of the best footballing sides in the division.

No room for sentiment in this game? Not if a so-called friend steals both your glory *and* your job, as Sammy McIlroy had done to Harvey. Morecambe have some of the best supporters in this league, but McIlroy and his side have at least one less friend in Hereford.

On a brighter note, a story with an already happy ending. Just over a year ago, four Bulls fans endured an horrific car crash and a spell in Intensive Care. All will be in the Walkers Stadium on Saturday for a match between the same two sides they were planning to watch on the day they almost lost their lives.

Lads, we've never met, but if anyone deserves a promotion party, it's you.

Estimates are that if it is the Bulls who are celebrating on Saturday, 10,000 people will be joining them inside the crisp-bowl, outnumbering Halifax by two to one. Fifteen thousand supporters plus a few neutrals would make for a cracking atmosphere, and the biggest day in the lives of sixteen players, most of whom were just beginning their careers. They would take the field in Leicester with 90 minutes in which to lay to rest thirty years of under-achievement. A large majority of Bulls fans had known only tepid, fleeting success, and many had known only non-league football, much of which had been desperate, awful fare. Here at last was the opportunity to put all of that behind them, and open another chapter of a little club that, like Accrington, wouldn't die.

Now some logistics. Tickets were arranged by my father, whose only words on being asked to buy twenty-three of them, were simply 'Don't tell your mother I've got the cash for that many'. Transport was courtesy of Woody and British Rail, as surprisingly, there were no volunteers to drive to Leicester. And Friday night entertainment was magnificently co-ordinated by fellow Twickenham White John, who came up with the perfect start to a big weekend.

'My boss is going back-packing for a year, his leaving party is a match in Brentford and we need a keeper.' 'Fine, count me in', I replied. 'Five-thirty kick-off, Griffin Park, bring your gloves.'

You beauty. Twenty-five years after numerous scouts had mysteriously overlooked my shot-stopping abilities, there I was, finally playing in a Football League Stadium. For the first time in a week my mind wasn't wandering to Leicester every few minutes, and credit to Brentford, they didn't hold back on the extras. Rob, a Brentford fanatic for whom the match was arranged, was in his own personal heaven, especially as he prepared to take a dubious last-minute penalty. To score on the same ground as his heroes would be the ultimate going-away present, all that remained was to find the net from twelve yards.

Twelve little yards, however, proved too much, and his scuffed kick was deflected away. Heads were in hands as just thirty seconds remained. Time enough for the first decent corner of the evening to find its way onto the head of our centre-half, who thundered it into the net. Rob had his goal, along with a fabulous shirt-over-head celebration, before being buried under a scrum of team-mates and many of the fifty supporters present. Usually the most eloquent of men, Rob was almost lost for words as he later received the match-ball. Whilst Brentford aren't a fashionable or glamorous club, they are and always had been Rob's team, and with a little help from his friends had given him a night he would never forget.

Whilst a dream come true for Rob, it was also a huge privilege for the rest of us. I had a feeling, however, that for two of us it wouldn't even be the highlight of our weekend.

Fast-forward sixteen hours to the station bar at St. Pancras, where six men in Hereford shirts were joined by six more in the blue and white of Halifax Town. A generation ago this would have been an accidental meeting almost guaranteed to end in carnage, but today it ended with a civil handshake and a cheeky wish of good luck.

Next season, in the Conference, that is. According to our Yorkshire friends, disappointment was heading our way in the form of John Grant, who would steal a win for his team. Yes, the same John Grant, the complete striker in all aspects bar the most important one, was now at Halifax, having once been surplus to requirements at Hereford, and a few other clubs in between. Grant against Superman? Do me a favour.

Next stop Leicester, and the first sighting of fifty Bulls fans in custom-made Superman shirts. All bright blue and bearing the inverted triangle, but closer inspection revealed that the S had been replaced with two words. Wayne Brown. Fabulous work, chaps, I'm sure Wayne will love them.

From a Superman to a super stadium, or at least a comfortable, if somewhat characterless bowl. A home for 30,000 people looks a little odd when half-full, particularly when a bank of seating the complete length of the pitch is empty, but for 10,000 Herefordians packed into a stand and a half, the effect of part Mardi Gras, part Marie Celeste was to generate a stunning atmosphere. Five years previously, nearly four thousand had assembled a mile down the road in the more modest surrounds of Filbert Street. There they witnessed the greatest moment enjoyed by the Bulls in their Conference life, when Leicester City were twelve minutes away from humiliation. That night saw a fabulous contribution by the Bulls support, but today saw another level of passion and noise. Horns, flags, black and white afros, painted faces, fifty Supermen and, bizarrely, a couple of inflatable women wearing only Hereford scarves, had assembled to support their team. A fleet of buses were parked outside, having deposited perhaps 15 percent of the City in Leicester. As someone remarked earlier today, would the last person to leave town please turn off the light.

Matt, my Chelsea-supporting friend, enjoying his second Bulls match, and used to crowds much bigger than this, was visibly moved. 'This is phenomenal. I've never seen such passion.' To be honest, neither had I, and the players weren't yet on the pitch. Whilst many present wouldn't have seen the Bulls more than a handful of times, it seemed that everyone had been infected with the emotion of the day, carried by the tidal wave of support for Hereford. 'Still confident?' asked Rich. I was. Somewhere, buried inside all of the excitement, was a little ball of calm, quietly saying that everything would be alright.

I still don't know why, but I believed it. John wasn't so sure, but then he never is, convinced that to assume victory would guarantee defeat. I left him to his disappearing fingernails as the volume moved up to eleven. I could only see the back of Tamika's head as he led the players onto the pitch, but to me he looked cool, calm, and ready for battle.

'Look, Tam isn't worried, you can tell', I offered. 'He knows we'll be OK.' Utter bollocks, of course, you would need ice in your veins to remain cool on a day like today, but Tam was indeed calmly going about his business with the assembled dignitaries. As for the rest of them, let's just say they were a little fidgety.

The first question was who would settle the quicker, and the answer was without doubt Halifax. Several forays toward Superman's goal withered, until on nine minutes a cross was delivered from the right flank. Most of the 15,549 pairs of eyes present clearly saw Tam handle the ball, but those that mattered, belonging to Dean Whitestone, didn't.

It was a huge escape, but Halifax continued to press, and on twenty-seven minutes Lewis Killeen collected a mis-hit clearance and from twenty-five yards gave Brown no chance.

Shit. Killeen is one of the few unproper players deserving of a bigger stage, and was asking all manner of questions of the Bulls' defence, and to be honest, the goal was coming. The depression, however, was temporary.

Within seven minutes, Lisa's pin-point cross found the diving head of Willo. Volume up to twelve, as Hereford's favourite teenager levelled the scores. The Bulls were back in the game, and for fifteen minutes either side of half-time dominated their Yorkshire opponents, culminating in a Purdie run being brought to a clumsy halt inside the Shaymen's penalty area. Mr. Whitestone, perhaps mindful of his first half mishap, indicated a goal kick. Whilst a blatant penalty had again been denied, justice had, in a way, been done, but Halifax made the most of their good fortune. In the best move of the game, Killeen crossed for substitute Grant to deftly plant in Wayne Brown's goal.

Yes, the same John Grant, the pacy, athletic striker who couldn't hit a cow's arse with a banjo had as predicted come off the bench to haunt us. Football is full of little ironies, but we had seen Grant in a similar position a hundred times, and the ball in the Meadow End car park an identical number. Eighteen minutes remained, and as Bulls' supporters rallied, GT and Tucka were at work. It was once again Ipoua time.

An exhausted but clearly upset Willo made way, but if anyone could rescue us, it was Ipoua. Over the season he had barely completed a match, but had repeatedly shown both his class and his big-game temperament, most recently just nine days ago. It was the perfect stage for the man from Cameroon to deliver his cameo.

Straight into the fray, Guy was demanding the ball like a man possessed, Halifax suddenly jittery, unsure of how to deal with this twinkle-toed giant. Winning possession on the edge of the Shaymen's box, Ipoua fed Trav, who returned a perfect cross. Before the ball had reached Guy's head, we were up, knowing exactly what would follow. A bullet header whistled past Jon Kennedy, and for the second time we were level.

Within four minutes of stepping onto the pitch, Ipoua had delivered the goal which we believed would take us to the promised land, for now GT's men were the ones with energy and ideas to spare. Full-time came, along with Fleetwood and Jenny, and urged on by a manager rarely seen this animated, Bulls fans, incredibly, upped the decibel level yet again. Hereford pushed and probed, still looking the more likely, with Halifax seemingly prepared to take a gamble on penalties, but with twelve

210

minutes of extra-time remaining, the prospect of a spot-kick lottery faded dramatically.

Ryan Green found himself with a little too much time on the corner of the Halifax penalty area as the ball fell toward him. Here, the very right-footed Green looked up and curled an exquisite left-footed shot into the opposite corner of the Halifax net. Jon Kennedy was every bit as stunned as the thousands of Bulls fans, as the goal of this and many other seasons was recorded by the most unlikely of sources. Green, when the mood takes him, is capable of sublime football, but just where this dipping, venomous strike came from, delivered with a foot until today used only for standing on, is anyone's guess. Certainly it was Ryan who had delivered, but it was more Giggs than Green.

Sheer unadulterated bedlam erupted, as Green followed up his wonder strike with a fabulously passionate celebration. Off came the shirt, thrown far into the crowd, followed by the corner-flag, hurled javelin-style back into the turf. Joy is a small word that can sometimes say a lot, but this was beyond ecstasy, the faces of his team-mates saying it all. For the first time in a match of five goals Hereford were in front, and whilst Green barely noticed the yellow-card his Olympian celebrations attracted, there was now the small matter of holding the lead for twelve minutes.

Which lasted a mere twenty. Superman bravely claimed a ball at the feet of a Halifax forward, and was knocked unconscious for his troubles, and with all three subs used, there could be no Mawson. An anxious debate followed, and as physio Wayne Jones worked on Brown, it was Andy Ferrell who discovered just what a brute Maws really was, lost inside a shirt at least four sizes too big. It was vital that Brown woke up. Which he eventually did, to the sound of 10,000 voices singing Wayne Brown is Superman. If Browner was possessed of special powers, he looked a long way from being in control of them. It was now up to his team-mates to protect him, which they did with a mixture of desperation and style. The desperation coming from nine of them, the style from just one, as Guy gave a master-class in ball-shielding, ball-juggling and ball-hiding, single-handedly winning four corners in succession, and almost alone occupying those last precious minutes.

His yellow-card for time-wasting was met with a trademark Ipoua smile, and as the arena echoed to his name, it became a smile that could light up not just a room, but a whole stadium. Guy knew as we did that finally, it was time to celebrate.

3,199 days after the whistle that began Hereford United's loan to the Conference, Dean Whitestone blew the one that ended it. It had been some journey, but the Bulls were back.

It was a strange, almost surreal experience, standing in the midst of thousands of the happiest, noisiest, most relieved people that could ever have been to a football match. Emotion was everywhere, and in many different ways. There were some who couldn't stop screaming, and others trying but unable even to speak. There were tears and hugs from the most macho of men, whilst a few sat in a daze, overwhelmed and unable yet to fully comprehend what had happened.

As for me, it's not easy to put into words quite what I was feeling. Elated, definitely, but there was more. A deep satisfaction perhaps, and pride that my crappy little team had finally delivered something tangible, and not such a long time after finding themselves just one match, one goal even, away from becoming another football club that no longer existed.

But isn't it just a little insane, how 22 men kicking a bag of air around a field inspires such emotion, when all they had achieved was the privilege of doing it again in August, the only difference being a few new fields to enjoy it in?

Tosh, and any proper football fan will tell you so. I, along with Justin, John, Rich, Alan and the rest, had invested so much of ourselves in following our team over the years that we were more than just observers.

Part of each of us was out there in that victory.

Whilst ten thousand Bulls fans went happily ballistic, a small group of sportsmen did exactly the same, joined by GT's backroom staff. A Cameroon flag was draped around Guy, DCB found himself in a Superman shirt, whilst a Union Jack with Newcastle United written large covered Ferrell.

It was a beautiful sight, in stark contrast to the scene at the far end of the stadium. The players and supporters of Halifax Town saluted each other in what must have been a heartbreaking ordeal. Our opponents had played an equal part in a fabulous game, and one which had no right to be quite so entertaining, given the prize at stake. The Yorkshire men and women hadn't however come to Leicester to be entertained, they had come, like us, to see their team win a football match. On the day, and equally so, over the season, there had been little to choose between the two sides, and the tears shed by the players and supporters of Halifax Town could so easily have been ours.

But they weren't. A stage was placed in the centre-circle, and was the setting for two poignant images. The first was of Graham Turner counting the medals in the tray as they were handed to his team. Every squad player got a medal, as did John Trewick, Wayne Jones, even the lad who brought on the water. Only when certain everybody had their piece of silver did GT take one for himself.

The other was of the figure standing beside Tamika as the trophy was presented. Here was a player whose season had been plagued by injury and loss of form, but a player who over eight years and some 300 matches had done more for his club than anyone. Tony James deserved to have his hand on that trophy every bit as much as Tamika, a point which Tam appeared keen to make, and when together they lifted it toward the Bulls supporters, it was a picture I will never forget. Fireworks and champagne flew, as the players danced and the supporters sang.

'We are going up, say, we are going up.' Four little words had never sounded so good, and with each repeat felt even better. Yes, we are going up.

Some say that it is better to travel hopefully than to arrive. They may well be right, but our journey was over. On many occasions along the way, hope was all that we had but finally, the Bulls of Hereford had arrived.

We were a proper team again.

I met my father outside the ground for a lift back to Hereford, for this was a weekend when my spiritual home beckoned so much louder than my adopted one.

Usually the most phlegmatic of characters, he was, in a more restrained way, every bit as thrilled as the rest of us, for GT and his troops had delivered their prize on a special day.

'That's some sort of present, isn't it, Dad?'

The Bulls had ended their nine year odyssey on my father's seventieth birthday.

Final Words

That's it, journey's end, Hereford are once again a Football League Club, and a new chapter will begin in August. Some refer to our Conference experience as the wilderness years, but I don't agree. Certainly we had been to many footballing backwaters, but a large part of me is glad to have made that journey. There is a school of thought that the Conference was the best, perhaps only place where GT could slowly rebuild a football club ruined by years of neglect, and they may well be right.

When Graham Turner was appointed, Hereford United was an accident waiting to happen. Now it is a small but viable home for a couple of thousand die-hards, and a whole host more who will occasionally pop down to the Street to check up on their team. Whilst GT is in charge there will be no return to the days of spending money the club doesn't have, but as a man who placed his own home on the line for the sake of the Bulls, I think he's allowed a little prudence.

Our Conference journey had been an incredible roller-coaster ride, on occasions being minutes from disaster, on others, minutes away from glory. From humiliation at Hayes to glorious failure at Filbert Street, from scoring with a swede to scoring a goal at Dover that probably saved the club. From the palatial surrounds of Rushden's Nene Park to the near-derelict austerity of the Gump and their Lawn, and from the misplaced passes of electricians and schoolteachers to the breathtaking skill of two lads who would become Welsh Internationals, we had pretty much seen everything.

But apart from the bricks and mortar of Edgar Street, there is one constant who stood firm through it all, and without whom Hereford United would almost certainly not exist, at least in its present form. Whilst Joan, the ROK, Tucka Trewick and particularly the handful of supporters who refused to go quietly had all done more than their share, on 20th May 2006 a football club manager earned a promotion more richly deserved than any Premiership or Champions League Trophy.

A more genuine football man than Graham Turner would be hard to find. Graham, you kept the faith when the only sensible option was to walk away, and delivered a promise made nine years previously. 'I took this club down, I'll take them back up again.'

I'm sure there were times when thoughts of promotion were the furthest thing from your mind, and others when you questioned your sanity, but you put a smile on the faces of a few thousand people who care for that little team almost as much as you do.

Thanks for that. It's been a blast.

Believe it or not, it isn't only me who became a little emotional on the 20th May. Below are just a few of the hundreds of entries on the various Bulls message-boards that weekend:

Words cannot describe how proud of you we are. For all of us who stand on the Meadow End, for the early Saturday mornings on a mini-bus to travel hundreds of miles with a hangover in the rain to cheer you on….WE ARE SOOOOOO PROUD OF YOU!!!!!

Thank you so much for making 20th May the best day of our lives, and for a fantastic memory that will last forever.

Janie and Tibzy.

Just got back from a 7,000 mile round trip to the Walker Stadium. The question everyone has asked is 'Was it worth it?' The answer after that fantastic game is a resounding yes. I don't think I'll ever get tired of watching the goals and if I didn't have a flight to catch, I would have watched them all night.

Jensen - Trumansburg, New York.

Most true football fans are delighted for you. Yesterday's result gave me more pleasure than any other this season. As a Brighton fan, I am delighted to see Hereford back in the League - where you belong. Well deserved, congratulations.

Zamoraisagod.

Matthew 'Pogo' Fowles, a Forest lad that moved to Hereford, worked at Sun Valley, some of you may know him. Sadly took his own life a few days before the 9-0 game. FOD Bull placed a Hereford shirt on his grave before leaving for the final.

Pogo, yesterday was for you.

Buzz the Bull.

Can't begin to tell you what a wonderful day Saturday was, the biggest emotional roller-coaster of my life. I'm not ashamed to say that at the final whistle we all cried, such was the incredible joy and relief. The many years of 270 mile trips for home games suddenly became wonderfully worthwhile this weekend. I am so incredibly proud to be a Hereford fan it is hard to describe. I am visiting Stamford Hospital later this week to have the stupid grin I have permanently on my face surgically removed!!!

Stamford Bull.

I've been going to Edgar Street since I was 14, for nearly all that time with the same three friends, and it became our second home. Two of them died last year, the other is now housebound with illness. I hadn't been to an away game in years, but felt that if I didn't go to Leicester, I would be letting down my friends. It was the right thing to do, an incredible day I shall never forget.

Terry, Angus and Ray, this was for you as well.   Anonymous.

Welcome back to the Football League!
Rob, a Sunderland and Ronnie Radford fan.

Postscript

Twelve months on from that fabulous day in Leicester, re-reading my scribbles still brings a little tear to the eye. Many things have changed, whilst some have stayed the same. The Bulls, after a brief mid-season push towards the play-offs, faded badly to a safe but unremarkable sixteenth place in League Two. Whilst taking points off the best sides in the division, there was never enough class or commitment to seriously threaten another promotion, and another summer of rebuilding is underway.

Tamika, Ryan Green and Willo are now League One players, whilst Ben Smith and Stevie G have returned to the Street, hopefully to be as prodigious as they have been prodigal.

Stabby Backilroy spectacularly didn't fail with Morecambe, winning the first New Wembley Play-Off, joining Conference Champions, and by a mile, Dagenham, as proper football teams. See you in a few weeks, chaps.

Entering the wilderness were Torquay and, would you believe it, Boston United.

Yes folks, there is indeed a god of football, and one with a sense of humour. The Boston Cheaters, along with Steve (guilty as charged) Evans, swapped places with the Daggers, righting a scandalous four-year-old miscarriage of justice. Belatedly overwhelmed by guilt, the Conference Board have indicated that Boston, along with their shiny new CVA, aren't all that welcome, and have placed them in Conference North. Sow and ye shall reap, and whilst I feel for the few genuine fans of Boston United, the truth is, you were never really a *proper* team.

Jimmy Harvey, esteemed gentleman of Hereford and Morecambe has a new job, and with coach Jenny Pitman is looking after the Gump and their brand new stadium.

As for Steve Perrin, he is enjoying life in the British Gas Business League, with Chippenham Town. The Gump also enjoyed the services of

Guy Ipoua, but not for long. Just two matches were enough for Jimmy to see that Guy's best days were behind him. Whatever the dancing Cameroonian is up to now, I suspect there is a smile on his face, and if he were to show it in Saxtys, I doubt he would need to buy his own beer. Tony James, having followed the money to Weymouth, will now be charming the purists at Burton, Weymouth having become Nouveau Poor even more quickly than they became Nouveau Riche. Here is one chap who really should have been a proper footballer, and maybe one day still will.

And some other old friends? The ROK is at Donny Rovers, Gavin Mahon is captain at Watford, Neil Grayson is approaching his 2,000[th] match as a professional (or somewhere near), Dodge is still a physio, whilst Snapper and Wrighty are the sparkies for the Take That Reunion Tour. Andy deBont runs a pie shop in Bournemouth, Elmo is Secretary of State for Education, the goal-machine is a policeman, and at least one former Bull apparently served a few months at Her Majesty's Pleasure in Gloucester nick.

And at least half of the above are true.

Two favourite sons of Stevenage have also moved on. Eldinho came to ES with Stockport and scored, whilst Graham Westley was 'relieved of his duties' by Rushden shortly after enduring a similar fate at Broadhall Way. Where he is now I neither know nor care.

And the Conference itself?

Nine former League Clubs will battle with the great unwashed of unproper football in a division dramatically different from the one in which Welling humiliated the Bulls ten, or was it a hundred years ago? It is now a division much closer to proper football, with barely a part-timer to be seen and many of the sides enjoying bigger support than half of League Two. The pool may be the same size, but there are more big fish in it, and it is a place that I suspect is now nowhere near as much fun.